Self-Defeating Behaviors

Self-Defeating Behaviors

Free Yourself from the Habits, Compulsions, Feelings, and Attitudes That Hold You Back

Milton R. Cudney, Ph.D.,
and Robert E. Hardy, Ed.D.

■ HarperSanFrancisco

A Division of HarperCollins*Publishers*

To my wife, Mildred, my sons, Tyren, Kurt,
and Cameron, my mother and extended family,
and to the memory of my son Kevan, whom we
all loved very much.

MC

To the people I love: my mother, Pearl, my
daughters, Tasha and Heather, and my beautiful
Diane. Also to Loren Brink for his endless support
and encouragement.

And to the memory of Walter H. Schwartz, Jr.

RH

FIRST EDITION

Library of Congress Cataloging-in Publication Data

Cudney, Milton R.
    Self-defeating behaviors : free yourself from the habits,
compulsions, feelings, and attitudes that hold you back /
Milton R. Cudney, Robert E. Hardy. — 1st ed.
      p. cm.
    Includes index.
    ISBN 0-06-250169-0
    1. Conduct of life. 2. Self-defeating behavior. 3. Behavior
modification. I. Hardy, Robert Earl. II. Title.
BF637.C5C83 1991
158'.1—dc20
                                          90-84903
                                            CIP

91 92 93 94 95 RRD(H) 10 9 8 7 6 5 4 3 2 1

This edition is printed on acid-free paper that meets the American National Standards Institute Z39.48 Standard.

Contents

Acknowledgments

This book would not exist in its current form were it not for the talent and persistence of Randy Schwartz, our co-writer for the project. We relied heavily not only on Randy's skills as a writer but also on his ability to design a sound structural framework for the concepts we wished to present. He added both richness and complexity to our behavioral model, yet in other instances managed to articulate clearly the more abstruse concepts we felt it necessary to discuss. The results of his efforts are evident, we believe, on each and every page of the book. Quite literally, Randy gave voice to our ideas. For this, and for his faith in us and in himself, we offer our thanks.

During the course of this project, we had the good fortune of working with several other talented professionals. Jonathan and Wendy Lazear of The Lazear Agency believed in the manuscript and spent much time and effort finding the best home for it. Kathy Erickson, also of The Lazear Agency, believed in our manuscript, fielded our numerous questions, and kept our spirits up throughout the rounds of submissions that led eventually to publication. We are indebted to her for her professionalism and her ongoing encouragement.

Tom Grady of HarperSanFrancisco saw considerable merit in our work. His suggestions helped us clarify our own thinking and added substantial value to the book. His editorial insights, coming at a time when we were much in need of them, proved invaluable.

To all of the people mentioned above—to Jonathan, Wendy, Kathy, Tom—and, especially, to Randy—we say thank you for bringing our dream to life.

Although the events, locales, and personalities described in this book are accurate, the names and identifying details of the individuals have beeen changed in order to protect their privacy.

Introduction

Most of us choose the kinds of lives we lead. Although we may not be aware of it, each day we make choices that determine whether we will be happy or unhappy, healthy or ill, creative or barren. We make the majority of these choices on an unconscious level, guided primarily by a sense of what has happened to us in the past and what might happen to us in the future. This apparently automatic process of decision making tends to hide the fact that we are making choices constantly. Most of us do not recognize, for example, that we choose to turn left instead of right at a particular corner on the way home from work, that we choose to light a cigarette at a given moment, or that we choose to avert our eyes rather than to look into the face of a person we pass on the street. Over time, we lose the sense of making a choice at each new moment of life; as a result, we come to believe that a vague external force—destiny, fate, luck, or God—determines how we live, what we accomplish, and sometimes, how we die.

The approach you'll be reading about in this book is based upon the notion that at each new moment of life, a person makes choices that lead, ultimately, either to self-defeat or healthy growth. Our belief here is that all people, regardless of age, sex, income, or personal history, have within themselves an undamaged and fully operational set of mechanisms that, if allowed to function, will provide them with a good chance of achieving health, happiness, and fulfillment. At each new moment in life, people choose to behave in one of two ways: They opt for either a *self-defeating* or a *life-enhancing* behavior. Self-defeating behaviors are, essentially, any actions that separate the individual from his or her healthy core of attitudes, beliefs, feelings, and values. Life-enhancing behaviors, on the other hand, are actions or stances that either establish or affirm the individual's connection with his or her intact and life-giving essence.

This is not to say, of course, that any single self-defeating or life-enhancing behavior—choosing to have one drink too many at a party, for example, or deciding to greet a new employee at the office—will, of itself, lead directly to unhappiness or fulfillment. All of us at least occasionally choose a self-defeating behavior over a healthier alternative, and few of us go through a day without choosing at least one behavior that could lead in the direction of an enhanced life. It's extremely unlikely for the results of a single self-defeating or life-enhancing behavior to be alarming, exhilarating, or even noticeable. But a series of life-enhancing behaviors will, over time, lead to the sort of breakthrough that comes when our minds, bodies, attitudes, and actions are integrated into the wholeness that is the source of our creativity, insight, usefulness, and contentment. On the other hand, a series of choices in favor of self-defeating behaviors will, if left unchecked, bring on physical illness, nervous collapse—and, in extreme cases, even death.

We believe, in short, that at each new moment of life, an individual faces a choice between a road that ends in self-defeat and one that brings him or her closer to a breakthrough. We realize that this statement may seem dramatic, but we stand by it nonetheless. In our combined years of practice, we have time and again found ourselves faced with clients who have asked, in one form or another, the same question: "Where did I go wrong?" These clients—among them have been prostitutes, substance abusers, juvenile delinquents, and distressed military veterans, as well as people with less "advanced" difficulties—have all sought to identify the single event or choice that sent them down the road of discomfort, failure, and defeat. "If only I hadn't married Harold," such a client will say wistfully, or "I made my big mistake when I joined the Marines." Another client will tell us that she would be successful and happy had she not chosen to drop out of college; still another will tell us that his life would have been completely different had his father and mother not divorced. While we can appreciate each person's desire to simplify (and, as a result, to understand) where things have gone wrong, we have eventually had to make it clear to the client that his or her difficulty has usually resulted not from a single occurrence or decision, but rather from a series of choices and reactions linked together to form a path that leads to frustration and defeat.

Why, you might be asking, would anyone choose a behavior that would clearly lead to defeat when an alternative behavior was available? The answer to this question is simple enough to be summarized in a sentence, yet so complex that we have written this book to explain it fully. The simple answer is that for all its virtues, our culture is in many ways toxic to humans, and that the by-products of its systems and structures impose negative experiences on most people. These experiences are painful — so painful that once a person has had one, that person may well spend the remainder of his or her life attempting to avoid similar experiences. This individual lives in constant fear and at each new moment of life chooses a behavior that he or she believes will protect against additional hurt or disappointment.

But these behaviors, which may have helped the person cope with the event that led to the initial fear, are often inappropriate at new moments of life. At this point, a curious phenomenon begins to occur: behaviors intended to protect the person from whatever it is that he or she fears tend to bring on the very consequences that the person is trying to avoid. Fearing weakness, a man behaves in ways that place a tremendous burden on his physical and mental resources: hence, he is weakened. Afraid of loneliness, a woman grasps avidly at the men she meets: the men recoil from this desperation, and the woman finds herself alone. In each case, the fear of a certain consequence leads to behavior that virtually assures the consequence. This is the way in which self-defeating behaviors are born and nourished.

Note that in the last sentence, we used the word "nourished." We did so to suggest that unless self-defeating behaviors are fed by the negative experiences they create, they soon will waste away. In addition to nourishment, however, self-defeating behaviors require exercise to survive. If the person who has developed the self-defeating behavior does not practice it regularly, the behavior will atrophy and eventually wither away. It takes work to nourish and exercise a self-defeating behavior. The exhaustion or weariness often felt by people who have spent a long time on the self-defeating road is the result of this ongoing and fruitless labor.

If you doubt that it takes hard work to practice self-defeating behaviors, imagine for a moment a totally healthy, integrated human being. Now imagine how hard (and how long) this person would need to work to bring about some sort of physical or mental calamity. Or imagine how much effort this person would have to expend to deplete his or her resources to the point where he or she needed to be incarcerated in a treatment center for "rehabilitation." Here again, the terminology we use to describe the consequences of self-defeating behavior is unknowingly revealing. We speak of "massive strokes," "mental breakdowns," and "total nervous collapse." In each case, we are talking about what has happened to a person who has finally buckled beneath the strain required to practice self-defeating behaviors on a regular basis.

Fortunately, there is available to each of us an alternative to a life of struggle, disappointment, and eventual breakdown. As you might guess, this alternative is the regular practice of life-enhancing behaviors. These behaviors will not only unite you with your best (and truest) inner self but also liberate your creativity, your wisdom, and your capacity for fulfillment. To achieve this breakthrough, however, you must learn to identify, understand, and abandon your personal self-defeating behaviors. The remaining sections of this book will help you understand the following:

- *How self-defeating behaviors are born.* In this section, you'll see how the interaction between a person's life-enhancing internal systems and the by-products of the toxic culture gives birth to a typical self-defeating behavior. You'll see how this interaction shapes basic self-defeating conclusions, which, subsequently, provide fuel for the fear that keeps people locked in patterns of unhappiness and defeat.

- *Why self-defeating behaviors are perpetuated.* To be sustained over time, self-defeating behaviors need to be nourished and exercised. In the second section of this book, you'll see how and why people repeat their patterns of self-defeat. You'll discover how the conclusions people draw from hurtful experiences give rise to the fears that guide their choices at new moments of life.

- *How self-defeating behaviors are practiced.* The third section of this book provides you with a detailed picture of what happens when a person chooses a self-defeating behavior over a life-enhancing alternative. You'll see how at each new moment of life, a person must make the choice to practice a self-defeating behavior. You'll also see how this choice inevitably forces the person to pay certain prices: consequences that must be minimized and, ultimately, disowned to perpetuate the cycle of erroneous choice and self-defeat.

- *How self-defeating behaviors can be replaced.* Once you've recognized why and how you hurt yourself, you can choose to stop. But if you try to stop practicing a self-defeating behavior without a healthy alternative to replace it, you're likely to revert to your old pattern. The final section of this book suggests a step-by-step approach that you can follow to break your self-defeating patterns. It shows you how to find and practice the kinds of healthy, life-enhancing behaviors that you can use in place of the habitual techniques that lead you down the road to self-defeat and unhappiness.

Thousands of clients who have come to us have used this approach not only to correct what has been "wrong" with their lives but also to discover the energy and strength that lies untapped within them. We are confident that you, too, will be able to gain insight from these pages and to use this insight to stop hurting your hidden—yet most precious—self.

Dr. Milton R. Cudney, Ph.D.
Dr. Robert E. Hardy, Ed.D.

Part One

How
Self-Defeating
Behaviors
Are Born

*After years of hard work, a successful businessman
finally took an ocean cruise he had been dreaming of
his entire life. He spent his days walking the deck of the
huge ocean liner, smelling the fresh sea air and lifting
his eyes to contemplate the vast and clear horizon. One
day, however, a violent storm blew up suddenly. Before
the man could take shelter, a blast of wind blew him
against the deck railing. A second gale caught him
before he could gain his balance, and he tumbled over
the top of the railing. As he fell overboard, though, he
reached out to grab something—anything—he could
hang onto. And luckily, he caught the tine of a heavy
anchor suspended from a link chain on the side of the
ship. He grasped at the anchor with both hands and
squeezed its tines until his knuckles turned white. As the
storm winds buffeted him from side to side, the man
clung to the anchor, holding on for dear life. . . .*

Chapter 1

What Is a
Self-Defeating Behavior?

Lynn was visibly distraught. Only a few months past her thirty-second birthday when she first visited our office, she looked at least ten years older, mostly because of the frown lines that seemed cut into her forehead and the tight set of her mouth. A slightly overweight woman, she wore an expensive-looking and conservatively tailored business suit. She told us that she was an office manager at a regional insurance firm, adding somewhat huffily that the company considered her a "top performer."

Why, we asked, had she come to see us?

"Because I have no life," she said grimly.

"Are you saying that your energy level is low?" we asked.

"That, too," Lynn replied. "But what I really mean is what I said: *I have no life.* I get up in the morning and I go to work. Then I come home, watch television for a few hours, and go to bed. That's what I do every day, week after week, month after month, year after year: work, eat, sleep. And if I didn't have to support myself, I probably wouldn't work, so that would leave food and sleep. And, of course, the TV."

We asked if she had friends or family. "No family," she replied. "I was an only child, and my parents are dead." Here Lynn paused to light a cigarette, which she smoked while formulating the rest of her answer to our question. "And as for friends," she said after a few moments, "well, I don't have many of them, either. None, really. There are a few women at work I go to lunch with, but they're married and have kids, which doesn't give them time to socialize outside the office. There's Ingrid, I suppose," Lynn continued. "She's single, but she claims she's allergic to cigarette smoke. Going out with her is more trouble than it's worth."

It's difficult to deal with a complaint as general as Lynn's seemed to be, so we moved on to ask her to describe in detail a typical day in her life. "They're all pretty much the same," she replied, "but, well, there was last Friday. . . . " On that day, as Lynn explained, her supervisor had complimented her on a project that her department had recently completed. But the elation she experienced upon hearing this praise dissipated soon enough. Driving home from her office, she felt a sadness creep over her, a mood she linked with the realization that she faced another Friday evening—and, worse yet, an entire weekend—alone and with nothing to do. To combat her despondency, she sought out a familiar remedy: she stopped at a convenience store, where she bought enough candy, snacks, and cigarettes to sustain her through another evening in front of the television.

At this point we sensed that the lack of life that Lynn had justifiably been complaining about was nothing more and nothing less than an ongoing sequence of self-defeating behaviors. Her life had become an arduous and repetitive ordeal—so much so that she felt best when she felt nothing at all. And like any bright and sensitive person in a similar circumstance, she had felt uncomfortable with this situation—enough so that she had sought help in an attempt to find out what she was doing wrong.

The Big Question

In our years of practice, we have come to notice that many of our clients make statements and display attitudes similar to Lynn's. The refrain we've heard most often from the people we work with goes something like this: "I keep hurting myself, but I don't understand why." We have heard these words so often that we've concluded that despite differences in age, sex, and financial circumstances, most of the people who come to us share a common problem. They simply are locked into the habit of making choices that do not work for them. Acting on these misguided choices, they say or do things that virtually guarantee dissatisfaction and unhappiness. These people (and millions like them) are caught in a cycle of *self-defeating behavior* and feel that they are doomed to lives of failure, misery, and disappointment.

What, exactly, is a self-defeating behavior? On the surface, it would seem that we could categorize as self-defeating any attitude or gesture that thwarts a person's healthy desire for love, acceptance, fulfillment, or tranquillity. And while it is true that self-defeating behaviors effectively distort the individual's best and healthiest response to a new moment of life, they have another key characteristic that distinguishes them from other behaviors:

> A true self-defeating behavior is an action or attitude that *once worked to help an individual cope with a hurtful experience* but that now works against the individual to keep him or her from responding to new moments of life in a healthy way.

When attempting to identify and eliminate your own self-defeating behaviors, it's extremely important to keep this definition in mind: to be truly self-defeating, a behavior must have worked for you at one point or another in your life—or, at least, you believed it worked for you. Why is this so? Because, we believe, human beings are profoundly rational creatures. Uncontaminated by false conclusions (which, as you'll see, are the toxic by-products of our culture), they will respond in a healthy and rational way to any situation or circumstance. This innate coping mechanism will work until, one day, an unfamiliar and threatening situation arises. At this point, people will instinctively do whatever is required to eliminate the threat and maintain equilibrium.

When an individual manages to cope successfully with a threat, the behavior that he or she has used to deal with it will become imprinted within that person's memory. Because the behavior has worked to eliminate a threat, it is stored within the individual's memory as an effective means of dealing with other threatening situations. Each time the individual encounters a situation that is unfamiliar or ominous, he or she will react with the behavior that tamed the original threat. But because the new situations often bear only faint or superficial resemblances to the original hurtful experience, the behavior that the individual chooses will almost always be inappropriate. The individual's logic is still working flawlessly—which, paradoxically, leads him or her to repeat time and again a behavior that simply doesn't work.

Some Common Self-Defeating Behaviors

The negative and counterproductive thoughts and actions that we refer to as self-defeating behaviors appear in many forms. Some of these forms do not seem to define a particular type of behavior at all but seem instead to point to character traits, moods, or attitudes. Do not be misled, however: all self-defeating behaviors, including those listed below, are chosen and practiced responses to new moments of life. Below we've listed some of the more common behaviors that fall into this category:

- Procrastination
- Defensiveness
- Abuse of alcohol and other substances
- Depression
- Worrying
- Compulsive/ritualistic actions
- Alienating
- Shyness
- Overeating
- Smoking
- Hostility
- Suspiciousness
- Impotence/frigidity
- Perfectionism

Although this list is far from comprehensive, we'd venture to guess that the great majority of people practice at least one of the behaviors we've mentioned. If you see on the list any behavior that you use to defeat yourself, you need to look into how you acquired the behavior and what you can do to replace it or, at the very least, to reduce its control over your life.

From Momentary Solace to Enduring Malady

How are self-defeating behaviors acquired and nourished? The conversation that occurred near the end of our first meeting with Lynn sheds considerable light on these insidious processes. Once it became clear that her primary complaint had to do with the oppressive loneliness she experienced, we chose to focus on this particular aspect of the existence she so wanted to escape.

"Lynn, why are you alone?" we asked.

Before responding, Lynn began to laugh: a low, hesitant chuckle undercut by a deepening of the frown lines that crossed her forehead. "That's easy," she said. "It's because I'm . . . you know . . . fat."

We quickly pointed out that while she was somewhat overweight, her categorization of herself as "fat" was, in truth, a demeaning exaggeration. We added that in light of the fact that many heavy people enjoy happy and active lives, her physical size was probably not the sole source of her discomfort. Then we repeated our question. Why, we asked, was she so alone in the world?

Now Lynn became defensive. "Look, I don't see where this is going," she complained. "Why am I alone? Who knows? I've never been much of a socialite, if you want to know the truth. I'm not one for small talk. I like to take care of business, then move on. It's just the way I am."

"Were you always that way?" we asked.

"For as long as I can remember," she replied a little sadly. "You know, people have these ideas of how a woman should act. And I guess I've never been able to act that way . . . to live up to stereotypes and expectations."

Because our meeting was nearing its conclusion, we explained to Lynn that neither we nor she could do much to change people's expectations. We should focus, we told her, on the steps that she could take to learn to feel comfortable with her place in the world. We then gave her an assignment. We asked her to think of a time in her life when she felt relatively happy and productive, and to try to remember what happened to change her view of herself and the world.

At the start of our next session, we brought this matter up immediately. Initially, Lynn seemed unwilling to talk about her past, claiming she'd been too busy at work to brood over what she termed "ancient history." But then, almost as an afterthought, she mentioned that she hadn't always been alone and aloof. "Back in my junior high days, I was outgoing almost to a fault," she said. "I joined clubs, had all sorts of friends, even got involved in student government. I was busy all the time, it seemed."

"When did things change for you?" we asked.

"I'm not sure," Lynn replied. "But by the time I got to high school, everything was different. We all grew up, I guess. The kids I hung around with, I mean. All of a sudden we were in this school with a bunch of strangers . . . it was a nightmare. All that mattered was how you looked, who you knew, how much money you had. Ambition and brains didn't seem to count for much."

"How about the clubs you belonged to? And your participation in student government? Did you stay with that through your high school years?"

"No," Lynn said. "I sort of burned out on all that, I guess. There was this election for student council treasurer when I was in the ninth grade . . . I ran, and I lost."

We asked Lynn to talk more about this episode. And talk she did: for the first time, she seemed to speak spontaneously and with feeling. She told us that she'd felt confident that she'd win the election, even after learning that her opponent would be the daughter of a prominent school board official. She'd had reason to feel confident; all of her numerous friends had told her she was by far the better qualified of the two candidates. Still, she campaigned vigorously; she asked classmates for their support, and they assured her they'd vote for her. So on the Friday afternoon when the election results were announced, Lynn felt the weight of the world crash down on her. She'd lost by nearly a two-to-one margin. She fled her sixth-period class in tears and left the school immediately, wanting never to return.

For the next two hours she wandered alone on the streets of her neighborhood, ducking behind cars and buildings to avoid contact with anyone who might have heard of her humiliation. She didn't want to go home and admit to her parents that she'd failed to win the election, and because she no longer trusted her friends — most of whom, she believed, had double-crossed her and voted for her opponent—she found herself with no place to go and no one to talk to. Eventually she ended up two miles from her home, standing in front of a drugstore. By then it was almost dark, so she went into the store and took a seat at the soda fountain—just to kill time, she told herself. Then she ordered a double chocolate malted, and, as she drank it, she felt its sweetness flow into her, filling the desolate void that losing the election had created. By the time she was finished, she felt better, calmer, and once again able to deal with the world. She went to a pay phone and called her mother for a ride home.

"That's quite a story," we told Lynn when she had finished. "Did it give you any sense of how you developed your fondness for sweets and snacks?"

"Oh, you mean that I eat to fill the emptiness I feel?" she replied derisively. "I mean, really! That's such a cliché."

"It's not that simple," we explained. "Yes, it is possible that you use junk food—and maybe cigarettes, too—as a substitute for friends and family, and for the emotional and intellectual stimulation that others can provide. But what seems more significant is that you seem to mistrust the world and all that it offers. You relate to it only on your own terms, then retreat from it before it can do you harm.

"Besides," we added, "it's not written anywhere that self-defeating behaviors have to be complex, clever, or original. All they really have to be is temporarily effective."

The Nature of Self-Defeating Behaviors

Those of us who practice self-defeating behaviors (and rest assured, most of us do) can learn much from Lynn's experiences. From our initial meetings with her, we were able to discern that she practiced on a regular basis at least six self-defeating behaviors: depression, overeating, smoking, defensiveness, hostility, and suspiciousness. Although at first this might seem like an extraordinary degree of counterproductive thought and action, we've found behavior patterns like Lynn's to be fairly typical. Whether we're aware of it or not, the majority of us—and here we are talking about allegedly "normal" people, not only those who have been labeled as "losers," "malcontents," "chronic failures," or, most unfortunately, "mentally ill"—act and think destructively several times a day. Repeatedly we react inappropriately to new moments of life, then wonder why happiness and success elude us.

Lynn's story reveals a good deal about what a self-defeating behavior is and why this sort of behavior is destructive. Like the mutable creatures in science-fiction and horror movies, self-defeating behaviors are deceptive. We find them in one form, and they appear to be our friends. Only later do they reveal themselves as harmful and devious intruders. And when this time comes—when, if you will, a self-defeating behavior finally shows its teeth—we want to flee or cry out for help. If we understand the true nature of self-defeating behaviors, however, we can learn to spot and get rid of them before they can do us harm. But to do this, we need to be aware of the general characteristics that all self-defeating behaviors share.

We've already mentioned the first of these characteristics: *at one point or another, a self-defeating behavior works to help an individual deal with a hurtful or threatening situation.* Looking at Lynn's situation, we can see that this is true. When her loss in the student election violated and threatened her healthy inner self, she sought solace in any form available to her. She found it by withdrawing from others and indulging in sweet, temporarily satisfying snacks—and, later in life, in the cigarettes she began to smoke in an attempt to control her weight. Withdrawal, overeating, and smoking became her means of dealing with psychic discomfort. Each of these techniques helped her to maintain a tenuous emotional equilibrium; they did nothing, however, to help her achieve any sort of stable peace of mind. None of Lynn's techniques constituted a *life-enhancing behavior* that she could have used to cope during uncomfortable moments of life.

This last point leads us to the second characteristic that is common to all self-defeating behaviors: although a self-defeating behavior at one point or another works to help the individual cope with a threat, *it is never the best behavior that could be used in a particular situation.* Let's face it: when she fled her school in tears on that Friday afternoon, Lynn did not make the wisest behavioral choice available to her. When she learned that she'd lost the election, she could, for example, have sought out and congratulated the winner, a gesture that might have bolstered her damaged self-esteem. To deal with the pain she was feeling, she could have talked to her friends, her parents, or a school counselor, thereby avoiding the danger that arises whenever strong and legitimate emotions are masked or buried. In addition to these measures, she might also have used her experience to test some of the faulty beliefs she apparently harbored: that life is always "fair," that others invariably behave honorably, and that as a "good" person she had a right to expect never to be hurt or disappointed. As we'll discuss later, these beliefs—we call them the *sweet poisons* inadvertently exuded by an essentially toxic culture—were at the core of her subsequent self-defeating actions. Her loss in the election was merely a triggering event.

The third (and perhaps the most insidious) characteristic of a self-defeating behavior is that, eventually, *it guarantees the consequences that the individual is trying to avoid in practicing it.* Again, Lynn's example is instructive. Having given of her healthy inner self, she ended up hurt and apparently betrayed. At that point she formulated a faulty behavioral conclusion, deciding, in effect, that if she withheld her healthy responses and acted instead in a destructive way, she'd be able to avoid the pain of rejection. When we asked her why she ran from the school that afternoon, she told us that she feared that no one would want to talk to her following her defeat. She went on to reveal that during her adolescent years, her single greatest fear was that she'd be ostracized, exiled from the world of happy and healthy people. Yet over the years that followed her defeat in the election, this is the very consequence that her behavior guaranteed. By her own admission, her popularity waned in high school: she put on weight, became increasingly suspicious and withdrawn, and developed a hostile personal style to keep others from getting close enough to betray or otherwise harm her. These behaviors persisted during her college years, when the demands of higher education exacerbated her sense of her own brittleness, inferiority, and isolation from others. And finally, she continued to practice her self-defeating behaviors in the workplace, thereby earning the reputation of a brusque, efficient, and hard-shelled administrator: a person who achieved results but who was something less than likable. As a result, she ended up in our office, complaining of loneliness, emptiness, and virtual isolation from the bustling sort of life she believed that other people enjoyed. She did not realize, however, that the self-defeating thoughts and actions she began to nurture as a means of warding off rejection virtually guaranteed that her worst fears would be realized.

As you read this book and attempt to identify the ways in which you are hurting yourself, keep this notion in mind. Look for the ways in which the people you'll meet eventually found themselves faced with precisely the consequences they tried to circumvent by way of self-defeating thoughts and actions. Above all, never lose sight of the fact that self-defeating behaviors are both dangerous and deceptive. They come into your life as apparent friends who offer comfort and protection in moments of distress. They help you through these threatening moments, and for this you are grateful — so grateful that you come to believe that you cannot live without their devious company. Sooner or later, though, these behaviors reveal their true nature. At that point, you must face the realization that your self-defeating behaviors have been unworthy companions and untrustworthy guides. The comfort that these behaviors offer is false. If you rely upon them too long, they will lead you away from the road of health, growth, and life. Self-defeating behaviors will, in the end, take you precisely where you didn't want to go.

Chapter 2

Your Life Systems

A few years ago, we worked for an extended period with a client whom we will here call Rachel. A slim, attractive professional woman, Rachel came to us because, she said, she was having trouble during her free hours. During the week, she went to her job and per-formed effectively—and, at times, even superbly. She performed her tasks and socialized with her co-workers; she earned raises and pro-motions. Off the job, however, Rachel was, in her own words, "a completely different person." She spent her evenings and weekends alone in her apartment, where she wrote letters that were never mailed, organized and reorganized her possessions and personal papers, and scrubbed and vacuumed her floors repeatedly. At thirty-one, Rachel had never been on a date with a man. Nor had she ever had—or, she claimed, even wanted to have—a sexual experience with either a man or a woman.

Several months of counseling did little to change this situation. Finally, in a fit of frustration, Rachel came to us and said she had discovered the source of her difficulty. "The other day, my mother told me that she has been frigid all her life," Rachel announced. "She said that my aunt is frigid, too. So I guess I inherited this thing from the women on my mother's side. It's in our blood."

We were quick to assure Rachel that her compulsive behavior during her free hours and her apparent lack of any sexual appetite had less to do with any inborn or genetic trait than with the set of aberrant and self-defeating behaviors she had learned and main-tained to cope with the fear of where her sexuality might lead her. Some of these behaviors, we conceded, may have had their origins in her family life. It was likely, we said, that Rachel might have learned certain behaviors from her mother or her aunt, both of whom might have acquired the behaviors from their own mothers. But we would not agree that any of Rachel's difficulties were evidence of a genetic disposition toward sexual dysfunction.

Nevertheless, Rachel's willingness to attribute her problems to genetics or "bad blood" made us think about our own theory of why people choose self-defeating behaviors over healthier alternatives. We had been aware for some time, of course, that this theory stood in direct conflict with much of the psychological, philosophical, and religious thinking that has shaped Western culture. For centuries, this culture has been largely grounded on the belief that human beings are inherently flawed and disposed toward evil. Traditional Christianity, for example, is based on the notion that humans are conceived in sin, are born into evil, and can be redeemed only through confession, repentance, and self-denial. Sigmund Freud, whose theories have had a profound influence on the way in which we view our world, believed, essentially, that anatomy is destiny— that each person is stamped at birth with indelible psychic and biological tendencies that must eventually surface and be acted upon. While we, as perceptual psychologists, could not endorse these views, we knew that we needed to take them into account and to propose a viable alternative. We needed, in other words, to develop an alternative to the theories and beliefs that condemned human beings to lives of misery, hopelessness, and self-defeat.

It was around this time that we became aware of the theories of Professor Ross L. Mooney. Professor Mooney, who spent much of his career attempting to identify the sources of growth and creativity, developed a simple but elegant model of how life renews, nourishes, and propagates itself. To describe this model, Professor Mooney chose the metaphor of a vast and continuous circulatory system through which feelings, thoughts, and actions are continuously exchanged and processed. We have adapted Mooney's metaphor of a *life circulatory system* as a basis for our theories of how and why people choose either self-defeating or winning behaviors in new moments of life.

The Life Circulatory System

Professor Mooney, in his article "Evaluation in Higher Education," depicted the relationship between individuals and their culture as a pair of interrelated infinity symbols.* To illustrate this relationship, we will use an adaptation of Mooney's original model:

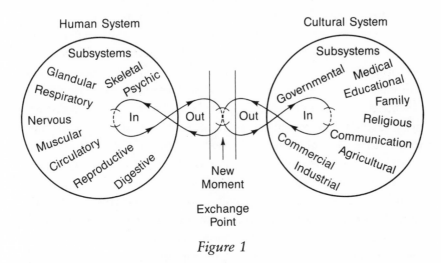

Figure 1

In looking at the model, you'll notice that the circle on the left depicts the individual's human system, while the circle on the right represents the cultural system within which he or she functions. The extended infinity symbols within each circle trace the path along which messages and actions travel from the individual to the culture, and vice versa. The point at which the two infinity symbols intersect represents a new moment of life: a juncture where the individual and his or her culture exchange information and gestures, or requests and responses. Each message or action that is transmitted through this juncture is, in turn, processed within either the human system or the cultural system.

You'll notice, however, that within both the human and the cultural system, there are several *subsystems*. The role of each of these subsystems is to process what is received at the new moment of life. But because the human system and its cultural counterpart are linked at the new moment, the function of each internal subsystem

---

*See Ross L. Mooney, "Evaluation in Higher Education," an address reported in the Bulletin for the Michigan Association of Colleges and Universities for its Fifth Annual Conference (November, 1967).

affects not only its own larger system and subsystems *but also the opposite system*. This concept will play an important role in our discussion of how a cycle of self-defeating behavior is enacted.

To see more clearly how these relationships work, let's consider a relatively simple example. Within the system of a human infant, the role of the skeletal subsystem is to provide structure for the body. To perform this function, the skeletal subsystem needs calcium so that its individual bones can grow in both size and strength. The skeletal system, therefore, sends a message to the digestive subsystem—which, in turn, sends the message to the psychic subsystem. As a result of these interactions, the infant feels hunger and cries out to be fed. At this point, the message moves from the infant's inner system to the cultural system. A representative of this system—usually the child's mother or father—processes this message, and the infant is fed the milk that fulfills the skeletal subsystem's request for calcium.

Suppose, however, that the dairy farmers of a particular culture develop an economical processing technique that reduces the cost of a carton of milk but that also removes most of the calcium from the product. If, over an extended period of time, the infants who function within the culture were fed this calcium-deficient milk, an epidemic of the disease known as rickets could conceivably spread through the culture. The skeletal subsystem within each infant would be unable to function properly; its bones would warp and grow brittle. The parents of the infants affected by the disease would, no doubt, notice its symptoms and report them to the medical subsystem within the larger cultural system. When enough cases of rickets had been brought to the attention of the medical subsystem, it would take action (in conjunction, probably, with the governmental subsystem) to inform the agricultural subsystem—that is, the dairy farmers—that it had better find a new way of processing the milk it produced.

In one way or another, each subsystem within the human and cultural systems transmits its messages to several or all of the other subsystems. This intricate and powerful life circulatory system enables life to flourish and reproduce itself. But as we'll discuss shortly, the power of this marvelous system can work toward bad ends as well as good. When toxic or inappropriate messages or material enter the system, the consequences can be disastrous for both the individual and the culture.

We Are Born Whole and Sound

Before we move on to look at how the interaction between an individual and a culture can result in either a self-defeating or a winning behavior, we need to pause for a moment and look at only the left half of the life circulatory system. If we were to pull our representation of this human system out of its larger context, it would look like this:

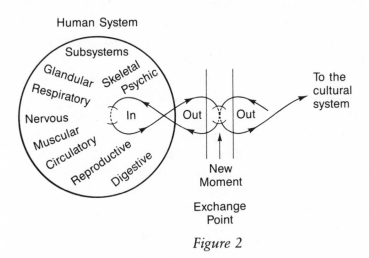

Figure 2

When a healthy human being—that is, an individual who comes into the world free of birth defects or damage caused by improper prenatal care—is born, his or her subsystems are fully functional. These subsystems are poised to respond appropriately and naturally to any circumstance the new human being encounters; they are prepared to do what is right and necessary if the individual is to grow and prosper.

As we illustrated earlier, each of the subsystems is dependent on one or more of its counterparts. No single subsystem can do its work properly without support and assistance from the other subsystems. When, for example, the organs that make up the digestive subsystem require oxygen to survive, they send a message via the nervous subsystem to the circulatory subsystem. The circulatory subsystem, in turn, sends oxygen-rich blood to each organ. In order to obtain the required oxygen, however, the circulatory subsystem must send a request—again, via the nervous subsystem—to the respiratory subsystem. At this point, the respiratory subsystem uses the nervous subsystem to tell its organs to perform their functions. The lungs expand and contract. The individual breathes, and as oxygen is drawn into the body, the requirements of all the subsystems are met.

This, then, is how life and health are maintained. As long as each subsystem sends and receives the appropriate messages, performs its many functions, and has its requirements met, the larger human system remains in harmony with itself. It fulfills its purposes in the universal scheme; it is inspired to create, to grow, and to reproduce itself.

In a perfect world, this state of equilibrium would always be maintained; each subsystem would have all its requirements met appropriately and immediately. As we well know, however, our world is far from perfect. At some point or another, one of our internal subsystems will issue a request, and the response to that request will be unsatisfactory, or perhaps even toxic. If, for example, an infant cries out for food and, in response, is fed sawdust, the infant's internal subsystems will reject the toxic material through the mechanism of regurgitation. These subsystems are prepared to cope with unsatisfactory responses to their requests. They will do whatever is required to keep the infant healthy and to ensure its growth.

Unless it is overwhelmed by massive or repeated assaults or traumas, the human system will remain perfectly functional until the natural consequences of aging wear out one or more of its subsystems. This system is programmed at birth to keep human beings alive, well, and at peace with themselves. Only through an insidious process of reprogramming can the human system be forced to perform in a way that is contrary to its original and natural purpose. And only through the workings of the psychic subsystem can this sort of reprogramming be accomplished.

The Special Nature of the Psychic Subsystem

Each subsystem within the larger human system performs numerous functions and is involved in a set of complex and interdependent relationships with its counterparts. For this reason, the great majority of the functions of each human subsystem are automated within the nervous subsystem. If this were not the case, we would need to make conscious decisions to breathe, to make our hearts beat, to manufacture new cells, and so on. Our conscious minds would be constantly occupied with the chore of telling our bodies how to function. Under these conditions, none of us would survive for long. Our minds simply could not work fast enough to tell our bodies how to operate.

One of our human subsystems, however, includes a conscious component. This, of course, is the *psychic subsystem*. Our psychic subsystem is, in effect, the conscious monitor of all the other human subsystems. The psychic subsystem enables us to bring messages from the other human subsystems and the cultural system to the level of consciousness. At this level, we make choices and decisions. These choices and decisions, in turn, reconcile the requirements of the other human subsystems with the messages that are sent by the cultural system.

Because it bears most of the responsibility for our ongoing behavior, the psychic subsystem — or, more accurately, its conscious component — is tremendously busy. Fortunately, the psychic subsystem includes additional components that perform certain routine tasks for the conscious component. In addition to its conscious component, each person's psychic subsystem includes a preconscious and an unconscious component. The relationship of these two components to the conscious component of the psychic subsystem can be represented like this:

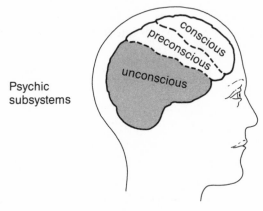

Psychic subsystems

Figure 3

The conscious component of the psychic subsystem, as we mentioned earlier, makes conscious decisions and choices. The *unconscious* component of the psychic subsystem, on the other hand, is responsible for the unconscious choices and decisions we make. The *preconscious* component acts as a mediator between the conscious and unconscious components. It processes ideas, images, and connections that have not yet been brought to the light of consciousness. People most often experience the workings of the preconscious component immediately before going to sleep or after waking up, or during meditation or while under hypnosis.

How does the unconscious system work? The process begins when the conscious component finds itself too busy to deal with all the choices and decisions it needs to make. At this point, the conscious component sorts through the millions of choices it faces and assigns the more basic and repetitive choices to the unconscious component. Because the conscious component is continuously being asked to make higher-level choices, it continuously assigns lower-level choices to the unconscious component.

Say, for example, that while driving home from work, you are trying to decide whether or not to make a major financial investment. While the conscious component of your psychic subsystem is processing all the information surrounding this decision, the unconscious component of the same subsystem is making the decision to apply pressure to the brakes of your car when you approach a red light. In this way, the unconscious component enables the conscious component to deal with complex choices that involve new information, new messages, and analytical thought. It also retrieves and brings to the level of consciousness information thought to be buried or forgotten, and in this way is the source of insight and inspiration.

This sophisticated and efficient division of labor that enables us to solve problems and perform complicated tasks. (If—as sometimes happens—the conscious component of your psychic subsystem were preoccupied with such basic and routine choices as whether to sit or stand, or fold your arms or put your hands in your pocket, then you would find it difficult to concentrate on solving an algebraic equation or on writing a letter.) When the conscious and unconscious components of your psychic subsystem are working hand in hand, your psychic subsystem operates at the height of its considerable power. This power, however, can work either for or against an individual. When faulty choices based on toxic input are assigned by the conscious component to its unconscious counterpart, a pattern of unhappiness and self-defeat is readily established.

A Dangerous Notion

For all its complexity, the psychic subsystem operates on the same principle as do the other human subsystems. It sends out a request or message, receives messages or material from the cultural system, and then moves on to the next new moment of life. This exchange works beautifully—as long as the messages or material the cultural system sends to the individual are healthy and appropriate. As we well know, however, this is not always the case. Our cultural system and its representatives send out numerous messages that are toxic to individuals. And once one of these toxic messages enters an individual's human system, a potentially disastrous cycle is initiated.

When toxic material enters an individual's human system, the subsystems within the larger system do what they can to expel or adapt to the intrusion. Our physical subsystems, such as the digestive and respiratory systems, have various ways of dealing with toxic input: coughing, regurgitation, fainting, and so on. Like these physical subsystems, our psychic subsystem does its best to deal with threatening intrusions. The mechanisms that the psychic subsystem uses to deal with toxic input, though more sophisticated than coughing, sneezing, or passing out, can pose a considerable threat to our overall well-being.

If, at a new moment of life, our psychic subsystem receives from the culture a message that is deemed to be threatening, a state of internal tension results. The psychic subsystem recognizes that this tension is not healthy, so it does whatever is necessary to reduce the tension as soon as possible. Almost always, the tension is reduced or eliminated. At the same time, however, an extremely dangerous notion is imprinted within the individual's psychic subsystem. Simply put, this notion goes as follows:

> It is not good enough to respond to the outside world, or to make requests of it, in a natural and healthy way. Instead, I must do

(whatever reduced the tension) whenever I encounter a threatening situation. What I need to do is to put a buffer between my healthy inner self and the toxic world.

To make matters worse, the busy conscious component of the person's psychic subsystem almost immediately shares this notion with its unconscious counterpart. Hence, the choice to do whatever it was that initially reduced the person's internal tension becomes the responsibility of the unconscious component. A self-defeating behavior is born — often without the conscious awareness of the person who gave birth to it.

"It Just Came Naturally"

Once a choice to behave in a self-defeating way has been delegated to the unconscious component of our psychic subsystem, the behavior starts to seem natural and automatic. The very fact that the choice is made on an unconscious level causes people to believe that the resulting pattern of self-defeat is simply part of their nature. "I never chose not to be sexual," complained Rachel, the woman we mentioned at the beginning of this chapter. "It never occurred to me that I was different until I got older and started hearing about all these terrible urges other people were constantly fighting with."

From the time we met Rachel, however, we were convinced that she had, in fact, learned to deny her sexuality through a series of increasingly sophisticated self-defeating behaviors. During one of our meetings with her, she described an event that took place when she was fourteen years old, an age at which many of us first experience and need to deal with our sexuality. Rachel was quite attracted to a boy in one of her classes at school. Actually, she was more than attracted to him; she developed a full-blown adolescent crush on him, and she wanted him to return her feelings.

When the boy did not overtly demonstrate any special feelings toward her, Rachel decided to take a risk. She composed a long, florid note to him; she told the boy that she loved him and wanted him to love her, too. She shoved the note through a slot in his locker and waited for him to respond.

For a few days, nothing happened. Then, a week or so after she delivered the note, Rachel walked past the boy and a group of his friends in the hall.

"Hey, Rachel," the boy called out, "I got your note."

Rachel paused and looked down at the floor, hoping that the boy would express some sort of affection for her.

"You can forget it," the boy continued, while his friends giggled and poked at him. "I mean, you're really ugly!"

The pain and humiliation Rachel felt at that moment came back to her when she described the incident during one of our sessions. Her voice broke as she came to the end of the story; her cheeks reddened, and she even shed a few tears. "I just don't know how or why anyone could be so cruel," she said. "He could have just ignored me, or told me privately that he didn't want to be my boyfriend."

We asked Rachel how she dealt with the boy after the incident. "Oh, I just shut him out completely," she said. "I acted as if he didn't even exist. And it wasn't just him I wanted to hurt—it was all the boys in the school. I turned into this quiet, aloof, and snotty kid who did well in school and didn't go on dates. It just came naturally for me."

At this point, it became clear to us that Rachel's healthy human system, in an attempt to deal with the internal tension she felt over being rejected by the boy, had chanced upon a temporarily effective behavior: an aloof withdrawal from members of the opposite sex. In responding to the hurt of the rejection, her conscious mind had come to the conclusion that if she pretended not to need the affection and attention of others, then she could not be hurt. The resultant behaviors—a superior distancing of herself from others, combined with an almost compulsive concern over her schoolwork —served, in effect, to short-circuit the connection between her reproductive subsystem (the source of sexual desire) and her other subsystems.

In one sense, these behaviors worked: Rachel was never again rejected or scorned by a boy or, later, a man. But in another sense, Rachel's self-defeating behaviors guaranteed that her primary fear would be realized: she would be alone and cut off from her sexuality.

Her aloofness and feigned superiority led her, at the age of thirty-one, to spend her leisure time alone and isolated, performing empty rituals to keep herself busy and invulnerable to pain.

Fortunately, we were able to show Rachel how she *chose* the behaviors that led to her current unhappiness. We showed her, too, that now that she was aware of her choices, she could choose different behaviors—attitudes or actions that could reverse completely some of the results of her self-defeating choices. Perhaps most important, we were able to convince Rachel that she was not condemned by some dubious genetic accident to a life devoid of intimacy or purpose.

We do not—and let us repeat the point here for emphasis—believe that any human being comes into the world programmed for a life of discontent, suffering, and disappointment. Nor do we believe that any human, for reasons of self-preservation or simple perversity, chooses without cause or motivation to adopt a self-defeating behavior. Before a person can choose a self-defeating behavior over a healthier alternative, some sort of toxic input from the cultural system must work its way into the individual's human system. And as we will discuss in the next chapter, toxic input from our culture is a plentiful commodity—so plentiful that each of us is guaranteed more than his or her share.

Chapter 3

The Toxic Culture

Our culture has performed wondrous feats. It has built schools, roads, and churches. It has developed a form of government that administers effectively and (more or less) fairly to the needs of vast numbers of people. It has brought about technological and medical advances that were undreamed of at the start of this century and has linked itself to the rest of the world via an intricate communications network. No culture in the history of the world has provided as many benefits to as many people as our culture has. We are, for the most part, adequately sheltered, well fed, and properly educated. People from other cultures look at us with envy. From their perspective, we all should be happy and contented.

For all of its virtues, however, our culture virtually guarantees that we will develop and practice self-defeating behaviors. In a culture where food is abundant, for example, some young women willingly choose to starve themselves. In a land of economic opportunity, millions choose to do nothing and must be sustained by our welfare, penal, and mental health systems. Why is this so? The answer lies in the very nature of our cultural system. It is made up of huge and powerful subsystems, each of which has its own functions and goals. To do their work, these subsystems function as efficiently, tirelessly, and indiscriminately as a vast, throbbing machine. And like many machines, our cultural subsystems produce toxic waste materials. Just as internal-combustion engines produce exhaust fumes that can poison living organisms, or nuclear plants generate deadly radioactive waste, our cultural subsystems send out toxic messages that eventually enter our human systems. These toxic by-products of our culture are the ultimate sources of self-defeating behaviors.

The Cultural System Versus the Human System

To see how the cultural system pollutes our individual human systems and creates self-defeating behaviors, let's return for a moment to a part of our diagram of the life circulatory system.

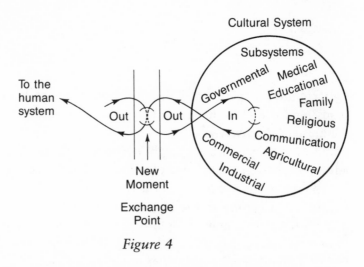

Figure 4

At a new moment of life, an individual's human system interacts and exchanges information with the cultural system. As long as this information is healthy for the individual, he or she will maintain equilibrium without resorting to a self-defeating attitude or action. When, however, an individual receives from the culture a message that is threatening or toxic, he or she is inevitably drawn into a cycle of self-defeat.

Why, you might ask, would the cultural system want to send out toxic messages to the individuals who interact with it? The answer is that it doesn't, any more than a gasoline engine "wants" to send noxious carbon monoxide into the lungs of people in its vicinity. In terms of good and evil, or morality and immorality, the cultural system and its subsystems are, essentially, neutral. When they are established, these systems are given a complex but monolithic task to perform; they are directed, for example, to educate the population, or to regulate the exchange of goods and services within the culture. *The sole concern of any cultural subsystem, therefore, is to accomplish the task it has been assigned and, in so doing, to per-*

petuate itself. In pursuit of this end, cultural subsystems will do whatever is necessary to accomplish the assigned task: they will displace people from their homes, label people as sick or inferior, or even wage war. These subsystems, which were intended to serve people, in many cases end up serving only themselves and the tasks to which they are unfailingly loyal.

Think for a moment about the educational subsystem within our larger cultural system. The task that has been assigned to this subsystem is to educate the population so that people might fill jobs, read signs and signals, and pay bills and taxes. The fundamental purpose of the educational subsystem, therefore, is to bring as many people as possible to the minimal level of literacy that the culture requires. Because even this apparently limited task is, in reality, a tremendous undertaking, the educational subsystem has found it necessary to adopt across-the-board standards and to prescribe, in effect, a way of thinking that will enable individuals to achieve those standards. The educational subsystem hasn't the time or resources to analyze each individual's thought processes and personal history for the purpose of designing a program of learning that meets the person's unique needs. It simply decides in advance what the needs are and meets these assumed needs as best it can.

In terms of accomplishing its assigned task, the educational subsystem is, by and large, successful. But in achieving this success, it generates numerous by-products that are toxic to people. Individuals who do not, for whatever reasons, answer standardized questions in the prescribed way are labeled "slow learners," "learning disabled," "disturbed," or, unfortunately, "dumb." When the educational subsystem communicates these toxic messages to persons who have been unable to fit into its prescribed program, they must find a way to cope with the implied notion that they are less valuable to the culture than are their friends or siblings. All too often, these individuals choose a self-defeating behavior and enter a cycle of despair that may never end.

More Toxic Messages

As we noted earlier, the nature of our cultural system causes it to generate a limitless flow of hazardous messages. In a very real sense, this means that we as individuals suffer so that our cultural system might continue to live in the manner to which it has become accustomed. During much of its evolution, our cultural system has been focused on the accomplishment of such monumental tasks as the building of a civilization out of a wilderness, the creation of an industrial network, and the establishment of an economic position in the world. The values that led most directly to these results—an emphasis on hard work, competition, self-denial, and personal sacrifice—have not necessarily been in harmony with the best interests of living and growing human beings.

These values have persisted to the present day, when we no longer are faced with the task of building a civilization from scratch. In this sense, they may have outlived some of their usefulness. But they are still with us, and their toxic fallout continues to flow from the cultural system into each of our human systems. To get an idea of the range and number of toxic messages that individuals regularly receive from the cultural system and its subsystems, consider this list:

Toxic Message	Source
"To remain pure and worthy of blessing, you must deny your sexuality."	Religious subsystem
"There is only one way of solving a problem or finding the truth."	Educational subsystem
"It's a good idea to borrow money to buy things you can't afford."	Financial subsystem
"Unless you are a certain height and weight, with a certain set of facial features, you are unattractive."	Communication/commercial subsystems
"To protect your family and way of life, you must go to foreign countries and harm the people there."	Governmental subsystem
"If you feel uncomfortable or anxious, take medications."	Medical subsystem

These are only a few of the literally thousands of toxic messages to which we are exposed every time we interact with our cultural system. Is it any wonder that our psychic subsystems veer off track in attempting to cope with the flood of life-denying input that pours through them each day?

The Unique Role of the Family Subsystem

In the last chapter, we pointed out that within our human systems, the psychic subsystem plays a unique role: it monitors and regulates the functions of the other human subsystems. Within the cultural system, the family subsystem performs in a similar manner. This special cultural subsystem acts as a filter through which the messages sent by the other subsystems must pass. The family subsystem, in other words, is capable of either suppressing or reinforcing the opinions and attitudes that are expressed by the other cultural subsystems. It is this capability that causes particular strengths or maladies to appear across the generations of a family subsystem.

Say, for example, that from one cultural subsystem or another, a child picks up the notion that people of one race are inferior to those of other races. When the child brings this idea into the environment of his or her family, the family can, through the statements and actions of its members, suppress the racist notion. But the family also is capable of validating this toxic message: if the child's parents or siblings are racists, they will let the child know, in one way or another, that it is appropriate to view and treat people of a certain race as inferiors. Through his or her interaction with the family subsystem, in combination with one or more of the other cultural subsystems, the child becomes disposed toward either tolerance or bigotry.

In terms of an individual's growth and development, the family subsystem has a profound influence. To a large extent, the family system determines how the developing individual eventually perceives good and evil, and right and wrong; we would even suggest that the family subsystem is responsible for the way that an individual feels about his or her god. Through a combination of reinforcement or suppression, the family subsystem also exerts a major influence on how the individual makes behavioral choices. The family subsystem "tells" the individual, for example, whether it is appropriate to cry when hurt or to flee when threatened. It's not surprising, therefore, that when the family system is healthy and whole, its individual members tend to make winning or effective behavioral choices—or that, conversely, individuals who come from a toxic family subsystem choose, eventually, to behave in ways that reflect the subsystem's dysfunction or fragmentation.

Like all great power, the power of the family subsystem brings with it the potential for tremendous abuse. Sometimes, this abuse comes about as a result of conscious choices, as is the case when children are verbally or physically attacked by their parents. In cases such as these, the connection between people's eventual self-defeating behaviors and the toxic environment in which they were raised is clear. In other cases, however, the relationship between people's unhappiness or failure and their family subsystems is not as clearly defined. This is especially true when family subsystems give their members toxic messages that are sent with the best of intentions. We've come to think of these kinds of messages as the *sweet poisons*. A sweet poison is a toxic message that is sent to an individual to help him or her avoid or cope with a potential difficulty, but that ultimately serves only to create a new problem or make a current problem worse.

Sweet Poisons, Bitter Antidotes

We did not fully understand what a sweet poison was or how it contributed to self-defeating behavior until we began to work with Lynn, whom you met in chapter 1. Lynn, a successful professional in her early thirties, complained that her life was devoid of happiness and purpose. She claimed to have little or no meaningful contact with other people and bemoaned the fact that her existence was made up largely of working, eating, watching television, and sleeping. Holidays and weekends were particularly bad times for her. While the rest of the world seemed to be relaxing or celebrating, Lynn sat alone in her house, using junk food, cigarettes, and occasionally alcohol to combat the depression that she feared might overwhelm her.

What struck us as unique about Lynn's situation was that, unlike the great majority of people who practice self-defeating behaviors, she did not seem to have received any overtly toxic messages from her family. An only child, she was born when her parents—now deceased—were in their early forties. In Lynn's own words, her mother and father "absolutely doted" on her. They saw to it that she seldom went without anything she wanted, whether it be money, toys, clothing, or, when she reached her teens, a new compact car. But it would be wrong, as Lynn quickly pointed out, to believe that their generosity was limited to giving her material goods. Rather, they praised and encouraged her constantly, assuring her that because she was a bright and personable girl, she would readily achieve whatever goals she set for herself.

"When I think of my mother now," Lynn reported during one of our meetings, "what I remember most is her voice. That, and what she always used to say to me. 'Keep up the good work,' she said. 'If you apply yourself, you can be anything you want to be.'"

In Lynn's mother's words, we saw the very essence of the type of toxic message we later came to recognize as a sweet poison. A message of this sort is communicated by a parent or family member who has the best of intentions: he or she wants only to build or strengthen a child's self-esteem. In attempting to do so, however, what this adult inculcates in the child is a hopelessly idealistic or simplified notion of how the world really works. The child is told that he or she can reasonably expect constant success; that justice always prevails in the world; that compromise is never necessary; and, more often than not, that a single idealized virtue ("hard work," "good sportsmanship," or "a positive attitude," to name only a few) is the key to perpetual happiness.

Though they can hardly be viewed as abusive, such messages as these can prove every bit as toxic as denigrating comments or a stony withholding of affection. Why? Because eventually, a person suffused with a sweet poison will run headlong into the insensitive workings of the larger cultural system. This is precisely what happened to Lynn. When she decided to run for the office of student council treasurer, she did so with the belief that she was by far the most qualified person for the job. She campaigned diligently but still lost the election—even though everyone she had talked to had assured her that she had victory all but locked up. The loving but toxic message she'd received from her family did not allow for the fact that the "best" people do not always win at the game of life.

Nothing her parents had told her led her to believe that the less qualified of two candidates is often victorious in elections and other contests, perhaps solely on the basis of a more pleasing physical appearance, more influential friends, or a general misunderstanding on the part of those who determine the outcome.

The main problem with sweet poisons, as we see it, is that they inevitably lead people to what we view as *bitter antidotes*. A bitter antidote is simply a sweetly poisonous message stood on its head. The lay term for turning a sweet poison into a bitter antidote is "black-and-white thinking," a pattern of thought demonstrated by people who, for example, move unhesitatingly from a hearty endorsement of buccaneer capitalism to a fervent advocacy of radical socialism. Such a person, whose thinking has invariably been distorted by a sweetly toxic message, ventures out into the cultural system thinking, "The world is a fair place, and I am a good person. Therefore, I'll always get what I want."

What happens, though, is that this person eventually finds him- or herself in a situation that reveals this conclusion to be false. Lynn found herself in such a situation when she lost an election that she believed she had every right to win. Because it is impossible for people to believe what they know from experience to be false, Lynn quickly formulated an outlook consistent with what she now saw as reality. Believing that she had been cheated out of a hard-earned victory, she unconsciously replaced her original conclusion with its opposite: "The world is an unfair place, and I'm not a worthy person. Therefore, I'll never get what I want."

This bitter antidote was no more accurate than the sweet poison it replaced. But because it seemed to resolve some of the psychic tension Lynn was experiencing, and because it contained a few grains of "hard truth" about the world, it quickly took the form of an irrefutable "fact." As such, it served as the basis for a protracted pattern of self-defeating thought and action.

As we've noted, the family subsystem is a source of many of the sweet poisons we receive from our cultural system. The other cultural subsystems, however, are equally capable of sending out messages that make us feel good but do not stand up to the test of reality. When our governmental subsystem tells us, for example, that ours is a wonderful country that has only a few minor difficulties, it is feeding us a sweet poison. Similarly, when the medical subsystem tells us that doctors are omnipotent—that they have, in effect, a cure for whatever ails us—it is comforting us with a sweet poison. We accept these toxic messages because they often seem to confirm our most optimistic vision of ourselves and our culture. But when truth clouds this vision, the sweetness of the well-intentioned message disappears, and its poison goes to work. At that point, we may, if we are not careful, become bitter and cynical, and choose behaviors that guarantee additional unhappiness.

Culprits and Accomplices

We're aware, of course, that our cultural system is not the sole source of the kind of disruptive input that gives rise to self-defeating behaviors. Certain events that are common to all cultures—death, disease, natural disaster, and so on—can cause people to adopt self-defeating behaviors when they attempt to cope with catastrophe. By and large, though, the great majority of self-defeating behaviors are caused by the toxic messages that our cultural system sends into our human systems. There seems to be little doubt that if we examine how our personal self-defeating behaviors were born, we will more often than not find that our culture is the culprit.

Each of us, however, is an accomplice in our own pattern of self-defeat. Our culture may cause us to develop a particular self-defeating behavior, but once that behavior is in place, we *choose* to maintain it. We believe that we have found an antidote to the toxic messages we receive from our culture; and though the antidote tastes bitter, and may even make us sicker than the toxin, we continue to swallow it. In this way, we compound the effect of the original toxic input. When faced with a new moment of life—an opportunity to grow and, at the same time, to be reunited with our own best selves—we instead choose to withdraw from people, become depressed, take drugs, overeat, or fantasize about how good life might be, if only we (or the world) were different.

Because of the way our human systems interact with the cultural system, we can do only one of two things if we want to break out of patterns of self-defeat: we can attempt to change either the cultural system or the way we react to its toxic by-products. But the first of these alternatives—to try to change the way our culture works—is, for the most part, a futile endeavor. Perhaps a few religious and social reformers have found fulfillment in the quest for some sort of comprehensive cultural change; by and large, however, attempts to change our cultural system are doomed from the start. Cultural systems do indeed change, but only over long periods or through great strife and upheaval. If we assume that we can break away from our self-defeating behaviors only when our cultural system ceases to encourage them, we condemn ourselves to lives that are not really lived, but, rather, simply endured.

So we are left with only one option: we must change the way we respond to the toxic messages that our culture sends out. To do this, we must learn to make healthy and clear-headed choices at new moments of life. First, however, we need to identify the specific pattern that our self-defeating behavior tends to follow. We must challenge the fears that we carry like lead weights from moment to moment. And before we can challenge our fears, we must expose the false conclusions on which these fears are based. We must realize, in short, that behind every self-defeating behavior lies a misguided belief about what we must do to avoid discomfort or sorrow. Once this belief is corrected, our fears tend to fall by the wayside, and we are free to make choices that lead us toward the road to a productive and fulfilling life.

Chapter 4

It Starts
with the Conclusion

We've suggested that a self-defeating behavior is conceived when an individual receives toxic messages from the cultural system. This exchange leads, at new moments of life, to experiences that are hurtful or threatening to the individual. To reduce the internal tension created by these experiences, he or she chooses—seemingly at random—a behavior that temporarily reduces the tension. This behavior may not be the best or healthiest alternative available, but it works for the moment—and that, really, is all the individual is concerned about.

A self-defeating behavior is not truly born, however, until the individual connects in his or her mind the painful experiences and the behavior that eased the hurt or anxiety. When this connection is made within the person's unconscious mind, a *conclusion* is reached. This conclusion, in turn, becomes a basis for the way the individual chooses to behave in the future. The formula by which the person reaches this conclusion can be expressed as follows:

Experiences + Behavior = Conclusion

This formula—or, more accurately, the specific information that is substituted for each of its variables—is stored in the individual's memory. Each time the individual approaches a new moment of life, he or she unconsciously consults this formula and chooses a behavior that closely resembles the behavior used to reduce internal tension at the moment when the conclusion was reached. In this sense, the individual has become programmed for self-defeat. To try to protect him- or herself from further hurt or anxiety, the individual returns again and again to the behavior that was chosen when the conclusion was first formed.

Before they understand how self-defeating behavior patterns work, people often contend that their "feelings" are to blame for their destructive thoughts and actions. They say that they behave in certain ways not because of a belief or an attitude—but, rather, because they become nervous, fearful, bored, or lonely under particular circumstances. Our response is to point out that although the line that divides a "feeling" from a conclusion is a fine one, feelings such as anxiety, boredom, fear, and emptiness are in most cases physical or emotional reactions to the faulty messages that conclusions express. The negative feelings that we sometimes experience at new moments of life are not, therefore, the cause of the self-defeating behaviors that we subsequently practice. Instead, they are signals that indicate that we've retrieved a faulty conclusion and are in the process of acting upon it. These feelings are neither good nor bad, right nor wrong. The conclusions that underlie them, however, are sometimes faulty. It's far more productive, therefore, to focus on the conclusions that are the basis for our behavior than on the feelings these conclusions may produce.

The Promise of Protection

Why do self-defeating conclusions exert such power over our behavior? The answer is simple: our self-defeating conclusions offer *the promise of protection* from hurt, pain, and anxiety. That this is a false promise does not matter, because within the individual's memory, both the self-defeating conclusion and the behavior it produces are completely logical.

Consider the case of Eva, who, when she came to us, for the past three years had been trying to stop smoking. She had started practicing her self-defeating behavior as a freshman at a small liberal arts college. During her first semester at school, she experienced a considerable degree of loneliness: she found it difficult to make new friends and felt rejected by her new environment. These feelings threatened her and led her to question her self-worth. Then, near the end of that first semester, a woman with whom she was casually acquainted asked Eva to attend a party with her. Thinking she had nothing to lose, Eva agreed to go. As it turned out, the party was a gathering of a small group of students who fancied themselves the avant-garde of the student body; there were lots of black clothes and dark glasses in evidence, and the air was dense with cigarette smoke. At first, Eva felt out of place and conspicuous. She stood alone at the edge of a small group whose conversation could scarcely be heard over the bizarre music that boomed from the stereo speaker behind them. There must be something wrong with me, she remembered thinking, if even these people don't want anything to do with me. Then, caught up in a state of silent panic, she did an impulsive thing. She tapped a young woman standing next to her on the shoulder and asked to borrow a cigarette. She lit the cigarette, drew on it, and exhaled the smoke without inhaling it.

Then, in Eva's own words, "the most amazing thing" happened to her. The group on whose fringes she'd been standing opened up to her, and within minutes she was engaged in enthusiastic conversation with several of its members. Before the night ended, she was pleasantly surprised to realize that she'd made four new friends. She remained close to each of these people throughout her college years. But unfortunately, by the time she graduated she was smoking a pack of cigarettes a day.

Within Eva's unconscious mind, this experience took the following form:

Experience	Behavior	Result	Conclusion
1. I felt alone and rejected.	I suffered.	My self-esteem was threatened.	I had to take action to save myself.
2. I felt alone and rejected.	I started smoking.	People accepted me.	Smoking protected my inner self.

Having lived through these experiences, Eva's second conclusion—that because it brought social acceptance, smoking protected her endangered inner self—seemed perfectly logical. That she later learned that smoking had little to do with why her new friends accepted her had no bearing on this faulty but logical conclusion. Nor did the fact that in later years, many of the people she met were put off by her self-defeating behavior. Intellectually, she knew her conclusion about smoking was ridiculous. Yet she continued to light cigarettes whenever she felt the slightest degree of uneasiness or social discomfort, until finally she became emotionally and physically dependent on tobacco.

How Self-Defeating Conclusions Influence Behavior

We know that people operate from their beliefs about the world and how it works. We know, too, that when tested against reality, many of these beliefs prove to be false, absurd, and downright self-destructive. The question we need to answer, then, is why so many of us allow our behavior to be shaped and influenced by beliefs (or conclusions) that simply aren't true.

Recall that in chapter 2, we described how our psychic subsystems operate. We suggested that each individual's psychic subsystem is made up of three parts: a conscious component, a preconscious component, and an unconscious component:

Psychic subsystem

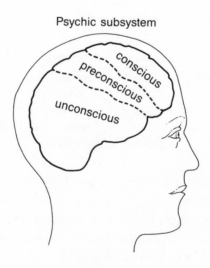

Figure 5

We went on to point out that because the conscious component of our psychic subsystem is so busy processing new information and making choices, it delegates much information and many choices to its unconscious counterpart. At this unconscious level, however, information and the choices based on it are not scrutinized, tested, or evaluated. Information is simply recalled, just as choices are more or less automated. This process of delegation and automation, we contended, is designed to keep us from exhausting ourselves in the attempt to keep up with the constant flow of information and requests that we receive.

What does this mean in terms of how we choose to behave? It means, simply, that if the conscious component of our psychic subsystem delegates a faulty conclusion to the unconscious, that conclusion will be programmed into our memory. If, for example, in our conscious mind we determine that smoking, drinking, overeating, or withdrawal protects us from the hurts that the outer world occasionally inflicts, this conclusion will almost instantly be delegated to our unconscious mind. It will remain unquestioned and untested, and it will continue to thrive on its own undeniable logic.

Experiences plus behavior equals a conclusion. When we choose a self-defeating behavior in response to a painful experience, and when, subsequently, our internal tension is reduced, we are sending to our unconscious mind the conclusion that the behavior is a healthy and productive one. In this sense, the notion of lying to oneself takes on an added dimension. When we send a faulty conclusion to the unconscious component of our psychic subsystem, we are telling ourselves, essentially, that a behavior that hurts us is a good one. Instead of telling ourselves a truth that bears up to the test of reality, we are programming ourselves for defeat.

Conclusions and Feelings

The relationship between faulty conclusions and the responses that people recognize as their feelings is complicated. It involves a series of interactions between the individual's psychic subsystem and one or more of the other human subsystems. Once a faulty conclusion has been retrieved, the other subsystems respond appropriately: the individual may experience a sensation of panic, fear, or despair. But these "feelings" are not the cause of the behavior that the individual chooses in an attempt to eliminate his or her discomfort. It is the conclusion behind the feeling that initiates a cycle of self-defeating behavior, not the physical or emotional response that the individual experiences. So when an individual reports, for example, that he or she smokes to eliminate nervousness in social situations, that individual is revealing a deeply held belief about the calming effects of nicotine. It is this belief—not the anxiety experienced at parties, restaurants, or night clubs—that is the root cause of the subsequent self-defeating behavior.

Nevertheless, when a person describes the "feeling" that allegedly causes a self-defeating behavior, he or she often reveals the conclusion on which the behavior is actually based. A client of ours named Alice, for example, contended that she went on destructive shopping sprees because she often "felt bored" in the afternoon. "Sometimes when I get off work, this feeling of total boredom comes over me," she told us. "It's as if life has no meaning, and the only way I can work up any enthusiasm at all is to go to the mall and buy something. If my life were somehow more exciting, I'm sure I could stop charging things that we can't afford."

What Alice was describing was a belief that certain new moments of life were meaningless to her: that these particular moments were devoid of challenges, opportunities, and options. She discovered that she could temporarily fill these empty moments with new possessions, which would sustain her mood until another cloud of boredom or purposelessness descended upon her. In focusing on the "feeling" that appeared to motivate her destructive spending sprees, however, she distracted herself from the faulty conclusion that repeatedly led her to perpetuate her self-defeating actions. To change her behavior, she needed to look behind her feelings of emptiness and purposelessness and examine consciously the conclusion that spending money is a viable means of keeping at a distance some of the fundamental questions that each of us must ask about our lives and how we live them.

Behind every self-defeating behavior lies a faulty conclusion about ourselves or our world. If we ignore this fact and focus our attention on how our minds and bodies respond to the erroneous beliefs we carry within us, we'll find it difficult to determine why we choose behaviors that lead us away from our healthy inner selves. Worse yet, we may succumb to the temptation of disowning our behavior, blaming it on mysterious "feelings" we can neither understand nor control.

Conclusions That Kill

Most of us would agree that smoking is a self-defeating behavior: it not only offends and irritates others, but it also virtually guarantees that we damage our physical health. A good majority of the self-defeating conclusions that many of us maintain can, in fact, harm, limit, or even kill us. Here, for example, are only a few of the relatively common faulty conclusions that many of us rely upon to guide our behavior:

- If I act aloof and uninterested, people won't be able to hurt me.
- If I remain miserable and unfulfilled, God will recognize my suffering and look favorably on me.
- If I worry constantly, nothing bad will happen to me.
- Attacking other people, either verbally or physically, will bring me admiration and respect.
- If I am always tense and alert, no one will be able to take advantage of me.
- If I get drunk at social events, people will like and respect me.
- If I smoke, I'll be viewed as a calm, sophisticated person.
- Being overweight keeps me from having to deal with many of life's problems.
- If I never even try to do something I want to do, I'll never experience failure.
- Behaving just like the other members of my family will guarantee me acceptance and security.

Remember: because conclusions such as these are stored in the dark, unconscious component of the psychic subsystem, they will continue to be drawn upon at new moments of life, regardless of how absurd they seem in the light of the conscious mind. The smoker, for example, knows (or at least should know by now) that cigarettes often cause irreparable damage to the lungs and cardiovascular system. Yet this conscious awareness is easily overridden by his or her subconscious conclusion that smoking will calm the nerves or convey an image of sophistication and composure. Similarly, the compulsive worrier knows, on a conscious level, that constant brooding and nervousness will not, in fact, keep an unpleasant event—an accident, say, or a surprising change in circumstances—from occurring. Yet within his or her unconscious mind there lies the conclusion, born of experiences in which worrying became linked with the avoidance of pain, that if you worry about some unpleasant event, it's bound not to occur. In conscious and realistic terms, the conclusion is obviously false. But within the individual's unconscious mind, it stands unchallenged as a powerful and potentially deadly determinant of behavior.

Faulty conclusions guide us toward behaviors that guarantee, ultimately, that we will be unhappy or unwell. We rely on them because we are not consciously aware of what they are telling us and because we believe that they will keep us from feeling pain or tension. Perhaps more important, we trust our self-defeating conclusions because they promise that if we act upon them, they will help us remain in control of our lives.

The Illusion of Control

When Daniel came to us, he claimed to be depressed. As a matter of fact, he claimed to have been depressed for more than five years, during which time he had dropped out of college, failed to hold three different jobs, enrolled in college for a second time, and then flunked out. He had been unable to maintain a relationship with any of the women who had been interested in him, and, on three occasions, he had been arrested for driving while drunk. He blamed this series of unpleasant experiences on his depression, which, he claimed, hung over him like a cloud, ready to pour dark rain on him the minute he felt happy or at ease.

We traced Daniel's unhappiness back to the end of his first year in college. When he returned home after successfully completing final exams, he was met at the door by his sobbing mother. She told Daniel not to bother to unpack, because his father, a forty-six-year-old businessman, had suffered a major heart attack. He was in the intensive care unit of a local hospital, and Daniel and his mother needed to get there immediately.

"I've been through a lot of bad times," Daniel told us, "but the three weeks while my dad was in the hospital was far and away the worst time of my life. Day after day I sat in the waiting room, worrying that any minute he might die. It got so bad that I even started praying, telling God that if he let my dad live I would never ask for anything again."

Although Daniel's father eventually recovered, his health forced him to retire and, from time to time, to return to the hospital for tests and checkups. The following autumn, Daniel dropped out of college and got a job selling stereos. After three weeks, he was fired for absenteeism, after which he went to a bar, drank too much, and, on the way home, was arrested for the first time for drunk driving.

"It was like, I was nervous and miserable all the time," Daniel recalled. "I did whatever I could to get out from under the cloud, but it just kept following me wherever I went."

It soon became clear to us that at the time of his father's heart attack, at an unconscious level Daniel had come to the conclusion that as long as he was miserable, his father would not become ill again. This crippling conclusion took shape according to the following logic:

1. I was happy after getting done with final exams.

2. Because I was happy, my father had a serious heart attack.

3. I worried and felt miserable while he was in the hospital.

4. My father recovered and did not suffer another attack.

5. Therefore, as long as I am worried and unhappy, my father will not have another heart attack. My ongoing misery is keeping him alive.

What Daniel had done, essentially, was to link two behaviors (happiness and misery) with two corresponding experiences (his father's heart attack and subsequent recovery) to create the logical but faulty conclusion that his own moods and feelings controlled his father's health.

During the years that followed, Daniel repeatedly drew on this conclusion to make himself miserable, because he believed at an unconscious level that his misery kept him in control of what happened to his father. This control was, of course, a total illusion, especially in light of the fact that Daniel's father avoided another heart attack by retiring from his job, losing weight, and seeking frequent medical care. Yet it was an illusion that Daniel clung to tenaciously, because he feared that he could not survive another surprise as traumatic as his father's initial illness. He could not see that this illusion of control had cost him an education, several jobs, more than a few personal relationships, and his own sense of health and well-being.

If you check back over the list of self-defeating conclusions we provided earlier, you'll note that each of them included the verb *will*. For the holder of these and similar conclusions, the faulty conclusion is, in essence, a distorted attempt to control the future. The experience that led to the conclusion created so much tension that the individual was willing to do virtually anything to avoid a recurrence of the original discomfort. Distorted and absurd though it might be, in each case the conclusion offers a promise of what will happen, if only the individual chooses to behave in a certain way. As Daniel's situation showed, most of us are more than happy to follow any program that gives us a sense of being in control of what happens to us. That this sense of control is a total illusion does not keep us from choosing behaviors that limit our growth and, in the end, do us far more damage than the recurrence of a hurtful experience ever could do.

Bringing Conclusions to Light

If a self-defeating conclusion, along with its promises of protection and control, remains stored within the unconscious component of our psychic subsystems, it will continue to exert its considerable

power over the way we act and feel. In this dark region of
the conclusion will survive as long as its own flawless logi
in place. To eliminate a self-defeating behavior in this earl
its development, therefore, we must retrieve from our unconscious
minds the conclusion on which the behavior is based. Once we have
brought the conclusion to the level at which we make conscious and
informed choices, we can put it to the test of reality and reveal it for
what it is: a distorted perception of how life works and of what must
be done to avoid pain.

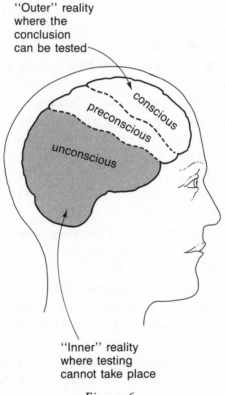

Figure 6

Say, for example, that Daniel had been able on his own to articulate his self-defeating conclusion at a conscious level. Almost at
once he would have suspected it to be false, and he might have taken
steps to test this suspicion. He might have chosen, for example, to

stop worrying and feeling depressed for a certain period of time, during which he would periodically check on his father's health. If, as is almost certain, his father had not had another heart attack, Daniel would have been able to expose on a conscious level the faulty logic of his conclusion. Why? Because he felt good and behaved spontaneously for an extended period of time, and still his father did not become ill again. Armed with this information, Daniel could then have formed a *winning conclusion:* namely, that the best thing he could do for both his father and himself would be to choose healthy behaviors and, ultimately, to experience both the pain and the joy of being alive.

How do we bring our self-defeating conclusions to light? The first step is always to identify the conclusion and to connect it with the behavior it inspires. If, for example, you find yourself on the verge of leaving a job at which you have been quite successful, you need to ask yourself about the conclusion that is leading you to make what might be a self-defeating choice. You need to ask yourself why you believe it is necessary to leave a job once you've demonstrated that you can perform the required tasks successfully. Do you believe that all success is a prelude to failure? Or do you feel that you can do a job well only when you are afraid of failing at it? Until you identify your particular self-defeating conclusions, you'll continue to behave in a way that confirms them.

Once you've identified a self-defeating conclusion and, therefore, brought it into the light of your conscious mind, you can test the conclusion against reality. You can, for example, gather more information about whatever it is that frightens you; if you believe that you must quit a job before you are eventually fired from it, you can ask your superiors how they feel about both your current performance and your future with the organization. Feedback from others is a fertile source of information that can be used to challenge self-defeating conclusions. Friends, co-workers, and therapists can all give you valuable information that you can use to test the validity of a belief or conclusion that continues to lead you to defeat.

Another way of challenging a self-defeating conclusion is to study yourself. If you keep an eye on your behavior and take note of what makes you feel good (as well as what doesn't), your healthy internal subsystems will provide you with clear guidance as to what works for you and what doesn't. You'll find that although it may give a momentary sense of security, behavior that is based on a self-defeating conclusion does not, in the end, feel good to you. Winning behavior, on the other hand, will reunite you with your best and truest self. This sort of behavior will lead to experiences that will form the basis for new, healthy conclusions: winning conclusions that, in turn, will keep you at peace with yourself and on the road to growth and success.

Over the years, we have become convinced that if you want to stop hurting yourself, you must change the conclusions that underlie your self-defeating behaviors. Through this process, you can use the considerable power of conclusions to your advantage, rather than to your detriment. Here we've touched on the first step in the process, which requires you to bring your self-defeating conclusions to the level of consciousness and to test them against reality.

But this step alone will not lead you to a new conclusion. All conclusions, including those that lead to winning thoughts and actions, are based on an interaction between an actual experience and the behavior you choose to respond to experience: again, experience plus behavior equals a conclusion. To replace a self-defeating conclusion with a healthier and more realistic belief, you must choose winning behaviors in response to new moments of life. In later chapters, we'll show you how you can start to make these winning choices. We'll show you how to choose actions and attitudes that will help you grow—rather than shrink—from the many new experiences you encounter during each and every day of your life.

Chapter 5

The Model of Self-Defeat

Although they lead us to failure, unhappiness, illness, and even death, self-defeating behaviors are, in their own limited way, as alive and dynamic as any other part of the life circulatory system. Each of our self-defeating behaviors has what we might think of as its own life cycle: once it is born, it must develop, assert itself, be challenged, and, sadly enough, be renewed. To establish itself firmly as a basis for our thoughts and actions, a self-defeating behavior must pass through all phases of this cycle. If it is arrested at any point in the cycle, however, it will turn on the conclusion that lies at its heart and will, in effect, self-destruct.

What does this mean in terms of the way in which we can choose to either perpetuate or eliminate our self-defeating behaviors? It means, simply, that at each new moment of life, we can choose to sustain or abort any behavior that will lead us to self-defeat. When we claim to be caught in a rut or pattern that we can't escape, we are really saying that we continue to make the same kind of choice at new moments of life. And having made this original self-defeating choice, we are propelled along a course of thought and action that will nourish and renew our self-defeating behaviors.

Before we move on in the next section of this book to discuss how each of us perpetuates his or her self-defeating behaviors, we feel it would be helpful to look at the overall model through which a behavior must develop if it is to survive. We introduce this model here as a preview of what is to come in later sections of the book and also to suggest for the first time how much effort is required to keep a self-defeating behavior alive and functional.

What a Self-Defeating Behavior Looks Like

Imagine that we could freeze a new moment of life in time and look at it under a microscope. If we were to represent a person who is approaching this new moment with the [ ] symbol, what we would see through our lenses might look like this:

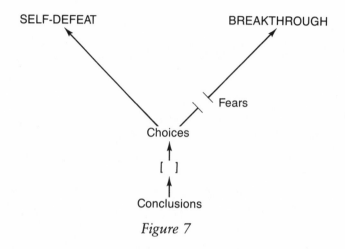

Figure 7

As this simple diagram suggests, each new moment of life would resemble the letter *Y,* with the upper branches of the letter representing the two routes or paths available to the individual at the new moment. This moment itself would occur at the point at which the three branches of the letter meet.

When an individual approaches the new moment, he or she brings a conclusion about what will happen if a particular thought or action is chosen. This conclusion, as we suggested earlier, is a logical and unconscious belief about life and reality. It is formed when the individual receives from the cultural system a message that leads to internal tension and, subsequently, chooses at random a behavior that, for one reason or another, serves to reduce the tension and eliminate the threat.

Fears and Choices

Each self-defeating conclusion that a person brings to new moments of life is, as we'll explain in the next section, an expression of a basic *fear:* a conclusion built on an *apprehension of what will happen if a particular self-defeating behavior is not chosen at a new moment.* Eva, who started smoking in order to gain the acceptance of a particular social group, serves as a case in point. Fearful of rejection, she asked to borrow a cigarette and subsequently found herself included in a lively conversation. In her mind, smoking became paired with a feeling of belonging to a group. Later, at gatherings that included any of her new friends, she continued to puff on cigarettes, fearing that if she didn't she would reveal herself as unsophisticated, vulnerable, and unworthy of attention.

Self-defeating conclusions and the fears on which they are based exert a dramatic influence on the choices that people make at new moments of life. In the absence of a conclusion and its accompanying fear, an individual would approach a new moment of life with a clear and unbiased view of the choice that lies ahead. But once a conclusion has been formed, the fear on which it is based blocks off the road that might lead to winning behavior and eventual breakthrough. The individual who is approaching the new moment believes, therefore, that he or she has no choice but to follow the path that leads to self-defeat.

Looking back at Eva, we can see how her conclusion about smoking and its accompanying fear limited her choices when she found herself in the company of people she didn't know well: she feared that if she didn't smoke, she'd be viewed as immature, shy, or otherwise unworthy of acceptance. So each time she got together with her friends, she faced at an unconscious level the choice of not smoking or lighting a cigarette. This choice, in effect, was no choice at all: she would either smoke or return to a state of loneliness and misery. Because she feared what would happen if she did not smoke, she found herself smoking whenever she felt momentarily threatened, bored, or insecure.

Self-Defeating Techniques

To illustrate further how a self-defeating behavior develops and sustains itself, we need to add another component to our basic model. We must consider the specific *techniques* a person uses to put his or her choice into practice.

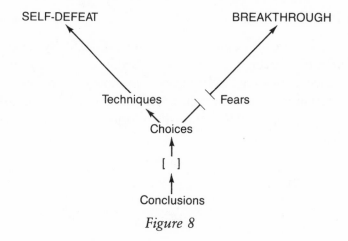

Figure 8

Techniques are the means by which individuals express their self-defeating choices to themselves and the world. A technique may take the form of an *attitude* or an *action*. Regardless of the form it takes, a self-defeating technique bears the individual's personal stamp; through the development and practice of techniques, the individual customizes his or her way of responding to new moments of life.

While people who carry within themselves similar conclusions tend to have similar fears and to make similar choices at new moments, each individual develops personalized techniques for putting his or her choices into practice. When fearful of losing control of external circumstances, for example, one person will throw a temper tantrum, another will overeat, and still a third person will withdraw into a cocoon of numbness.

Eva, for example, used smoking as her primary self-defeating technique. This technique was a means of putting into practice her belief that she needed to "enhance" (and, simultaneously, to hide and protect) her inner self by way of some pseudosophisticated or devil-may-care gesture. Another person in similar circumstances might have chosen instead to crack a snide joke, sip an alcoholic drink, or speak untruthfully about his or her wealth, skills, or accomplishments. Techniques, in short, tend to be individualized, even though they may be driven by common conclusions and fears.

Prices

Because they are based on misguided choices and faulty conclusions, self-defeating techniques inevitably produce unhappy results—consequences that tend to be identical to those the individual feared when forming his or her initial conclusion. We call these unpleasant consequences *prices*. Here's how these prices fit into our model for self-defeat:

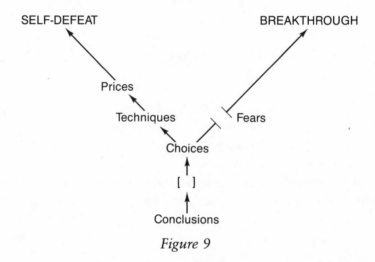

Figure 9

What are some common prices we pay for our self-defeating choices? The list of potential prices is as long as the list of choices and techniques that lead to these consequences. Prices can be as minor as momentary discomforts or short-lived episodes of physical pain; the price for choosing to hold your finger over an open flame, for example, is a burning sensation that will soon disappear if you remove your finger quickly. Other prices—the kind we're talking about here—are not so trivial. Included among the major prices people pay to perpetuate their self-defeating behaviors are loneliness, anxiety, failed careers, financial ruin, and physical illness. These and similar results occur when an individual repeatedly chooses to follow the road of self-defeat over an extended period of time.

As painful as they might be, however, prices perform a valuable service for us. They are the means through which our life circulatory system tells us that our conclusions are faulty and that our behavior must change. Prices, in this sense, are warning mechanisms. They let us know that we are on the wrong path and advise us to make necessary adjustments to the ways in which we think and behave.

During our meeting with Eva, for example, we asked her how she felt on the morning after the party where she had started smoking. "Awful," she admitted readily. "My throat was sore, my chest was congested, and I felt a dense, heavy pressure in my head—not pain, really, but a general stuffiness." Here we pointed out that these physical sensations were the initial prices she paid for smoking cigarettes. Uncomfortable though they were, we told her, they were in fact beneficial. They were her body's way of telling her that smoking was an unhealthy behavior, one that would bring on unpleasant consequences. Had she recognized these prices for what they were, she might well have chosen then and there to stop smoking for good.

In this way, prices alert us and guide us toward required change. If we experience fully the discomfort that comes with a price, we can at that point interrupt our cycle of self-defeating behavior. The danger comes, however, when we attempt to avoid paying a price in full: when we resort to the advanced techniques of minimizing and disowning.

Minimizing and Disowning

To complete a cycle of self-defeat, we must—and the *must* is important here—draw upon the advanced techniques known as *minimizing* and *disowning*. We call these techniques "advanced" because they can be learned only through an attempt to perpetuate a self-defeating behavior. They complete our model of self-defeat, as is shown in figure 10.

We minimize a price when, instead of acknowledging the tension or pain it is causing us, we tell ourselves that the price isn't all that bad. To avoid paying the full price for the behavior that has led to loneliness, for example, a cold and aloof person might say, "Being alone really isn't too much to bear. It would be worse to have somebody around constantly, watching your every move and looking for ways to find fault." Or a person such as Eva might, after the first night of smoking, conclude that the sore throat, stuffy head, or moderate depression experienced afterward was a small price to pay for the appearance

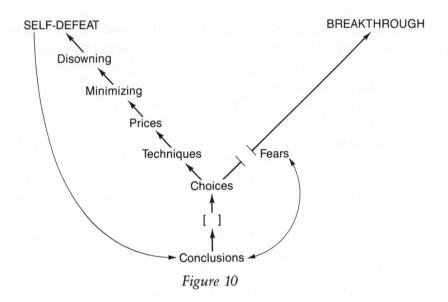

Figure 10

of increased sophistication and the social acceptance that this toxic behavior seemed to bring. As Eva told us: "Sure, I felt lousy. But a dull headache was a lot better than the way I'd been feeling before I went to that party. I'll trade a little discomfort for nagging loneliness any day."

But as Eva eventually discovered, it isn't enough simply to minimize a price that we are paying. Even a minimized price brings with it some pain or tension, so at this point the individual who is creating a cycle of self-defeat must disown responsibility for his or her discomfort. People find ingenious ways to accomplish this disowning: they blame their parents, spouses, jobs, lovers, friends, financial circumstances, genetic makeup, or even a factor as neutral as the weather. "If my parents had shown me any love," the lonely and isolated person might lament, "then I'd be able to show people how I feel about them, and I wouldn't be sitting here alone." Or, as Eva thought to herself once it was apparent she would not be able to quit smoking: "Okay, so now I'm a smoker. I don't really like smoking, and my parents and friends back home disapprove of it. What I should have done was picked a college that had more people with my background in the student body. If I'd done that, I wouldn't have had such a tough time fitting in." It is when we are minimizing and disowning that we do much of the hard work that is required to sustain our self-defeating behavior. If we do not minimize, we pay the full price for our behavior; the pain and cost involved instruct us to change both the behavior and the conclusion that underlies it. And if we do not disown, we must face up to our own responsibility for whatever misfortune has occurred. This, in turn, curtails the cycle of self-defeat, in that we must inevitably look at what we can do to keep the misfortune from happening again.

But if, as our model illustrates, we apply our minimizing and disowning techniques when faced with a price, we guarantee that the cycle of self-defeat will be repeated. Why? Because the unpleasant experience through which we have just passed will be stored within our unconscious mind as further evidence that our original conclusion was valid. This experience, once it has been fed into our original conclusion or, as sometimes happens, stored as a conclusion in its own right, will guide our behavior at the next new moment of life, because experience plus behavior equals a conclusion. We had an experience; we were faced with paying the price for our behavior. To reduce the tension or threat that accompanied the price, we chose a certain behavior: we minimized the price and disowned responsibility for it. Our disowning and minimizing, in turn, successfully blunted the impact of the price: it enabled us to feel less pain and responsibility. The conclusion we draw at an unconscious level from this sequence is that *self-defeating behavior limits the amount of pain, tension, and responsibility we must bear.*

You Can't Get There . . . from There

The model of self-defeat is, essentially, a recipe for failure. Take one conclusion and a dose of fear; make misguided choices; minimize prices; then add generous amounts of disowning. The result? Renewed self-defeat, topped with the notion that you were meant to fail and can do nothing to change. If you swallow this concoction, you'll take into your human system the most toxic message of all—namely, that you were born to fail and that you will never find peace or fulfillment in this or any other world.

Perhaps the most sinister feature of this cycle of repeated failure is that people tend to be most motivated to break out of it precisely at the points at which escape is impossible: when they are faced with a price, for example, or while they are attempting to minimize the price or disown the responsibility for it. Under these circumstances, people seek out the following imaginary route:

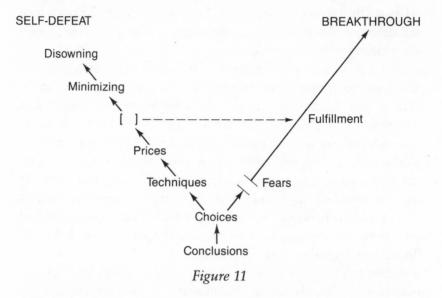

Figure 11

There's only one problem with this approach: *you can't get there (to the winning road) from there (the self-defeating road)*. The only point of access along the winning road is the point where choices are made. Once you've opted for a self-defeating action or attitude, you cannot leave the road to self-defeat until you reach a new moment in life. At that point, you can select a winning behavior and reap the benefits that come from this sound and healthy choice.

New moments in life, in other words, are the crucial transit points that enable you to avoid the cycle of self-defeat. These new moments are the "here" from which you can get to the "there" (or winning road) you want to travel. The ticket that will lift the barricade posed by fear must always take the form of a clear-headed, healthy choice. This choice is not always an easy one to make, but it's the only ticket that will take you where you want to go. Finding this ticket involves taking a long, deep look at your own conclusions and fears. We plan to help you take this look. You might be surprised at what you see, but we think you'll agree that the effort was well worth making.

Part Two

Why
Self-Defeating
Behaviors
Are Perpetuated

... At last the storm abated, and the man who had been thrown overboard, though he still clung to the anchor that had saved his life, was able to relax a bit. Soon enough, he thought, someone on the cruise ship would notice his absence and would send a crew out to rescue him. He did not know, however, that the chain from which the anchor hung had been damaged in the storm. One of its links was badly eroded, and the battering force of the wind had caused it to crack.

The sun had just reappeared when, finally, the damaged link gave way. Both the anchor and the terrified man who clung to it fell into the ocean and began to sink. As he plunged underwater, the sinking man had only one thought. "This anchor saved my life," he told himself. "If I let go of it, I'm sure to die. . . ."

Chapter 6

Living Fearfully

It comes as no surprise to most people—especially people who are upset enough to seek counseling—that they are locked in a pattern that fails to bring them happiness and peace of mind. These people are more than willing to accept the notion that in response to toxic messages from the culture, they have formed self-defeating conclusions about themselves and about life. They are willing to concede, too, that they often make choices that guarantee failure or unhappiness. But frequently, these clients take issue with us when we suggest that although they are not to blame for developing a self-defeating behavior, they bear sole responsibility for maintaining the behavior.

Behind this resistance to the notion of personal responsibility for self-defeating behaviors, we have come to suspect, is a lack of awareness of the fears we carry from moment to moment. To understand why you continue to choose behaviors that work against your best interests, you need first to recognize the degree to which fear shapes your thoughts and actions. Fear plays a role in all our lives; none of us could live for long without it. Fear tells us, for example, not to step in front of speeding cars or pet animals that might be rabid. Fear keeps us from eating or drinking substances we know to be poisonous; it tells us not to play with loaded guns or swim in turbulent waters. If we lacked a capacity for fear, our survival would be left to chance. We would live or remain healthy only as long as we didn't encounter a situation that might kill or harm us. Without our capacity for fear, once we did encounter such a situation—a vicious dog, for example, or a steep cliff—we would avoid disaster only if we were lucky.

The kind of fear we are talking about here is a healthy, protective fear: a feeling that motivates an appropriate response to a very real hazard. The primary purpose of this *real fear* is to help us deal with situations that might hurt us. In this sense, it is a life-preserving and life-enhancing response to the world. Real fear tells us, for example, to check the safety catch on a gun before we handle it, or to take shelter from flying debris during a tornado. The healthier a person is, the more responsive he or she is likely to be to the warning provided by real fear.

There is, however, a second type of fear, one that arises from the faulty and self-defeating conclusions we form when trying to cope with toxic input from our culture. It helps to think of this second type of fear—which, in contrast to real fear, is both limiting and destructive—as *mythical fear*. Until we recognize how our psychic subsystems react to both real and mythical fears, we will have trouble distinguishing between the two. This confusion about our fears and how they work is the primary reason we perpetuate and nourish behaviors that we know will hurt us. So to clear up this confusion, let's look first at a basic model of how all fear works, regardless of whether it is mythical or real.

How Fear Works

A few of our basic fears—such as the fears of falling and of loud noises—seem to be included in our makeup when we are born. The purpose of these fundamental fears is to protect newborn infants from danger during the period when their conscious minds are developing. With the exception of the few basic survival mechanisms, however, all of our fears, whether mythical or real, originate from our conclusions about ourselves and the world. We have an experience that brings us either pleasure or pain, and in reaction to these feelings, we behave in a certain way. If the pleasure continues or the pain abates, we form a conclusion about what we must do to maintain a good feeling or avoid a bad one.

As we mentioned earlier, real fear protects us and keeps us from hurting ourselves. The reason for this is that real fear, in contrast to mythical fear, is based on a *valid conclusion* about the world and how it works. If we were to look at our model for human behavior, real fear would occupy the position shown in figure 12.

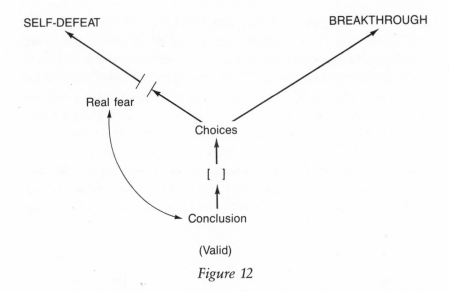

SELF-DEFEAT   BREAKTHROUGH

Real fear

Choices

[ ]

Conclusion

(Valid)

Figure 12

This version of the model illustrates an important concept about the way we think and act: it shows that *real fears close off the road to self-defeat and, hence, are powerful life-giving forces.* A real fear, which is always derived from a valid conclusion, can prevent us from choosing behaviors that will bring us harm, anxiety, or other discomfort.

To see more clearly how this process works, consider why you stop when you approach a red traffic light. The unconscious (but valid) conclusion you draw upon as you approach the light is that if you do not stop your car, it will collide with or be struck by a car moving across its path. Your real fear of being involved in a collision —which, you sense, will cause you to be injured—tells you to step on the brake and come to a stop at the light. In this instance, a real fear, born of a valid conclusion, protects you from injury or death.

We should point out, however, that each of us can, through the powerful process of making a choice, short-circuit the protective function that real fear serves. We can, for example, choose not to stop at a red light and—if we are lucky—can drive through the intersection without colliding with another vehicle. It is likely, too, that if we repeat this choice enough times and are fortunate enough not to have an accident, we will form a new conclusion about red lights: we will decide that there is no reason to stop when we see one. If we continue to make choices based on this faulty conclusion, however, we will eventually have an accident, at which time our original, valid conclusion about red traffic lights will be retrieved and consulted when we decide whether or not to stop at controlled intersections.

Mythical fears, as you might suspect, work in exactly the same way as real fears. The difference between the two is that real fears are based on valid conclusions about ourselves and the world, but *mythical fears always result from faulty conclusions.* If we look at mythical fear within the context of our basic behavior model, we see this:

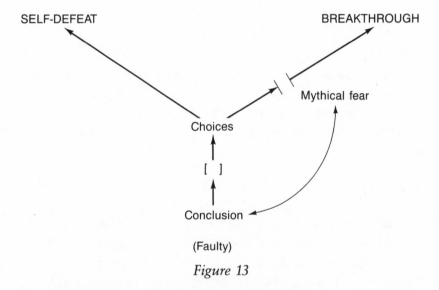

Figure 13

As this version of the model illustrates, the nature of the conclusion on which a fear is based determines not only whether the fear is real or mythical but also which of the two behavior roads the fear blocks off. While real fears protect us from choices that will lead to self-defeat, mythical fears block any potential progress we might make toward winning behavior and eventual breakthrough. Each type of fear, in other words, serves to limit our choices. But while real fear guides us toward choices in favor of life and health, mythical fear prompts us to make choices that will lead, ultimately, to self-defeat.

Earlier we introduced Eva, who during her college years came to believe on an unconscious level that smoking was the key to social acceptance and hence the remedy to loneliness. Her faulty conclusion—that smoking made her more attractive and less vulnerable to rejection—brought with it a fear of what would happen if she chose not to smoke: namely, that her new friends, and all the friends she made later in life, would recognize her unworthiness and abandon her. She came to believe, in short, that if she quit smoking she would again be friendless. This fear, which Eva herself came to view as mythical, limited the number of behavioral choices available to her in new moments of life. It kept her from choosing not to smoke and hence kept her from testing the validity of the conclusion on which her self-defeating behavior was based. While Eva's real fears—for example, the fear of developing lung or heart disease, or of alienating her nonsmoking friends and family members—would have protected her from the consequences of further destructive behavior, her mythical fears protected only the faulty conclusions of which they were part and parcel.

Faulty Conclusions, Mythical Fears: A Death Embrace

You've probably heard the term *death embrace* before. It's used to describe a situation in which two organisms or institutions relate to each other in a way that will ultimately destroy both, but that for the moment provides each with a false sense of security. People who are caught up in destructive marriages or relationships are, whether they will admit it or not, locked together in a death embrace. Each partner in a death embrace fears letting go of the other; to do so would seem to mean immediate destruction or, at the very least, the triumph of one partner over the other. This fear keeps both parties on a course of certain—but deferred—defeat. The parties sense this but refuse to let go. Often, they hope the extra time that the embrace allegedly grants them will bring a miracle or some form of external intervention.

The relationship between faulty conclusions and mythical fears is, in effect, a death embrace. The fear cannot arise unless the faulty conclusion is retrieved; the conclusion can exist only as long as the fear directs the individual toward the kind of negative experiences that appear to validate the misguided belief. Under these conditions, both the conclusion and the fear can flourish in a state of brittle but perpetual interdependence.

Faulty conclusions codify and express mythical fears; these fears, in turn, validate the conclusions to which they are bound. A mythical fear is nothing more and nothing less than a prediction of what will happen if a particular self-defeating choice is not made. If we examine some of the common faulty conclusions we talked about earlier, we can see this relationship clearly:

Faulty Conclusion	Mythical Fear
"If I act aloof and uninterested, people won't be able to hurt me."	"If I am open and amiable, people *will* hurt me."
"If I remain miserable and unfulfilled, God will recognize my suffering and look favorably on me."	"If I enjoy life and try to reach my potential, God *will* take note of my pleasure and condemn me."
"If I worry constantly, nothing bad will happen to me."	"If I stop worrying, something bad *will* surely happen to me."
"Attacking other people, either verbally or physically, will bring me admiration and respect."	"If I don't attack people, they never *will* admire or respect me."
"If I am always tense and alert, no one will be able to take advantage of me."	"If I relax or let my mind wander, people *will* take advantage of me."
"If I get drunk at social events, people will like and accept me."	"If I don't get drunk at social events, I *will* be shunned and rejected."
"If I smoke, I'll be viewed as a calm, sophisticated person."	"If I don't smoke, I *will* be viewed as tense and fragile."
"Being overweight keeps me from having to deal with many of life's problems."	"If I lose weight, I *will* be overwhelmed with a host of other difficulties."
"If I never even try to do something I want to do, I'll never experience failure."	"If I try to do something I want to do, I *will* certainly fail."
"Behaving just like the other members of my family will guarantee me acceptance and security."	"If I behave differently than the other members of my family, I *will* be cut off and alone.

As you can see from these examples, the role that the faulty conclusion plays in the death embrace is to provide a logical basis for thinking, feeling, and acting in a certain way. In return for this "support," the mythical fear closes off the road to breakthrough. It restricts the individual from making a choice that would lead to an experience that, ultimately, would expose and eliminate the faulty conclusion. In this way, the death embrace remains intact, while the individual moves miserably but inexorably toward collapse and defeat.

How We Make Mythical Fears Come "True"

It seems as though it would be easy enough for a person to break the death embrace between faulty conclusions and mythical fears. It would seem logical that if only a person would choose not to create the mythical fear, he or she would be able to expose and correct the faulty conclusion on which the fear was based. To an extent, this is true: if the individual is consciously aware of the relationship between fears and conclusions, he or she can systematically test the fear against reality at new moments of life and can use the resulting experience to invalidate the self-defeating conclusion behind the fear. But because most people do not have a clear sense of how and why they choose behaviors that lead them to defeat, they fall into a pattern that cements, rather than tests, the death embrace. They actually create a series of experiences that appear to confirm their faulty conclusions.

Why, you might ask, would anyone choose to behave in this way? Don't all of us seek acceptance, tranquillity, and a sense of well-being? Of course we do—on a conscious level, at least. But remember: faulty conclusions and the fears they promote operate within the unconscious component of our psychic subsystems. Within this dark arena, these conclusions and fears have only one function, which is to *protect the individual from harm or discomfort.* To perform this function, they draw on all of the intricate components of our model for behavior. They influence our choices, encourage us to minimize the prices we pay for our behavior, and tell us to disown responsibility for the behaviors we have chosen. Through these mechanisms, our faulty conclusions and mythical fears inspire self-fulfilling prophecies about what will happen if we choose self-defeating behaviors over healthier alternatives.

Take, for example, the case of Ted, a veteran of the Vietnam War. Ted was referred to us by the Veterans' Administration because, in addition to several other difficulties, he had been unemployed for three years. At our first meeting, we asked Ted why he believed he had been unable to find work.

"I can't get past the interview," he explained. "They read my resume and call me in, but during the interview they see how messed up I am because of the war. I mean, who wants to hire someone who might go psycho on the job?"

Ted had served in Vietnam for twelve months. In the aftermath of a particularly violent episode of combat—one during which two of his close friends had been seriously wounded—Ted began to behave erratically. He complained of headaches and imaginary wounds; he sometimes talked to himself; his hands shook so badly that he couldn't insert a coin in a soft drink machine. The military doctors he consulted labeled him as dysfunctional and arranged for him to be discharged.

Ted internalized the faulty conclusion he received from these doctors. He began to believe that he was severely and permanently damaged, and that this disability was obvious to everyone who met him. He feared that he would never again be accepted—that he would never be loved, treated with respect, or allowed to function normally. This fear, in turn, caused him to choose behaviors that would confirm the conclusion that he was irrevocably "messed up." He let his hair and beard grow long; he walked the streets in jeans and a fatigue jacket, with his shoulders slumped and his eyes on the pavement. He presented to the world the classic picture of the disturbed and potentially explosive Vietnam veteran—and the world, predictably enough, rejected him. His mythical fears came true.

As part of our treatment, we arranged for Ted to participate in a mock job interview. We videotaped the interview and, at our next meeting, asked Ted to watch the tape. He agreed, and afterward we discussed what he had seen.

"To begin with, I wasn't very well dressed," Ted said. "I had a tie on, but my shirt was wrinkled and my shoes hadn't been polished for a while."

"So why didn't you iron your shirt and polish your shoes?" we asked.

"What difference would it make?" Ted replied. "No one's ever going to hire a guy like me, anyway."

We asked Ted what else he saw on the tape. He pointed out, correctly, that he had slumped in his chair, had failed to look the interviewer in the eye, and had mumbled his responses to several of the interview questions. He noted, too, that he had compulsively folded and unfolded his hands, and that, all in all, he had acted tense and fearful, perhaps even trapped.

"Have you ever tried to change the way you act in these interviews?" we asked.

"Not really. I guess I really don't know any other way to act."

"How about just acting like yourself?" we suggested. "Like a healthy, normal twenty-eight-year-old man who is eager to find a job."

"You've gotta be kidding," said Ted. "If these people saw what I was really like, they not only wouldn't hire me—they'd probably call the cops."

It seemed clear to us at this point that Ted's faulty conclusion about himself—that acting like a dangerously demented war casualty would protect him from disappointment and failure—worked hand in hand with his fear of rejection. This conclusion and the accompanying fear, in turn, caused Ted to choose behaviors that led inevitably to hurtful experiences: rejection, unemployment, and suggestions that he seek therapy to "fix" what was wrong with him. These experiences not only validated the conclusion he received from the military doctors but also made real the perpetual rejection that Ted feared.

More on Mythical Fears

As Ted's situation illustrates, we get ourselves into real trouble if we allow our mythical fears to guide our behavioral choices. If we heed the counsel of these unreliable guides, we cannot help but choose behaviors that will lead us onto the road of self-defeat. Worse still, our mythical fears will point us toward the very experiences we most fear. In the wake of these negative experiences, we become even more convinced that our faulty conclusions are accurate appraisals.

To deal with our mythical fears and to reject the toxic "advice" they provide, we need to learn to recognize them. We need to learn as much as we can about the general forms in which our mythical fears tend to appear; we need also to look through these fears and see clearly the faulty conclusions they express. Only when we have developed this clarity of vision—or, if you will, this ability to look into ourselves and see clearly what is going on at the unconscious level where conclusions and fears embrace—will we be able to take effective steps to get past these obstacles, which stand between us and the road to breakthrough.

Chapter 7

The Forms
that Fear Takes

Trying to identify a point at which you can break out of a cycle of self-defeat is, in many ways, like trying to decide where a perfectly drawn circle begins. In both cases, any spot you identify not only curves backward toward an earlier point of initiation but also curves forward to still another potential beginning or ending. The circularity of self-defeating behavior patterns often frustrates people who are trying to move out of the cycle to take their first steps along the winning road. Behind each behavioral choice lies a fear; behind each fear, a faulty conclusion; behind each faulty conclusion, an experience and a behavioral choice. . . . How can anyone possibly find the place where it all begins? It's worse, even, than a complex maze, which at least allows a person seeking a way out to try different paths and, through a process of elimination, to narrow down the possible routes out of the trap. Within the circle, there seem to be infinite potential beginnings and endings—points of entry and departure that can change the moment we turn our heads.

One possible starting point for a person who wants to break out of a self-defeating behavior pattern is to recognize and understand his or her personal fears. These fears—and here we are talking about only the mythical fears that block the road to breakthrough—are, in effect, bridges that link our unconscious conclusions with our conscious choices. Our mythical fears translate, at the level of conscious thoughts, our faulty beliefs about what will happen if we behave in a certain way. For this reason, they can provide us with both insights about the conclusions we carry within us and explanations for the self-defeating choices we continue to make.

The more we are able to recognize and understand our mythical fears, the better prepared we will be to make winning choices at new moments of life. It seems worthwhile at this point, therefore, for us to talk more about the forms our mythical fears take. Understanding these various forms puts us in a position to categorize and understand our personal fears, and to avoid creating them at new moments of life.

Our experience has led us to conclude that virtually all mythical fears fall into one of two broad categories: (1) the fear of discovering something unpleasant about yourself and (2) the fear of what others might do to you. Because human thought and behavior occurs along a continuum, rather than along a rigidly segmented line, it's possible—and even likely—for any single fear to appear to belong to both of these categories. We find it helpful, however, to maintain the boundaries between the forms of fear, however shadowy those boundaries might be. Remember: we are trying to find a way in and out of a circle, which, by its very nature, resists both entry and escape.

The Fear of Discovering
Something Unpleasant about Yourself

It's amazing how many people continue to behave in self-defeating ways simply because they fear that if they don't choose a familiar but destructive behavior, they will find out something about themselves that they don't believe they can live with. The specific self-defeating behavior a person chooses is, in fact, often a reaction to an irrational but deeply held belief about his or her essence. People who choose to deny their sexuality, for example, often fear that if they didn't do so they would be overcome by the voracity of their sexual appetites: they would become, in their own words, "whoremongers," "nymphomaniacs," "prostitutes," or "perverts." Similarly, people who ignore their own needs and present a pose of caring or sweetness to the outside world often fear that if they assert themselves or ask for what they deserve, the will have to acknowledge the fact that they are "pushy," "hateful," or "self-centered."

What are some of the other "facts" that people are afraid to discover about themselves? Although this sort of mythical fear can manifest itself in truly exotic ways, we've found that it is most commonly found in one of the following forms.

If I don't continue to behave in self-defeating ways, I will find within me . . .

- a person I do not like.
- a stupid person.
- an incompetent person.
- a weak and vulnerable person.
- an inadequate person.
- an untrustworthy person.
- a greedy, ambitious person.
- an irresponsible person.
- a rebel.
- a conformist.
- absolutely nothing.

The last item on the list brings up an interesting variation of this particular form of mythical fear. We have encountered more than a few clients who believe that if they abandon a self-defeating behavior that has been leading them into difficulty after difficulty, they will cease to have any human identity whatsoever. People who express this particular fear, we've found, have usually ceased to communicate with their true inner selves at an early age and have practiced their self-defeating behaviors for almost as long as they can remember. We're reminded here of Roger, a client who sought counseling because his incessant drinking and carousing had made it impossible for him to succeed in either a career or any sort of lasting personal relationship. When we suggested to Roger that he would have to abstain completely from alcohol if he was to make any progress toward achieving his goals of personal happiness and professional success, he replied: "What, me quit drinking? You've got to be kidding! I mean, that's who I *am* — Roger, the original party animal. If I quit going out and partying, what would I *be?*"

The Fear of What Others Might Do to You

Aside from the fear of finding something unpleasant (or nothing at all) at the core of the self, the most common mythical fear that people fall prey to is the fear that if they don't behave in a certain way, others will attack, hurt, or ignore them. People whose behaviors are governed by this form of mythical fear often have no clear sense of who (or what) will act against them; the threatening force is sometimes identified only as "life," "God," "other people," or simply "they" (as in, "If I don't work at least fourteen hours a day, *they* will come and throw me out of my house"). People who live in fear of what others might do can rarely relax; they believe that tension, worry, and alertness are all that protect them from some sinister external agent. And while people will readily admit that this makes for a miserable life, they will quickly add that at least they are "secure."

Mythical fears of this sort are often behind what therapists refer to as "delusional" or "magical" thinking. What it really is, however, is *fearful* thinking. It's commonly expressed in one or more of the following ways.

If I don't continue to practice my self-defeating behavior . . .

- others will lose respect for me.
- others will reject me.
- others will make demands of me that I can't handle.
- others will take advantage of me.
- others will fall ill or die.
- others will see how terrible I really am.
- God will punish me.
- God will condemn me.

As the last two examples on this list suggest, this form of fear often appears in people who carry within them distorted or mistaken religious conclusions. If properly taught and practiced, religion can be a powerful, ongoing motivation toward winning behavior: toward growth, openness, regeneration, and hope. Taught for the wrong reasons or incompletely understood, however, religious teachings can easily be bent to work against, rather than for, the health and fulfillment of individual human beings. Once the concept of God as an inflexible and punitive judge of all thought and action is instilled in a person's mind, that person will inevitably find it difficult to challenge the resulting mythical fear of divine retribution.

One final note on this particular form of mythical fear: People who are caught up in it spend tremendous amounts of time and energy looking for evidence that will substantiate both the fear and the conclusion on which it is based. Conversely, they seem to be blind to any evidence that would alleviate the fear or invalidate the conclusion behind it. We once worked with a client named Celia, a young woman in her early twenties who was systematically starving herself to death. Behind this behavior lay the fear that if she gained weight, Dirk—her husband—would leave her. "Look what happened to my friend Carol," Celia told us. "She put on ten pounds, and the next thing you know, her husband left her for another woman." Later on in this same conversation, Celia revealed to us that her friend Carol had been involved in two extramarital affairs prior to her husband's leaving. Nevertheless, Celia remained convinced that Dirk would abandon her if she gained so much as a pound.

The Fears of Failure and Success

So far, we've presented what we believe are the two major categories into which most mythical fears fall. Within these categories, however, are two more specific forms of fear that prevent people from traveling the road to breakthrough. We're talking here about the fear of failure and the related fear of success. Because these two fears are so pervasive among people who practice self-defeating behaviors, we feel it's important to take a closer look at how each works to perpetuate destructive patterns of thought and action.

The Fear of Failure

Our cultural system places so much emphasis on what it calls "winning," regardless of the cost to the self or others, that a large segment of our population finds it difficult—if not impossible—to compete earnestly or to take risks. These people take on and cultivate a mythical fear of failure: a fear that, if left unchallenged, eventually comes to govern their lives. Around this fear they weave intricate and superficially logical patterns of self-defeating behavior. Although these patterns vary from individual to individual, they are directed toward a common goal. People whose behavior patterns are built around the fear of failure are trying to avoid situations in which they might be asked to put their best selves forward, only to be told that they are not adequate or that someone else has more to offer.

People whose jobs require a considerable investment of the self and a high level of risk are especially prone to this form of mythical fear. Performers, athletes, writers, artists, and salespeople, for example, are all judged on the basis of clearly observable results: a song, a touchdown, a book, a poem, a picture, a sculpture, a deal. Because the evaluation of their efforts is clear-cut, immediate, and apparently final, people who are expected to perform in these areas are prone to such self-defeating behaviors as perfectionism, escapism, and procrastination. The artist decides she can't work on her painting because "the light isn't right" and chooses instead to spend the day rearranging her furniture. The salesperson doesn't follow up on a potential lead, but instead devotes an afternoon to meaningless paperwork. The star athlete plays up to his or her billing when little is at stake but "chokes" during crucial games or matches. If you look closely enough, you'll find that behind each of these clichés lies a mythical fear of failure.

Individuals who fear failure develop, over time, a somewhat convoluted rationale for their behavior and the consequences it leads to. These people, in one way or another, withhold their best efforts or, in extreme cases, intentionally choose behaviors that will ensure failure. The *illusion of control* is at work here; these individuals believe that any failure they predicted (or caused) is not a true failure. Why? Because they knew all along that the failure was inevitable and, hence, either did nothing to change the outcome or behaved in a way that made success impossible. People who base their behavioral choices on the fear of failure are choosing to lose the game of life by forfeit. Later, they can always say, "If I had showed up to play, things would have turned out differently."

A young woman named Sally, for example, came to us after failing to pass a single course during her freshman year at college. In high school, she had been extremely successful, both academically and socially; her teachers and counselors all predicted that Sally would maintain her high level of performance when she got to college. The pressure of these predictions and expectations, however, caused her to develop an intense fear of failure. To deal with this fear, she concluded that she would not do well in college—but that she would fail on her own terms. She skipped classes, didn't hand in the required assignments, and refused to study for exams until it was too late. These behaviors gave her a sense of control over her situation and relieved her anxiety over the prospect of flunking out of school.

Once we realized what Sally had been doing to herself, we asked her how she felt about her dismal academic performance. Was she angry, or hurt, or disappointed, or scared?

"I really don't have any feelings about it, one way or another," Sally responded. "It's not like I really failed. I just sort of dropped out. If I had done my best and still flunked all those courses . . . well, that would have been a real wipe-out."

The Fear of Success

Less common (but no less limiting) than the fear of failure is the fear of success—or, more accurately, an apprehension of what are perceived as the negative consequences of success. The fear of success is a close cousin to the fear of failure: both are responses to high expectations, and both are developed through an attempt to predict (and hence, control) the future. People under the influence of this mythical fear believe that today's victory is little more than a deceptive prelude to tomorrow's defeat. They view success as a bait that will lure them away from the familiar comfort of a self-defeating conclusion. Once they have taken the bait, a return to "reality" is bound to come about in the form of an eventual failure or catastrophe. "The cream will rise to the top and then sour," is a sentiment we've heard from more than a few of our clients.

A person caught up in this mythical fear has what is essentially a complaint against life itself. Our existence is cyclical by its very nature; all of us experience both triumphs and defeats, just as we all must deal eventually with loss, change, calamity, and death. The person who fears success acknowledges this basic truth but then goes on to draw from it a faulty conclusion: because all of us are bound to be hurt or disappointed, he or she reasons, why bother to enjoy any accomplishment or good fortune that comes our way? Realizing that life guarantees none of us uninterrupted success or freedom from anguish, this person attempts to negotiate what amounts to a truce. "I won't try to succeed," he or she decides, "and that way, I'll never have to deal with a defeat or a loss that I can't handle."

What makes this fear all the more crippling is that it is often found, paradoxically enough, in people who are bright, accomplished, and ambitious. The career of one of our clients, a successful middle-aged advertising executive, illustrates this point dramatically. Jack had spent twenty-eight years in the advertising business without advancing beyond the level of middle management. He attributed this stalling to the fact that he changed agencies every three years or so. "You have to move around, keep looking for the right spot," Jack explained to us. "You can only go so far at an agency, and then you're dead in the water. That's when you know it's time to move on."

Through our subsequent conversations with Jack, we were able to identify his particular pattern of self-defeat. He would join an agency, and for the first year or so, he would apply all of his energy and creativity to the new job. At some point near the end of his second year at the agency, his hard work would begin to pay dividends; he would receive raises, promotions, or special recognition. Shortly thereafter, he would become disillusioned and would begin behaving in a way that made his lack of commitment obvious to his superiors. By the end of his third year, his reputation at the agency would have fallen, and he would no longer be treated as a rising star. This would be fine with Jack, because by this time he would have long since convinced himself that he was due to change jobs.

"How are things going at the agency where you work now?" we asked Jack during one of our meetings.

"Well . . . uh . . . pretty well, actually," said Jack. "Damned good, if you want to know the truth." Here he furrowed his brow and nodded. "As a matter of fact, I think it's time I did a little looking around. I don't want to be caught off guard when things turn bad at *this* place."

What Forms Do Your Fears Take?

Before we move on to look at how mythical fears influence behavioral choices, we'd like to suggest that you take a moment to think about the form that your particular fears take. Ask yourself if you're afraid of finding within yourself a person who is unkind, manipulative, ambitious, or inadequate. Or do you fear that if you abandon the pose you present to the world, you will have no identity or distinction whatsoever? Are you afraid of what others might do to you if you forsake your self-defeating behavior patterns? Are you fearful of failure? Of success? Of the ebb and flow of fortune that is life itself?

Perhaps the best way to identify the form in which your personal mythical fears appear is to ask yourself this: What do you feel that you are avoiding by continuing to behave in ways that hurt you? Along these same lines, ask yourself what you believe is the worst thing that might happen if you chose behaviors other than the self-defeating ones that you're most comfortable with. Then, once you've identified this *worst mythical consequence,* try to determine how likely it is that what you fear will come true. The information you gain from this brief experience can prove invaluable once you are well into the process of trying to make healthy and permanent changes in how you behave. It can help you see that it's much less risky to abandon your self-defeating behavior than to continue to practice it.

Remember: mythical fears express faulty conclusions. If you continue to be restricted by the death embrace in which your fears and conclusions are locked, you'll be hard pressed to find the freedom you need to make clearheaded, winning choices when faced with the opportunities for growth that each new moment of life affords.

Chapter 8

Making Choices

We've said it before, and now we must say it again: although an individual is not to blame for developing a self-defeating behavior, he or she *is* responsible for perpetuating the behavior and for allowing it to mature into a pattern. The conclusions and fears that give birth to self-defeating behaviors are, for the most part, imposed upon us; none of us come into the world, for example, with the belief that people are out to take advantage of us or that we lack the strength to do what life asks of us. The combination of experiences and behavior leads us to these conclusions and creates within us the fears that we bring to new moments of life.

Nevertheless, there eventually comes a point at which we can exercise control over how we behave. The mechanisms through which we exercise this control are known as *choices*. Through these choices, we each decide whether we will travel the winning road or the road to self-defeat.

A choice is required to perpetuate any thought or action that is not grounded in a physical reality. A physically crippled man does not choose to walk with a limp; the disease or trauma that has damaged his leg makes it impossible for him to walk any other way. If he averts his eyes and frowns as he moves along the sidewalk, however, it is because he has *chosen* this behavior; after all, it is possible for a crippled person to greet others with a smile. This is not to say that there is no relationship between the man's disability and his choice of behavior. But the fact remains that he has a choice with regard to the manner in which he presents himself. So if he chooses a pose that scares or alienates the people he passes on the sidewalk, he is responsible for both his behavior and the consequences it leads to.

The ongoing sequence of experiences that we call life is nothing more (and nothing less) than a series of choices. When a person makes a behavioral choice at a new moment of life, he or she is influenced not only by the immediate circumstances but also by each and every choice he or she has made prior to that moment. The behavioral choice the person makes at the new moment, in turn, has an influence on the choices he or she will make at subsequent moments. This means that any single choice an individual makes has the potential to determine the direction of his or her life.

This notion frightens many of us. It suggests that we must take total responsibility for what happens to us: we cannot blame our age, gender, physical condition, parents, or financial circumstances for the quality of our lives. Neither can we abandon ourselves to the workings of God, the fates, chance, or any other external manipulator of our fortune. The notion of free choice implies, in the end, that each of us must face him- or herself and say, without qualification and in total honesty, "I am what I have chosen to be."

We believe that there is no reason for people to be frightened or immobilized by the notion of free choice. Nor should we spend a lot of time and energy worrying about making the "right" choice in all situations. Each of us is born with an internal mechanism that, if allowed to function, will lead us directly to the choice that is in our best interest at a new moment of life. This mechanism is a part of our healthy inner core; it cannot be damaged or disabled. We can, however, learn how to short-circuit the workings of our internal guidance system. Once we have done so, the process of making choices becomes difficult; it seems as if we must remain constantly alert and deal with an ever-expanding range of behavioral options. We tell ourselves that this ongoing tension and uncertainty is the price we must pay for "sophistication"—when, in fact, it is nothing more than the price we pay for trying to second-guess our healthy inner selves.

Hard and Easy Choices

If the inner mechanism that guides our choices is allowed to perform its function—if, that is, we do not short-circuit the mechanism by retrieving faulty conclusions and creating mythical fears—it will guide us toward the thought or action that is most appropriate for us at a new moment of life. To see how this process works, we need only consider how we instinctively react when we are faced with real danger. If, for example, we are standing in the middle of a street when, all of a sudden, a speeding car screeches around a corner and heads in our direction, we instinctively move out of its path. We do not pause to analyze whether or not the car will stop before it hits us, or what type of injuries we will sustain if we are struck, or why the car is missing a hubcap, or what the driver is wearing. Instead, we get out of the way as fast as we can. Later we might wonder why the car was speeding or whether the driver intended to run us over, but at the moment of choice we do only what our inner mechanism tells us is the best thing we can do.

As we discussed earlier, however, toxic input from our cultural system eventually teaches us that our best response—the response that is natural and instinctive—is not, in fact, good enough for certain situations. From these painful experiences we acquire the notion that it is not adequate for us to respond spontaneously to new moments of life—instead, we must think of all the possible forms our response might take and then select from these possibilities the alternative that is most likely to ease our pain. Because this process requires so much thought and energy, our psychic subsystem develops a shortcut for dealing with new moments. It causes us to choose at an unconscious level whatever response has worked to ease the pain in earlier situations. At this level, it does not seem that we are choosing a particular behavior. We are deluded into believing that we are only doing what "comes naturally."

Nothing could be further from the truth. When we make a choice that short-circuits our healthy inner mechanism, we are putting forth a considerable amount of effort to avoid the tension or discomfort that we believe will result if we act spontaneously. We are doing this work at such a high rate of speed, however, that we are able to fool our conscious minds into believing that we have put forth no effort at all. When we practice a self-defeating behavior, we are constantly expending energy to make choices that run counter to the winning choices that require much less effort.

This explains, for example, why people who are depressed feel tired all the time. There is often no obvious explanation for their fatigue; they haven't been working or exercising or, as they will often admit, doing much at all. Yet below the level of consciousness, these people are putting most of their mental and physical resources into the effort required to make the self-defeating choices that manifest themselves as sadness or depression.

It's hard work, in other words, to continue to behave in ways that lead to self-defeat. People who practice self-defeating behaviors are often accused of taking the easy way out when faced with new challenges or demands. The truth is that they are doing a good deal more work than people who trust their inner mechanisms and make winning choices without depleting their energy.

Why Self-Defeating Choices Are So Difficult

There's a good reason why it takes more effort to choose a self-defeating behavior than it does to choose a winning behavior. To practice and perpetuate a self-defeating behavior, you must make several choices to maintain the internal logic of your thoughts or actions. If you choose to follow the winning road, on the other hand, you need only make a single choice: all you have to do at a new moment of life is to ignore or look past a mythical fear, and then choose a winning behavior. Once you have made this choice, your psychic subsystem is free to move on to other business. But if you opt for the road to self-defeat, you must continue to make choices. You cannot move on to the next new moment until an elaborate sequence of thoughts and actions has been enacted.

To see what this sequence of choices looks like, let's return to the model for self-defeating behavior. With a few enhancements, this model shows clearly how much work a person must do to make a self-defeating choice at a new moment of life.

As this enhanced version of the model shows, we need only make a single choice—represented here by the asterisk—to move onto the winning road and the next new moment of life. To travel the road of self-defeat, however, we must devote our energy to an ongoing process of thought, analysis, and selection. At the risk of getting ahead of ourselves, let's examine in greater detail the choices

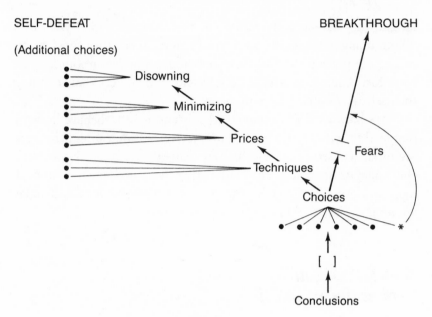

Figure 14

a person must make to perpetuate a cycle of self-defeat. Upon approaching a new moment of life, this person must do the following:

- *Retrieve a faulty conclusion.* If this conclusion is not retrieved at the new moment, the mythical fear that accompanies it cannot rise up to block the winning road.

- *Acknowledge a mythical fear.* Having retrieved a faulty conclusion, the individual must then choose to respond to the accompanying mythical fear in a way that legitimizes it as a basis for subsequent thought or action.

- *Choose a self-defeating behavior over a winning alternative.* In response to the mythical fear, the person must next make a choice to behave in a self-defeating way. If he or she chooses a winning alternative at this point, the cycle of self-defeat is broken.

- *Choose a technique that can be used to enact the behavior.* Next, the person must select from a wide range of techniques that can be used to make the behavior evident to the outside world. Should he or she withdraw or become depressed? Yell or scream? Drink too much or drive faster than the speed limit? Have sexual relations with someone he or she doesn't care for? Put off today's required tasks until tomorrow? At this point in the cycle, the individual must choose from among a virtually limitless list of potential techniques. (Advanced practitioners of a particular self-defeating behavior will have long since decided on a favorite or personalized technique that can be used to enact their behavioral choices. At this point, therefore, they can save time and energy by limiting the range of available techniques to the familiar favorite and one or two alternatives.)

• *Choose to minimize the price that must be paid for the behavior.* As we mentioned earlier, all people who practice self-defeating behaviors must pay certain prices. When confronted with these prices, however, an individual can choose either to pay the price in full (which, as we'll see later, interrupts the cycle) or to minimize it. The person who chooses to minimize the price of his or her behavior, however, must move on to make still another choice: he or she must select a *means* of minimizing the price. Some common means of minimizing are lying to oneself about the price ("it's really not that high"), using alcohol or another drug to modify one's perception of the price, and seeking the counsel of an alleged friend or expert who will help with the minimization.

• *Choose to disown responsibility for the behavior and its consequences.* Having minimized the price for the behavior to the extent that it can be paid with relatively little pain or anxiety, the individual still must deal with any remaining discomfort. To do this, he or she must disown responsibility for the behavioral choice that set the cycle in motion. Once the choice to disown responsibility has been made, however, still another choice is required. The individual must at this point decide who or what is responsible for the self-defeating behavior. Here again, a wide range of alternatives is available; the individual can, for example, blame his or her parents, the cultural system, God, genetics, fate, other people, or even the weather.

- *Use the entire experience as evidence in support of the faulty conclusion that initiated it.* The cycle of self-defeat cannot be completed until the individual chooses to interpret the entire experience as evidence that supports the faulty conclusion. If the individual does not make this choice, he or she will inevitably be forced to challenge the validity of the conclusion that initiated the sequence. When faulty conclusions are challenged, there is a good chance that they will be revised or abandoned. Should this occur, the cycle of defeat will be effectively interrupted, and the individual will find it difficult to replay a similar sequence of choices at subsequent new moments of life.

The sequence we've just described highlights only a few of the choices a person must make to perpetuate a self-defeating behavior; it suggests only a few of the options that are available at each choice point. The sequence we've outlined here, in fact, illustrates the simplest possible enactment of a cycle of self-defeat. In the majority of actual situations, however, more complicated variations of the cycle are put into play. An individual will often initiate a second cycle of self-defeat before the first is completed; the potential choices that must be made sweep over the person in waves, and the resulting confusion obliterates the fact that decisions are being made very quickly and that prices are constantly being paid. It's hard work to make all the choices that a self-defeating behavior demands. If we insist on depleting our energies in this way, our minds and bodies will eventually buckle beneath the strain.

"I Think I'll Just Stay Home and Relax"

A client of ours once described to us the sequence of choices he made one afternoon and evening to perpetuate a self-defeating behavior that had been interfering with his ability to enjoy life. Jim saw himself as a shy, withdrawn person. He believed that he lacked the social grace and inner warmth required to build and maintain friendships. We share his words with you here because they illustrate so clearly how much work it is to make the kinds of choices that nourish a cycle of self-defeat:

Last Friday afternoon, this guy at work, Henry, stopped by my desk and told me that he and his wife were having a few people over that evening, around seven o'clock. He asked if I wanted to join them.

I thought for a second, and it came to me that if I agreed on the spot to go to Henry's, I'd be as much as admitting I had nowhere else to go. I mean, I didn't want to give the impression that I was some kind of loser, sitting around with nothing to do, ready to jump at short notice. So I said to Henry: "Thanks, but I've had a rough week. I think I'll just stay home and relax tonight." When I got home that night, I turned on the TV, but I didn't pay much attention to it. I was thinking about the party over at Henry's: who would be there, what they'd have to eat, that sort of thing. I started feeling like maybe I should have accepted the invitation. I get sick of sitting home every night, you know. But it was too late. And besides, I've been to those parties with people from work before. They really aren't that much fun — just lots of gossip and drinking, and when it's over you worry that you might have said the wrong thing to someone.

At this point, we interrupted. "Did you think at all about calling Henry and asking if the invitation was still open?"

"Yeah, for a minute," Jim replied. "But that would have made me look like a real loser. Everyone would have known that I was sitting at home by myself."

He continued:

Anyway, I started getting pretty depressed about blowing another opportunity to get out of the house and talk with people, maybe even make a few friends. But like I said, no one is ever honest or open at those parties. It's all gossip about work — that, and everyone trying to impress everyone else. I can't stand that phony crap.

Finally, I got tired of worrying about it. I'd made my decision, and I'd just have to live with it. It's this pride thing of mine, I guess. Or maybe I'm just too honest for my own good. The way I am, though, get-togethers like the one at Henry's are just more work than they're worth. To hell with it, I decided. I really did feel like staying home and relaxing. I ordered a pizza, had a few beers, and went to bed. It didn't turn out to be that bad of a night, after all.

In Jim's recollection of this particular evening, we see evidence of self-defeating choice upon self-defeating choice. To begin with, we see him retrieving a faulty conclusion ("If I reject Henry's invitation, I'll avoid being labeled as a loser") and, at the same time, activating within his mind the fear that if he were to accept the invitation, his colleagues would view him in a negative light. Next, Jim chooses to withdraw from Henry's offer; he makes up an excuse about needing to go home and relax. When the price for this choice manifests itself in the form of the discomfort he feels while sitting in front of the television set, Jim refuses to pay it in full. He chooses instead to minimize the price by telling himself that he probably wouldn't have enjoyed the party, anyway. Having minimized the price to a level he can bear without too much trouble, Jim goes on to make still another choice: rather than accept personal responsibility for his displeasure, Jim disowns his behavior, blaming it on his "pride" and "honesty," as though these two qualities were somehow separate from his inner self. In the end, he can use the entire sequence of choices to validate his sense of himself as the sort of person who time and again sits home alone on Friday nights: in his own words, a "loser."

How much "relaxing" do you think Jim did as he sat in front of the television on this particular evening? Probably very little: he was too busy making the choices necessary to maintain his cycle of self-defeat. Had he made healthier—and, in the long run, easier—choices, he might have accepted the invitation, attended Henry's party, and come home feeling better about both his colleagues at work and himself. The winning choice in this situation, had Jim opted for it, would have left him far more relaxed than did his choice to stay home and perpetuate his cycle of self-defeat.

Toward Better Choices

Compared to self-defeating choices, winning choices are relatively easy to make. At a new moment of life, a person simply chooses a winning behavior over one or more self-defeating alternatives, after which his or her mind and spirit are free to move forward and to deal effectively with whatever challenge or choice the next new moment poses. This person does not need to struggle with faulty conclusions and the mythical fears these conclusions create, with the choice of an appropriate self-defeating technique, or with a range of options for minimizing prices and disowning his or her behavior. The individual who makes winning choices is not caught up in a cycle of recollection, fear, anxiety, and rationalization. He or she is alive and healthy in the present moment and does not need to worry about what might have been done better in the past or what might happen in the future.

A recent campaign against substance abuse caught on to this notion and used it as a theme. The campaign advised its audience—for the most part, young people—to "just say no" when the opportunity to use drugs presented itself. Although it was mocked because it was simplistic and naive, this message pointed to a basic truth. It suggested that the self-defeating behavior we know as substance abuse is best curtailed when an individual is at the initial choice point of a potential cycle of self-defeat. If the individual makes the simple choice not to use the drug at this point, he or she can avoid the series of difficult choices that lie along the road traveled by the substance abuser. People who can find it within themselves to "just say no" to drugs need not subsequently worry about how to pay for the substance, how to disguise their behavior from others, how to minimize the physical and mental prices the substance abuser must pay, or how to break out of the cycle of self-defeat that substance abuse inevitably creates.

Still, many people find it difficult to believe that winning choices can ease or eliminate much of the burden they place on their minds and bodies. Time and again, our clients tell us that in making a particular self-defeating choice, they were only doing "what comes naturally," or that they were "taking the easy way out." When we challenge statements such as these, we find that the people who make them do not really believe that self-defeating choices are easier to make than winning choices. Rather, they feel that in most new moments of life, they essentially have no choice with regard to how they behave. They are so caught up in faulty conclusions about themselves and the world and so restricted by mythical fears that they cannot believe they have options and alternatives. These people have adopted the belief that they have no power to choose. Until they have successfully challenged this conclusion, they will remain unable to see how much easier it is to travel the winning road than to struggle through successive cycles of self-defeat.

We believe that each individual is the sole determiner of the choices he or she makes. The individual's capacity for making winning choices can, of course, be compromised by one or more of the factors we'll discuss in the next chapter. Nonetheless, we believe that until people acknowledge their ability to make choices, they will find it impossible to break free from cycles of self-defeat. To deny the notion of free choice is to live under the tyranny that faulty conclusions and mythical fears impose. To acknowledge the ability to choose, on the other hand, is to declare oneself free to travel the road that leads to fulfillment and eventual breakthrough.

Chapter 9

Why People Choose to Defeat Themselves

If, as we've suggested, it is relatively easy to make winning choices at new moments of life, then why do people persist in making the kinds of choices that lead to self-defeat? To answer this question, we need to look at two things: the nature of choice itself and the mind of the person who is faced with a choice. Because of the way in which our minds work, it's necessary to make the great majority of choices rapidly and at a level below conscious thought. For this reason, many self-defeating choices seem to be not choices, but instinctive responses to situations we believe we have encountered before. And even in cases where we can slow the choice mechanism down enough to bring the choice to the level of the conscious mind, we often lack the information we need to see all of our available options. Hence we often find ourselves "choosing without choosing." A choice made under these conditions, as we'll soon see, will more often than not draw us into a cycle of self-defeat.

What we'd like to do here is to look at the factors that cause people to make self-defeating choices. We should say right at the start, however, that none of these factors make it impossible for a person to make winning choices. If we understand each factor, we can take it into account when we are faced with a choice; we can "neutralize" it and diminish the extent to which it can direct us toward choices that are not in our best interest. The first step in changing *how* we choose is to understand *why* we choose.

The Speed of Choice

In part 1 of this book, we suggested that the conscious component of our psychic subsystem delegates the majority of choices it encounters to its unconscious counterpart. If this were not so, our conscious minds would soon be overwhelmed by the number of choices that are required during each minute of the day. Once these choices have been assigned to the unconscious mind, however, they can be made very quickly—usually, within a fraction of a second. We do not need to "think" about choices made at this level. They are made and acted upon so quickly that our conscious minds record them as rapid, instinctive responses to familiar situations.

Suppose, for example, that you reach for the handle of a kettle that you have left boiling on the stove. If the handle is hot enough, you will immediately let go of it and draw your hand away from the source of the pain that you feel. You have no sense of having *chosen* to let go of the handle. You've simply responded naturally to your very real fear of being burned.

Yet in a sense, you have chosen your response. It is entirely possible (although certainly not natural) for an individual to continue to hold on to a piece of metal that is burning his or her hand. It's possible, in other words, to choose to subject oneself to pain. G. Gordon Liddy, the convicted Watergate conspirator, once held his hand over the flame of a blowtorch to demonstrate the strength of his will. While the relative sanity that Liddy displayed in this situation is open to debate, the incident nevertheless suggests that there is no natural law that makes it mandatory for a person to withdraw his or her hand from a source of high heat. (Those of us with less willpower than Mr. Liddy have, of course, long since learned that it is in our best interests to remove our hands from hot metal or flames as soon as we can.)

The point here is that any behavioral choice that has been delegated to the unconscious mind—and most behavioral choices have, indeed, been delegated to this level of the psychic subsystem—is made almost instantaneously. At a conscious level, we have no sense of making these choices; the unconscious mind simply makes them too quickly for us to notice. Say, for example, that while you are at work one day, your supervisor gives you what seems to be an overwhelming assignment. Within an instant, you may decide not only that you won't be able to complete the assignment, but also that you'll experience considerable anxiety over the prospect of your eventual failure. In the same instant, you may even have decided on the excuse you'll offer when the assignment isn't finished on time, and whom you'll ultimately blame for the problem. Within a second or two, you'll have determined your total reaction to your supervisor's request and will have selected the behavior you'll use to make this reaction evident. In the end, you'll have made a self-defeating choice without knowing or acknowledging that you've made any sort of choice at all.

A Lack of Information

It may be hard to believe that in today's information-saturated society, some people simply do not have available to them the information required to make winning choices. Most of us, in fact, have exactly the opposite problem: when faced with a choice, we seem to be surrounded by too many options and alternatives, and too much data. The vast amount of information we bring to new moments of life confuses us, making it next to impossible to make clearheaded choices. More often than not, we simply throw up our hands and choose to do what we have been doing all along.

However, there are cases in which people lack the information they need to choose a winning behavior over a self-defeating alternative. These situations tend to arise not as much from a person's lack of intelligence, curiosity, or education as from the degree of complexity our cultural system has created. We once worked with a client named Evan, for example, who spent four years at a college that did not offer a course of study in his area of interest. He initially chose this particular college because it was close to his home and because it offered him a generous scholarship. He remained at the college, however, because he believed he would be drafted into the military if he chose to drop out or transfer. Although the war in Vietnam was winding down, Evan, like many young men in his age group, did not want to risk being sent overseas and injured in a questionable cause. He was not aware that he could transfer to another college without exposing himself to the draft; when he asked his advisor about the possibility of changing schools, he was told that it wouldn't be wise to tamper with his deferment. So he continued to attend a college whose strengths did not match his interests. He did rather poorly in his courses, and, as a result, developed a negative self-image that stayed with him for several years.

Another client of ours who made self-defeating choices because she lacked the information to do otherwise was Greta, a woman in her mid-thirties. Her predicament, however, was more immediately dangerous than Evan's. She was married to a man who beat her at least once a week. The injuries she sustained from these beatings grew more and more serious, but she continued to live with her husband and endure his abuse. When we asked her why she had not sought refuge at one of the growing number of battered women's shelters in the area, she told us she didn't know that such places existed. She said she believed her only alternative to being beaten was to call the police and have her husband put in jail. She didn't want to do this, she said, because her husband was already on probation for another offense and could be sent to prison if she signed a complaint against him. If that happened, Greta explained, she would lose her source of income and would have to accept welfare to survive. Because she lacked the information to make what would have been a winning choice—that is, to get away from her husband as soon as possible—she chose to remain in the house she shared with him and to put up with his violent and dangerous behavior.

Tunnel Vision

We've all known people whose behavior seemed to be guided by tunnel vision. These people focus their attention exclusively on a single goal or purpose; they seem unable to see alternatives or to take detours, regardless of the benefits that a potential alternative or detour might offer. People who repeatedly make self-defeating choices suffer from a variation of this problem. Their attention is so keenly and constantly focused on a particular mythical fear that they find it impossible to look to one side or another for healthy alternatives to their self-defeating behavior.

Just as the person standing in a railroad tunnel focuses exclusively on the headlamp of the approaching locomotive, the person who makes self-defeating choices as a result of tunnel vision tends to focus on a single, huge mythical fear. A fear of this proportion often has to do with death, insanity, disease, or a similar calamity. The fear absorbs all of the person's energy and concentration; such people cannot even consider a thought or action other than in terms of the overriding mythical fear. Many of the people who are labeled as "hypochondriacs," for example, make the majority of their behavioral choices on the basis of whether a potential action will bring on or stave off the illnesses that they so dread. When we ask such people why they focus so exclusively on sickness and death, they often respond that if they drop their guard, one illness or another will sneak up on them and do them in.

Daniel, the young college dropout we discussed earlier, provides a clear example of how tunnel vision can cause a person to make repeated self-defeating choices. Daniel feared that if he made winning choices and, as a result, enjoyed life, then his father would die. So great was this fear that Daniel continued to make choices on the basis of whether or not a potential thought or action would sustain his unhappiness. He believed that if he remained unhappy, his father would not die. The prospect of his father's death became the locomotive rushing into the tunnel where Daniel found himself. He felt that he needed to focus on it exclusively to ensure that it would not run him over.

The Cycle Is Life

When we ask an alcoholic or a compulsive overeater why he or she continues to drink or eat excessively, the first response we often hear is, "I don't know, I guess that's just the way I am." Later, when we have managed to persuade this person that he or she in fact chooses to abuse food or alcohol, the person often responds by asking, "Okay, but if I don't drink (or eat), then what's left for me?" At this point, it becomes clear to us that for this particular individual, *the cycle of self-defeat has come to represent life itself.* And if the cycle of self-defeat is, in effect, all of life, then any choice that might break the cycle is a choice in favor of emptiness, oblivion, or perhaps death.

People who make self-defeating choices because they believe that their cycles of self-defeat are all that life offers have usually developed their self-defeating behaviors at an early age and have practiced these behaviors for a long time. Food and substance abusers tend to fall into this category, as do recidivist criminals and "therapy junkies" who move from counselor to counselor in search of a pat explanation of "what is wrong" with them. These people believe that their self-defeating behavior is an accurate reflection of their true inner self. To choose a winning behavior, by this logic, is to deny—perhaps even to obliterate—one's inner essence. If a person believes that a self-defeating behavior is the only means of presenting his or her true self to the world, then that person will find it very difficult to make winning choices.

Remember Roger, the self-described "party animal" we mentioned earlier in this section? For Roger, the self-defeating cycle of going to parties, drinking too much, and subsequently failing to hold jobs or maintain relationships had become life itself. This cycle represented to him the life he was meant to lead; he could not imagine how he might live if he stopped drinking. The repeated self-defeating choices he made were his attempts to be true to his inner self. "Don't talk to me about choices," Roger once said to us. "If you have the soul of a drunk, then you lead a drunk's life. All you can do otherwise is sit around and count the number of days you've been sober."

We do not mean to suggest here that it is impossible for people who view the cycle of self-defeat as life to make winning choices. Like all of us, these people choose to behave in accordance with the conclusions they have formed about themselves and life. Once they've identified and challenged the faulty conclusions that guide their lives, these people cease to look at their self-defeating behaviors as true expressions of their inner essence. They are then able to see clearly the many options that new moments of life offer and to choose behaviors that reflect, rather than distort, their healthy inner selves.

From Thought to Action

In this and the previous chapter, we have spent a good deal of time discussing how we make choices and why people persist in making choices that result in self-defeat. We have discussed this at length because we believe that choices play a crucial but often misunderstood role in determining our behavior. But the concept of choice is an elusive one. Of all the elements included in our model of self-defeating behavior, choices are the most difficult to isolate and analyze. Choices are made so rapidly and so often, and are influenced by so many factors, that it is hard to freeze them in time and describe accurately the functions that they perform. By looking at the elements that precede and follow self-defeating choices, however, we can gain additional insight as to how these choices shape our behavior.

Our psychic subsystem uses choices to build bridges between our conclusions and fears and the techniques we develop to respond to new moments of life. While we cannot observe a person's choices, we can identify the techniques he or she employs to put these choices into action. What's more, once we've studied these techniques, we can develop an accurate understanding of the faulty conclusions and mythical fears that lie behind them. So while choices themselves remain elusive, they can shed a good deal of light on the inner thoughts that shape them, as well as on the outer actions to which they lead.

Choices are mediators that carry information and guidelines back and forth between our thoughts and our actions. Through choices, we interpret new moments of life in ways that either validate or challenge faulty conclusions, and that either reinforce or undermine mythical fears. This is why it is crucial for us to recognize that as we move from moment to moment, we are constantly making choices. If we deny that we are making choices, or if we make choices without the required information or from a distorted point of view, we relinquish control over how we behave and how we live. When we find ourselves caught up in a cycle of self-defeat, we must try to slow down the speed at which we make choices and, then, to use the precious time we gain to obtain as much valid information as we can. As we'll suggest in the final section of this book, the process of making healthy choices at first requires work—or, to put it more accurately, conscious effort. Through practice and experience, however, the pattern through which winning choices are made will be programmed into our minds; it will be delegated from the conscious to the unconscious level of our minds. When we reach this point, we will not so much have learned how to make winning choices as we will have unlearned the process of perpetuating behaviors that bring us only misery, anxiety, and doubt. We will have discovered how to establish and nourish a healthy connection between our thoughts and actions. We will no longer need, in other words, to expend the repetitive and unproductive effort that is required to sustain a cycle of self-defeat.

Part Three

How Self-Defeating Behaviors Are Practiced

. . . As the anchor sank deeper and deeper into the ocean, the man who had been thrown overboard still continued to cling to it. He knew that he was sinking fast, but he also knew that hanging onto the anchor had saved his life. So he held his breath and allowed the weight of the anchor to carry him toward the ocean floor. He was aware that he was in danger, but the anchor, which had saved him once, might miraculously save him again.

"This really isn't so bad," the man thought to himself. "It's pleasant down here, once you get used to it. The water is warm, and there's a real sense of peace and quiet. It's not like being on a ship, where a storm can come upon you in a flash and throw you overboard."

Finally, the anchor came to rest on the ocean floor. The man, who still clung to it, was having difficulty holding his breath. His lungs burned, and his head filled with pressure. "What am I going to do to get out of this mess?" he asked himself, believing all the while that sooner or later a member of the ship's crew would appear to rescue him. . . .

Chapter 10

Self-Defeating Techniques

The choices we make when faced with our mythical fears initiate and perpetuate our individual cycles of self-defeat. These choices set the stage for self-defeating behaviors. They do not, however, put these behaviors into practice. The actual practice of a self-defeating behavior requires an additional mechanism—one that translates a choice into a conscious thought or an observable action. We call this sort of mechanism a *technique.*

A technique is a thought or action that is used to carry out a choice at a new moment of life. When an individual makes a self-defeating choice, he or she must also identify a technique that can be used to implement it. If no technique is identified, then the cycle of self-defeat is interrupted. People who practice self-defeating behaviors must therefore have at hand at least one technique that can be drawn upon at new moments of life. Without these techniques, people have no means for acting out their chosen responses to mythical fears.

The techniques that people use to put their self-defeating choices into practice fall into two categories: *internal techniques* and *external techniques.* Internal techniques are thought processes that are activated in support of self-defeating choices—for example, fantasizing, comparing yourself to others, or reviewing past hurts. External techniques, on the other hand, are observable actions that are used to act out misguided behavioral decisions. A list of the more common external techniques that people use to avoid their mythical fears would include such actions as crying or laughing at inappropriate times, withdrawing from challenges, and inflicting physical harm on themselves or others.

Some people use only internal techniques to practice their self-defeating behaviors. Others rely exclusively on external techniques. Usually, though, a person needs to use a combination of at least one external and one internal technique to put a self-defeating behavior into practice. The reason for this, as we'll discuss later, is that an internal technique that is used to implement a self-defeating choice often creates a level of tension that can be relieved only through the use of a related external technique. When techniques are used in this combination, people in effect subject themselves to what we call the "one-two punch."

Like self-defeating choices, techniques are brought into play at each point along the road to self-defeat. The individual who travels this road must make several choices; for each choice that is made, an appropriate technique must be identified. In the more advanced stages of a cycle of self-defeat—the stages in which an individual must contend with the prices of his or her behavior—advanced techniques are required. As we'll see later, the minimizing and disowning a person must do to avoid the full consequences of his or her behavior are nothing more than advanced techniques that are used to carry out self-defeating choices.

Techniques, Choices, Fears, and Conclusions

Each self-defeating technique that a person develops has a single, overriding purpose: to translate a behavioral choice into a conscious thought or an observable action. This choice has been made in an attempt to avoid a mythical fear—which, in turn, lies at the heart of a faulty conclusion that the person has formed. This means that within a cycle of self-defeat, a behavioral technique must reflect and support the distorted logic that the faulty conclusion imposes on a person's thought processes. The examples provided in the following chart demonstrate the relationships among the elements that make up a cycle of self-defeat.

Notice that in each of these examples, the self-defeating technique that is used not only enacts a choice but also reflects the fear and the conclusion on which the choice is based. The technique transforms the choice into a behavior and, at the same time, supports the logic by which the cycle of self-defeat operates.

Conclusion	Fear	Choice	Technique
Hiding my weakness will protect me from rejection.	If I am found out, I'll be hurt.	Hide the weakness.	Attack others.
Turning off my sexuality is good because it keeps me in control.	If I experience sexuality, I'll be overwhelmed by desire.	Deny my sexuality.	Ignore sexual feelings; label self as "bad."
Rigidity is good because it keeps me safe.	If an event catches me by surprise, I'll be devastated.	Worry to bring on depression.	Magnify changes beyond reality.
Smoking allows me to relax.	If I can't smoke, I'll be a nervous wreck.	Continued/ increased smoking.	Buy cigarettes; sit in smoking areas.
If I remain suspicious, people won't hurt me.	If I don't take steps to defend myself, I'll be exploited.	Mistrust people.	Suspicion, aloofness; look for reasons to withhold trust.
If I know what other people are going to do, I can keep them from revealing how inadequate I am.	If people are allowed to act freely, they'll expose my inadequacy.	I'll try to control the actions of others.	Manipulation.
Drinking enhances my life.	If I don't drink, my social life will collapse.	I'll keep on drinking.	Associate with people who drink frequently.
If I don't try to do anything, I'll never have to deal with failure.	If I put forth an effort, I'll probably fail.	I'll fail on my own terms.	Procrastination.
If I hide my true self, I'll be immune to criticism.	If I don't hide my honest responses, I'll be criticized.	I'll hide my inner self and my feelings.	Avert eyes; fail to speak up; avoid conversation.

Where Do We Get Our Techniques?

We are not born with faulty conclusions, mythical fears, or a disposition toward self-defeating choices. We learn these beliefs and
apprehensions through painful experiences and through the actions
we take to ease our discomfort. We are not born with self-defeating
techniques, either; the guidelines for using these techniques are not
genetically encoded into our thought processes. We *learn* our techniques and refine them through practice. At the unconscious level of
our psychic subsystems, these techniques are interpreted as hard-
won survival skills that are strengthened through repeated application. So natural do these thoughts and actions seem that we tend to
forget where—and how—we first learned them.

In talking with our clients about how they came to practice
their self-defeating behaviors, we have come to the conclusion that
people develop techniques in one of three ways: (1) through replica-
tion of the situation that originally gave rise to their mythical fears;
(2) through negative role-modeling; and (3) by accident.

Replicating a Situation That Bred Fear

When Molly was a child, she and her brothers were frequently
abused—both physically and verbally—by her father. "At first we
thought it happened only when he'd had a bad day at work," she
recalled. "But then it started happening more and more often—
instead of once a week we would catch it every other day, sometimes
every day. We knew when it was coming: we'd hear the door open
and close when Dad came home at night, and we'd wait. If he didn't
holler 'Hello' or call out to see who was home, we knew. One of us
was going to get smacked or screamed at."

Later, after she married and had children of her own, Molly
found herself falling into a similar pattern of child abuse. "I didn't
want to hurt them," she told us, "but it got to be the only way I could
keep from falling apart completely. I remember when it first began:
I'd had a terrible day at the office, and when I walked in the door the
first thing I saw was a stack of unopened bills—unopened because
we had no money to pay them. I heard the television blaring in the
living room, and Jennie was screaming at Robert . . . it seemed they
just didn't care about what I was going through to keep a roof over

their heads. So I . . . I let them have it but good, and I sent them both to their rooms. Afterwards I felt . . . not good, but more in control."

Within a few months, Molly was regularly abusing her two children. Although she never seriously injured either of them, the scene played itself out so frequently that Molly's neighbors eventually notified the police. "Toward the end, I was going after them all the time," Molly admitted. "Sure, sometimes I was upset for a good reason. But it got so that I hit them and screamed at them just because I was tired . . . or bored . . . or even because I got lonely."

What Molly had managed to do, in short, was to replicate the situation in which her own fears and faulty conclusions were born and bred. When her father lashed out at her and her brothers for no apparent reason, she began to believe that there was something wrong with her: something that disturbed her father and provoked his violent behavior. As an adult with children of her own, she continued to carry within her the belief that she was inadequate; and so, in a distorted attempt to please her absent father, she adopted his techniques. It is often said that imitation is the sincerest form of flattery. Molly carried this notion to an unfortunate extreme. To escape a self that she believed to be inadequate and worthy of abuse, she *became* her father, using the destructive techniques she had learned from him against her own children.

Negative Role-Modeling

Our culture tends to glorify individuals who have gained fame and notoriety despite the use of behavioral techniques that, for most of us, would lead inevitably to self-defeat. We are thinking here of rock stars who behave in violent or boorish ways, athletes who drink excessively or take drugs, financiers who achieve great wealth through manipulation and dishonesty, and other celebrities whose deeds and misdeeds captivate the public's attention and promote controversy. Such people serve as negative role models for those individuals who are looking for ways in which to implement their self-defeating choices.

We do not mean to suggest here that an individual must be successful or famous to serve as a negative role model. People can learn self-defeating techniques from almost anyone. Usually, though, the individual chosen as a negative role model is someone whose behavior provokes or irritates a person or institution that is viewed as a source of distress or tension. Children who are angry at their parents, for example, often adopt the self-defeating techniques of people whom the parents find objectionable. A similar phenomenon occurs even in group therapy sessions, where one participant, upon becoming frustrated with his or her progress, will begin to use the techniques displayed by another participant—usually one whose actions seem to provoke or irritate the therapist.

The first time we met with Chad, we suspected that he had acquired his self-defeating techniques from negative role models. At age nineteen, Chad was a sight to behold: his head was shaved, save for a thin purple band of hair running from the front to the back of his skull. A lavender butterfly was tattooed on his right cheek, and he wore a jacket made of scuffed black leather, with an obscene phrase spelled out in metal studs across the back. His vacant eyes seemed to look right through us. He spoke only in short, cryptic phrases and occasional bursts of profanity.

Once we were able to get past these behaviors, we learned how Chad had acquired his particular techniques. Both of his parents were successful professional people, and, as Chad moved into his early teen years, they repeatedly expressed disapproval over his lack of ambition and accomplishment. Often they compared him unfavorably to sons and daughters of their friends. Not surprisingly, Chad became extremely angry with his parents and began to look for ways to displease them. Eventually he noticed that the appearance and antics of certain punk rock groups seemed to irritate his parents to no end. Being an intelligent (as well as an angry) young man, Chad immediately saw how he might strike back at his mother and father. Within a week, he had a new haircut, and soon thereafter, the indelible tattoo on his face. His parents were predictably outraged.

"They didn't seem to like who I was," Chad told us once he had progressed past the techniques we saw during his first visit. "So I thought, okay, you don't like who I am, so how do you like *this?*" At which point he lapsed into the dead, wide-eyed stare with which he had first confronted us and allowed his tongue to dangle from the corner of his mouth.

Learning Techniques by Accident

By replicating the situations that bred their fears or adopting the behaviors of negative role models, most people are able to develop techniques that adequately implement their self-defeating choices. In some instances, however, a person acquires a technique almost spontaneously—or, as we prefer to think of it, *by accident.* This process begins when a person experiences a considerable amount of pain or stress and, quite by chance, finds a technique that alleviates the discomfort. The combination of uncomfortable circumstances, a self-defeating choice, and a need to express the choice lead the person to an appropriate technique—one that he or she will continue to use as a means of practicing a particular self-defeating behavior.

Consider the case of Bob, a middle-aged accountant who learned, apparently by chance, that by distorting feedback from others he could maintain a superficial sense of equilibrium. One day at the office, Bob's supervisor returned an audit report that Bob had finished a week earlier. "This looks good," said the supervisor. "But you might want to take another look at the net earnings in light of the new tax laws. The figure could change."

Now Bob's supervisor had often made similar comments, and Bob had always interpreted them as helpful suggestions. On this particular day, however, Bob was especially frustrated and more than a little angry. Earlier that morning, his wife had suggested that he look for a new job—a position that might pay more and give him more free time. Her remarks irritated Bob; they caused him to retrieve a faulty conclusion about his own inadequacy and to dwell on this conclusion all morning. He brooded over the notion that it was only a matter of time before his current firm found him out and dismissed or demoted him. By the time his supervisor arrived at his desk with the audit report, Bob had essentially chosen to leave his job.

When the supervisor delivered his evaluation of the report, Bob deliberately distorted the feedback he received. "He's putting me on notice," Bob said to himself. "He's letting me know what they really think of me around here. He's telling me it's time to wake up and smell the coffee." At this point, Bob began to feel better. His supervisor was a lousy boss, his firm was a lousy employer, he wasn't appreciated. . . . For the next several weeks, Bob continued to distort everything that was said to him at the office. All the while, he felt great; he was gathering more and more evidence to support his choice to quit his job, even though he hadn't yet begun to look for a new position. He had chanced upon a technique that would enable him to implement effectively his self-defeating choices.

Inner Techniques

As we pointed out at the beginning of this chapter, self-defeating techniques appear in two forms. They are either thoughts that articulate a person's faulty conclusions or observable actions through which the person carries out a self-defeating choice. We call the former *inner techniques* and the latter *outer techniques*. Some people use only inner techniques to enact their choices; others use a combination of inner and outer techniques. It's less common to find a person who practices only outer techniques, but such cases no doubt exist.

What are some of the conscious thoughts that we have been able to identify as inner techniques? The list we've provided below, although by no means comprehensive, identifies some of the more common thought processes that people use to carry out their self-defeating choices:

- Comparing oneself to others
- Holding back honest feelings
- Anticipating negative results
- Forming unrealistic expectations
- Distorting feedback
- Creating false limitations
- Blaming oneself or others
- Imposing guilt on others
- Reviewing past hurts
- Labeling oneself or others
- Blanking one's mind
- Fantasizing

- Intellectualizing
- Selective forgetting
- Magnifying real problems
- Rationalizing

Inner techniques such as those listed above produce deceptive results. Most inner techniques enable a person to feel more at ease, calmer, or more in control of his or her feelings—but only temporarily. Over time, inner techniques in fact create tension and anxiety, because they deny or violate the true inner self. Say, for example, that a person feels a need to write poetry but fears that he will not be successful. In response to this fear, the person chooses not to write a poem and uses several inner techniques to articulate this choice on a conscious level. The person tells himself that any poem he writes will undoubtedly be of poor quality. He reminds himself that years of training and practice are required to write well, and that he has had little experience or education in this area. Besides, he really doesn't have the time to write a good poem . . . or the right pen . . . or a quiet place to work. . . .

After drawing upon these inner techniques, the person achieves the desired results. No poem is written, and, moreover, the would-be poet takes superficial comfort in the choice not to write. If this same choice is made repeatedly, however, and if the same inner techniques are used to implement it, the person's true inner self will protest. He will feel miserable, tense, and unfulfilled and may even resort to a destructive outer technique that will relieve temporarily his ongoing sense of discomfort.

People who use only inner techniques to enact their self-defeating choices tend to be tense, irritable, depressed, and fragile. In our practice we see many individuals who suffer from chronic pain and use inner techniques to immobilize or limit themselves; they feel guilt, blame themselves and others, and dwell on the unrealistic expectation of a miracle cure that will rid them of their discomfort. As a result, these people become depressed, anxious, and fearful. Many eventually resort to outer techniques to reduce the internal tension that is with them during each waking moment of every day.

Inner techniques, in short, lead in one of two directions. Either they cause people to internalize completely their misery, or they cause people to choose an outer technique that will temporarily alleviate the distress. But outer techniques, as we shall soon see, serve only to compound people's difficulties and, in the process, to inflict discomfort on others.

Outer Techniques

Outer techniques are overt and observable actions that are used to carry out self-defeating choices. People tend to resort to outer techniques only when they have exhausted their inner techniques (or vice versa), or when they do not have available to them an inner technique that appropriately expresses a choice that they have made. An outer technique is the "behavior" that people often think of when they hear the term "self-defeating behavior." Because a true self-defeating behavior is a complex cycle of fear, choice, thought, and action, however, we believe that it is more accurate to think of an observable destructive action as an outer technique. A list of the more common outer techniques that people use to implement their self-defeating choices would include the following:

- Attacking others, physically or verbally
- Throwing temper tantrums
- Manipulating others
- Laughing when it is not appropriate
- Being late for appointments
- Arguing for the sake of argument
- Withholding sexuality in loving relationships
- Analyzing problems or situations when action is required
- Acting rashly in situations where thoughtful analysis is required
- Pouting
- "Nervous" tics or habits
- Failing to meet obligations

- Lying
- Crying at inappropriate times
- Making sarcastic remarks
- Engaging in promiscuous or unloving sexual activity
- Drinking too much
- Using drugs
- Engaging in racial or religious bigotry
- Smoking or chewing tobacco
- Spending money one does not have
- Gambling
- Stealing
- Acting "crazy" to acquire or maintain a diagnostic label

Quite a list, isn't it? We humans are nothing if not ingenious creatures. As we have developed as a species, we have devised (and continue to devise) a vast array of techniques that we believe will allow us to cope with the toxic input we receive from our cultural systems. But being ingenious is not the same as being intelligent. For as clever as they might seem, the outer techniques we use to implement our self-defeating choices serve only to delay the moment at which we are confronted with prices we must pay for violating ourselves and others.

The "One-Two Punch"

The phenomenon we refer to as the "one-two punch" occurs when people use a combination of inner and outer techniques to double the negative consequences of a self-defeating choice. What typically happens here is that upon making a choice, these individuals first attempt to implement it by way of an inner technique: they fantasize, rationalize, set limits, and so forth. This technique works for a while, but soon these people begin to feel the tension and discomfort that result when the healthy inner self is denied or persecuted.

Should this tension become unbearable, these individuals attempt to relieve it through the means of an outer technique: they hit someone, scream, break into tears, or attempt to numb themselves with drugs or alcohol. Like its inner counterpart, the outer technique affords temporary relief. Eventually, however, it leads to serious consequences; someone is physically or psychologically damaged, financially ruined, or even directly punished by society. In this way, these individuals effectively deliver to themselves a one-two punch. They are made miserable not only by the tension that accompanies the use of an inner technique but also by the consequences of the behavior that they choose as a means of easing the tension.

Unfortunately, many people fall into the habit of using the one-two punch to carry out their self-defeating choices. Consider Molly, the young mother who was abused as a child and, as a result, came to abuse her own children. When she arrived home from work the night she first employed this technique, she saw a stack of unpaid bills and heard the sound of misbehaving children. Having made the choice to practice a self-defeating behavior, she first chose an inner technique: she told herself that she was a failure, both as a provider and as a mother. These thoughts, in combination with the frustrations she had encountered earlier at work, created within her an unbearable level of tension — a state of misery she endured as long as she could. Finally, though, Molly resorted to an outer technique. She abused her children both physically and verbally, and — for the moment, at least — reduced her discomfort.

But what happened eventually? She began to rely on this technique to maintain her equilibrium, until finally her neighbors called the police. At this point, she was forced to absorb the second half of the one-two punch: she endured a tremendous humiliation when she was taken to the police station and charged with a crime, and a tremendous loss when her children were removed from her custody. Through a dangerous combination of inner and outer techniques, she managed to compound and intensify the consequences of her self-defeating behavior.

You Give What You Get

When we use techniques to carry out our self-defeating choices, we are in a sense attempting to give back to our cultural system at least a part of the toxic input that we've received from it. Our internal human system knows when it has received toxic information or material, and it does its best to eliminate it. The techniques that we use to perform this process of elimination, however, are often ill-chosen. As a result, they are almost always unsuccessful. Rarely do they completely purge the human systems of toxins. And more often than not, they guarantee that more toxic input will be received.

Why is this so? One reason self-defeating techniques fail is that they violate the true inner self. Hence, while they manage to cycle some of the toxic material back into the cultural system, they damage the inner self in the process. Using a self-defeating technique to rid your human system of toxins is a little bit like smashing a hole through one of the walls in your house so you can throw an obnoxious visitor through the opening. You may get rid of the unwanted guest, but you'll still have to deal with the damaged wall. And just as there are alternatives to ruining your house in the event that you want to evict an unwelcome visitor, there are better ways of dealing with toxic input from the culture than ejecting the poison by way of a self-defeating technique.

Self-defeating techniques also fail because they virtually ensure that additional toxic input will be received. Even people who use only inner techniques will eventually receive more toxic messages from the cultural system. People who are tense, moody, or irritable as a result of their inner techniques will eventually come to be known by these characteristics. Sooner or later, they will be told, in one way or another, that they aren't measuring up to the expectations set forth by the cultural system. This information cannot help but reinforce the faulty conclusion on which their self-defeating behavior is based. This toxic input, in turn, will initiate a new cycle of self-defeat, which will be repeated until they learn to make winning choices at new moments of life.

Fortunately, each of us has been provided with a mechanism that can guide us away from self-defeating choices and the behaviors we use to act out these choices. We have within us the ability to recognize the prices we must pay in order to practice our self-defeating behaviors. If we recognize these prices for what they are, rather than view them as unjust punishments for actions over which we have no control, we can break the cycle of self-defeat. Prices are reliable internal guides. They can show us how to learn and grow from our mistakes.

Chapter 11

Prices

If we practice self-defeating behaviors for any length of time, we must inevitably pay certain prices. The more overt and clearly defined forms of self-defeating behavior force us to pay unambiguous prices. The price of chronic overeating, for example, is obesity; the price of long-term smoking is lung and/or heart disease. When we practice a self-defeating behavior, we are interfering with the natural and healthy functions of our human systems, and these systems eventually rebel against our abuse of them. Through prices, they tell us that we are on an incorrect course and are moving in a direction that leads only to pain, unhappiness, or death.

For this reason, prices are both necessary and instructive. If our human and cultural systems did not exact prices for certain types of behavior, we would live in a chaotic and dangerous world. If, for example, our culture did not dictate that the thieves must pay certain prices after being apprehended and convicted, such crimes as burglary, robbery, and embezzlement would be committed much more frequently they are now. Or if, on the other hand, our physical subsystems allowed us to drink as much alcohol as we wanted without suffering any consequences, many people would be in danger of dying from alcohol poisoning. Prices, in short, tell us what we can and cannot do. They place limits on our behavior and keep us from injuring or destroying ourselves and others.

The prices we pay for our self-defeating behaviors take several forms. They appear most obviously in the form of the physical and psychic consequences that result when we behave in ways that violate our healthy inner selves. Prices also take the form of lost opportunities: new moments of life that we fail to seize upon because we are caught up in our cycles of self-defeat. What's more, we often are not the only people who must pay the prices associated with our self-defeating behaviors. Others must pay these prices, too; our families, friends, and colleagues are often forced to absorb some of the costs of our destructive behavior. If we rationalize our self-defeating behaviors on the grounds that we alone must pay for them, more often than not we delude ourselves and expose the people we care about most to needless pain.

If we pay attention to the prices we must pay and if we take an honest accounting from them, these prices can show us when and how to change our behavior. We should therefore be thankful that prices exist, and we should pay these prices fully. As we'll see in the next chapter, any attempt to avoid or reduce the prices associated with a self-defeating behavior serves only to guarantee that the behavior will continue to be practiced. And as the behavior is perpetuated, the price we must eventually pay for it continually increases.

Why Prices Are Necessary

People who refuse to acknowledge that they choose to practice their self-defeating behaviors have a difficult time dealing with prices. They tend to view prices as unjust punishments for thoughts or actions over which they have no control. "It doesn't seem fair," such a person will often say to us. "Why do I have to feel lonely all the time, just because I'm not an outgoing person?" Our response to this sort of statement is to point out that, in fact, prices are the very things that make life "fair." Prices link behaviors with consequences, and in this way help ensure that more often than not, people reap what they sow.

Without prices, we would have no guidelines to tell us that we were making behavioral choices that violated our inner selves. If we were to feel no guilt or endure no form of censure when we hurt other people, we might go through life doing great damage to ourselves and others. We might remain forever unaware that we had done wrong, just as certain sociopaths commit heinous crimes without any sense of violating themselves or others. A world without prices would be a dangerous and confusing place.

Physical pain, for example, is a basic and obvious price that protects us from harmful or self-destructive actions. Say you woke up angry and upset one morning and decided that a good way to express your displeasure would be to hit yourself on the head with a hammer. Upon carrying out this choice, you would feel a good deal of pain, the memory of which would probably dissuade you from choosing this behavior again. Without this pain, you might come to the faulty—but, in its own way, logical—conclusion that hitting yourself on the head is a good way of relieving anger or tension. Soon enough, however, this self-defeating technique would cause you to injure or kill yourself. In the absence of pain, you might never know what hit you—not, at least, until the consequences of your actions were irreversible.

Prices establish the basic rules according to which the game of life is to be played. When we violate these rules, we must face the consequences. This relationship between actions and consequences is the basic connection that gives direction to our lives.

Prices Make Life Meaningful

Think of a game you have played and enjoyed in the past: hide-and-seek, football, bridge, chess, or any other form of recreation that has brought you pleasure. Chances are that you enjoyed the game for two basic reasons: because it had a clear *objective* and because it had a set of *rules* that determined what actions were allowable in pursuit of the common objective of all its players. More than likely, the pleasure you took from playing the game stemmed from the challenge of achieving the common objective while at the same time observing the constraints imposed by the rules.

But think of what the game would have been like had it not had a sensible objective, or had there been no rules for playing it. Suppose, for example, that the objective of a game of checkers was to clear the board of all pieces as soon as possible, and that any player could win the game simply by knocking the board off the table. How enjoyable do you think the game would be to play under these conditions? A player might initially experience a feeling of anarchic glee upon upending the checkerboard and scattering the pieces across the room, but that feeling would soon pass. Without a sensible objective and a set of rules, the game would becoming meaningless, and few would be motivated to continue playing it.

Just as rules and objectives give meaning to games, prices lend meaning to life. Without the rules that prices enforce, all of our actions would be equally valid and appropriate. The act of kissing your child would be no better or no worse than the act of killing your mother; without prices, the consequences of both actions would be identical. Rising from bed each morning and accomplishing some sort of productive work would bring no greater benefit than sleeping all day. Life would be nothing but a series of meaningless choices and actions; we would never be punished, but neither would we ever be rewarded. Prices are necessary not only because they protect us from harm, but also because they tell us what life means. They enable us to distinguish healthy choices from unhealthy alternatives and to comprehend the consequences of each action we take.

How Prices Instruct Us

It is our belief that within the larger interaction of human and cultural systems, prices tell us when we are behaving in an unhealthy way and show us how we can correct our course of thought and action. In terms of our basic model, prices serve to block the road that leads to self-defeat:

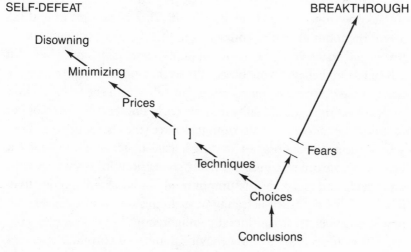

Figure 15

This version of the model shows us that if we recognize prices and pay them when they are due—if, in other words, we do not minimize them or refuse to take responsibility for them—we can interrupt our cycles of self-defeat. When we recognize and pay the prices of our self-defeating behavior, we create for ourselves a new moment of life: a moment at which we can choose to travel the road to health and breakthrough. "If you choose this behavior," our prices say to us, "then this is what will happen. If you want a different result, you must make a healthier choice—one that doesn't violate your inner self or bring distress to others."

Consider, for example, the predicament of people who chronically choose to overeat. These people are eventually confronted with several prices: weight gain, diminished physical endurance, pains in the muscles and joints, inability to wear certain types of clothing, and an outwardly unattractive appearance. If people who overeat acknowledge that they aren't happy with these consequences, and if they honestly experience the distress that their behavioral choices have brought to them, these people will be directed toward a way out of the cycle of self-defeat. The next time they sit down to a meal, they will be motivated to choose to eat less, or to eat healthier or less caloric foods. Their memory of the discomfort brought on by their overeating will direct them toward winning choices at new moments of life.

Prices do more, however, than guide us toward better choices. If we acknowledge and pay them fully—if, that is, we not only think about them but also allow ourselves to *feel* the distress they bring— prices will strike at the heart of the faulty conclusions on which our self-defeating behaviors are based. Prices that are not minimized challenge these destructive beliefs about ourselves and the world. These prices direct the light of reality into the dark, unconscious parts of our minds. If we follow this light from its source (the consequences of our self-defeating behaviors) to its target (the conclusions behind the behaviors), we can recognize our faulty conclusions for what they really are: fragile and misguided assumptions about what will happen to us if we don't behave in self-defeating ways. In this way, the prices we must pay for our behavior can literally enlighten us.

If we look again at the behavior pattern of chronic overeaters, for example, we might well find that their cycle of self-defeat is based on a faulty conclusion that goes something like this: "Being over-weight keeps me from having to deal with many of life's problems." The mythical fear that these people feel on the basis of this conclu-sion is that if they were not overweight, then their inability to deal with life would be exposed. Accordingly, they choose to overeat, in the unconscious hope of achieving and maintaining a state of obesity.

But what happens when the prices associated with this particu-lar self-defeating behavior present themselves? If these prices aren't minimized, overeaters must consciously deal with one or more of the following: an unattractive outward appearance, the culture's preju-dices against obese people, an inability to participate in certain types of physical activity, and the physical ailments brought on by carrying around too much weight. At some point, overeaters must ask them-selves if these are not real problems — and if, ultimately, their obesity has not in fact brought on, rather than warded off, discomfort and anxiety. This is the point at which fundamental behavioral change becomes not only possible, but likely. When people see their faulty conclusions in light of the prices that must be paid, their sense of what is healthy and logical will invalidate these conclusions and lay the groundwork for a change in behavior.

Different Types of Prices

At the beginning of this chapter, we suggested that prices tend to fall into two general categories: the *actual consequences* that self-defeating behaviors bring about, and the *opportunities that are lost* when people are too caught up in their cycles of self-defeat to live each moment to its fullest. We suggested also that actual conse-quences may be either *physical* or *psychic,* and that all types of prices are paid not only by the person who practices a self-defeating behavior but also by those around that person. To sharpen these dis-tinctions further, let's look at some of the specific prices people pay in order to continue to practice their patterns of self-defeat.

Physical Consequences

The most obvious prices we pay for our self-defeating behaviors are the physical consequences that sometimes result when unhealthy

techniques are practiced over extended periods of time. The following is a partial list of these observable physical consequences:

- Obesity
- Lung disease
- Heart disease
- Skin disease
- Sexually transmitted diseases
- Physical exhaustion
- Alcohol/drug-related physical problems (cirrhosis, hepatitis, etc.)
- Chronic anxiety
- Hypertension
- Chronic pain
- Premature aging
- Migraine headaches
- Stomach ulcers
- Stroke
- Bruxism (the grinding down of the teeth as a result of chronic anxiety)

We do not suggest, of course, that all of these consequences result
exclusively from self-defeating behavior patterns. We're aware that most
of the conditions listed above may have multiple causes, and that some
of these causes (for example, a hereditary disposition toward heart disease) are outside of the individual's control. Most doctors would agree,
though, that some form of self-defeating behavior contributes to the
development of each of the conditions we've listed above. We believe
that while self-defeating behaviors are not *solely* responsible for the
consequences we've listed above, the ongoing practice of these
behaviors can *influence* whether or not a person develops a particular physical ailment, along with the level of severity of the ailment.

Psychic Consequences

The psychic consequences that result when we practice self-
defeating behaviors are every bit as destructive and limiting as the

physical consequences that arise when these behaviors are perpetuated over time. And since our internal human subsystems are all
integrated with one another, it seems logical that the psychic consequences we suffer as a result of our unhealthy choices can eventually
lead to physical consequences, and vice versa. It's been clearly established, for example, that the ailments we have come to know as *psychosomatic illnesses*—ulcers, colitis, migraine headaches, and so
on—result from an interaction between our psychic subsystems and
one or more of our physical subsystems.

Even in the absence of an observable psychosomatic condition,
the psychic consequences to which self-defeating behaviors lead can
cause tremendous distress and place severe limitations on us. In
terms of psychic consequences, people who practice self-defeating
behaviors can expect to pay one or more of the following painful
prices:

- Loneliness
- Shame
- Loss of self-respect
- Alienation
- Loss of energy
- Rage
- Bitterness
- Humiliation
- Guilt
- Anxiety
- Helplessness
- Hopelessness
- Sadness
- Hatred

Those of us who practice self-defeating behaviors deal with
these psychic consequences on a regular basis. The specific consequences we experience vary according to the type of behavior we
choose to carry out our unhealthy choices. If, for example, we
choose to act in ways we know are harmful or wrong, we experience

guilt and shame. If we choose techniques that cause other people to punish or attack us, we experience rage, bitterness, and hatred. If we behave in ways designed to keep others at a distance, we experience loneliness, alienation, and sadness. And if we fail to recognize these thoughts and feelings as the prices we must pay for our behavior, we are doomed to endure them and to perpetuate an existence that bears little resemblance to the cycle of growth and fulfillment we know as life.

What's worse, a failure to respond appropriately to these psychic consequences can result in actions that contaminate other people. If we refuse to pay these prices ourselves, others end up paying them. When, for example, we respond to our rage or self-hatred by bringing on a financial calamity, we spread the consequences of our self-defeating behavior to our friends, families, and creditors. In an attempt to avoid paying the prices of our behavior, we spread the poison that is killing us. We become sources of the very toxins that initially caused us to develop our patterns of self-defeat.

Lost Opportunities

The physical and psychic consequences we suffer as a result of our self-defeating behaviors are in most cases easy enough to recognize. Not quite so evident, however, are the prices we pay in the form of *lost opportunities*. When we practice self-defeating behaviors, we spend tremendous amounts of time and energy thinking about the various unhealthy choices that such behaviors require. Our attention becomes focused on the techniques we use to carry out these choices, as well as on how we can minimize the observable consequences that these techniques bring about. Caught up in this cycle of self-defeat, we are often unable to recognize new moments of life that afford us opportunities to interact with ourselves and others in healthy, life-enhancing ways.

These lost opportunities are the hidden consequences of our self-defeating behavior patterns. It's difficult, therefore, to specify what our self-defeating behaviors cost us in terms of physical well-being, emotional growth, or material success. In dealing with our clients, however, we've observed that people who remain locked in cycles of self-defeat tend to miss out on opportunities for the following:

- Expressing the self creatively
- Achieving a sense of inner peace
- Achieving personal goals
- Improving personal relationships
- Experiencing the full range of human emotions, from deep grief to profound joy
- Advancing careers
- Developing friendships
- Continued learning
- Helping others
- Understanding different types of people and their cultures

People whose self-defeating behavior patterns block off these kinds of opportunities almost inevitably fail to achieve their full human potential. They can add up the physical and psychic consequences of their behavior, but the sum of these consequences rarely accounts for the sense of loss or incompleteness that they feel. When such people complain that there is "something missing" in their lives—an elusive wholeness that cannot be grasped or identified—they are often referring to prices paid in the form of lost opportunities. The healthy inner self knows its purposes and capabilities. When we make choices that thwart these purposes and capabilities, the inner self protests, and we feel the nagging sense of loss that accompanies a life not lived to its fullest.

Others Pay Our Prices, Too

It would be convenient, appropriate, and somehow fitting if we alone were forced to pay the prices associated with our self-defeating behaviors. In an attempt to minimize the consequences of their choices, many of our clients have tried to contend that this is indeed the case. "So what if I'm stuck in a pattern of self-defeat?" these clients argue. "I'm only hurting myself, and I can live with the consequences of my actions. So why do I need to change the way I behave?"

Our answer to this question is that very rarely are the prices of a self-defeating behavior paid only by the person who chooses to practice the behavior. As we suggested earlier, a self-defeating behavior is, in a sense, a person's attempt to send back into the cultural system some of the toxic input that he or she has received at an earlier time. Sadly enough, this attempt is often successful. And when it is, the people and the organizations around us are forced to absorb the consequences of our unhealthy behavioral choices.

Recall, for example, the case of Molly, the young mother whose self-defeating behavior we described in the previous chapter. Abused as a child, she grew up to abuse her own son and daughter. As a result of this behavior, she paid certain prices; she was shamed, humiliated, and deprived of the right to care for her children. But the children paid certain prices, too. They endured both verbal and physical abuse, and, eventually, were subjected to the trauma of being removed from their home and placed under foster care. It would have been ridiculous for Molly to contend (which, we are happy to report, she never did) that she alone suffered the consequences of her destructive actions.

Or consider Jack, the advertising executive who moved from agency to agency, changing jobs each time his fear of success forced him into a cycle of self-defeat. Jack could (and did) argue that he alone paid the price of his self-defeating behavior; it was he, after all, who found it impossible to advance beyond a certain level in his profession. Through a careful analysis of his pattern of self-defeat, however, we were able to show Jack that he was inflicting his prices on others. His wife, for example, was on several occasions forced to disrupt her life and move to a new city when Jack abruptly resigned from a job. The advertising agencies where Jack worked also paid certain prices as a result of his actions; they lost not only a talented employee but also the time and money they had invested in him. Moreover, these organizations no doubt suffered from the toxic messages Jack sent out to his colleagues as he prepared to take his leave.

The consequences of a self-defeating behavior are almost never restricted solely to the person who practices the behavior. Smokers who develop lung cancer, for example, hurt not only themselves but also the friends and family members who must watch them suffer and die. The medical costs of sustaining the smoker through a lengthy terminal illness must be paid by either an insurance company or a government agency—which, in turn, compensates for these losses by raising insurance premiums or personal taxes. In this way, the prices associated with a single individual's self-defeating behavior are distributed not only to his or her colleagues and relatives but also throughout the larger cultural system. Toxic input from the cultural system produces a self-defeating behavior, the equally toxic consequences of which are returned to the culture when the individual who practices the behavior inflicts his or her prices on others.

We Must Pay Our Prices

At the beginning of this chapter, we contended that prices were both necessary and instructive, and that without them we would have no means by which to make sense of life. Yet in the preceding section, we described the havoc that prices can wreak when they fall upon others and spread throughout our cultural system. You might be asking, therefore, whether prices are good or bad. If they are good, how can they possibly cause the amount of pain and disruption that they bring? And if they are bad, why are they necessary parts of a meaningful life? And, perhaps most important, how should we respond when we are confronted with the prices associated with self-defeating behaviors?

The answer to these questions is that if we recognize prices and *pay them fully* when they first appear, they will serve as reliable behavioral guidelines and will give our lives meaning and purpose. If, however, we attempt to defer these prices or to pass them on to others, they will eventually take on catastrophic dimensions. This is why it is essential that we avoid the advanced self-defeating techniques that are used to *minimize* and *disown* our personal prices. For, as we'll demonstrate in the remainder of this section, it is through minimizing and disowning that we complete our cycles of self-defeat. Through these two advanced techniques, we change the nature of prices. We transform instructive warnings into consequences that can kill.

Chapter 12

Advanced Techniques I: Minimizing the Prices We Pay

We feel that it's worthwhile here to pause for a moment and reflect on the predicament of those unfortunate individuals who continue to perpetuate their personal cycles of self-defeat. These individuals deserve our empathy and understanding, because they are trapped in what seems to be an inescapable dilemma. Upon approaching a new moment of life, their path is blocked on the one hand by the mythical fears that impede progress along the road to breakthrough, and on the other by the prices associated with a familiar self-defeating behavior. These people's options at this new moment appear to be limited to a choice between two evils:

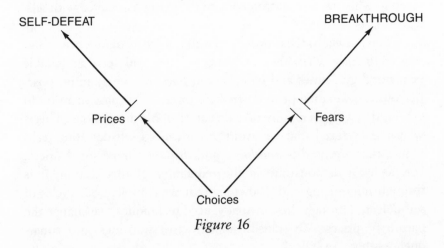

Figure 16

Faced with this choice, such individuals are understandably ill at ease. They know that a self-defeating thought or action will bring on less-than-pleasant consequences. Yet their mythical fears, often operating on an unconscious level, block out any awareness of the healthy alternatives that are available. And to make matters worse, they frequently must choose a thought or action within a fraction of a second, which does not give them time for deep reflection or lengthy analysis.

How do people who time and again find themselves in this situation resolve their habitual dilemmas? Sometimes, if their fears of having to pay the prices that lie along the road to self-defeat are strong enough, these people make healthy changes in the way they behave. More often, though, they make their behavioral choices "easier" by disrupting the balance between prices and fears. They do this through the application of an advanced technique known as *minimizing,* which distorts the role that prices play in guiding our behavior.

We call minimizing an "advanced" technique because it is nothing more (and nothing less) than *a self-defeating technique that is applied at an abstract level of thought and in moments of relatively high psychic urgency.* Minimizing doesn't occur until after an individual has already used at least one technique to carry out a self-defeating choice. Once this choice has been made and implemented, however, the individual *must* make use of a minimizing technique in order to maintain his or her cycle of self-defeat. If the individual does not minimize at this point, a new moment of life is created, and this person is in a position to make a positive change in the way he or she behaves.

Minimizing, in short, is a sophisticated means by which people alter the balance between prices and fears so that they can continue to practice their self-defeating behaviors. Through minimizing techniques, people tell themselves that their hurtful and destructive choices are appropriate and inevitable. They use their conscious minds to shore up the false logic that operates at the unconscious level where faulty conclusions are stored.

The minimizing techniques that people use to sustain their cycles of self-defeat are as varied as the primary techniques that are used to initiate these cycles. When they are first developing their self-defeating behaviors, however, most people use at least one of the common minimizing techniques—ignoring, comparing, numbing, joking, and so on—that we'll be discussing in this chapter. Later, when these initial attempts at minimization cease to accomplish their purpose, the individual who insists on practicing a self-defeating behavior must either find new ways of minimizing his or her prices or "enhance" an old minimizing pattern so that it can continue to distort the messages that prices are attempting to convey. And because no attempt at minimizing is ever completely successful, this individual must then move on to disown his or her behavior and to view its consequences as evidence that validates a faulty conclusion.

The Price-Fear Equation

As we demonstrated earlier, the basic behavioral choice a person makes at each new moment of life is influenced by two factors: the mythical fears that spring from the person's faulty conclusions about life and the prices the individual must pay in order to make a self-defeating choice. When these two factors are virtually equal—when the individual's mythical fears are as intense as his or her real fears of the consequences to which a self-defeating behavior will lead—the individual has (in theory, at least) a "free choice." But this sort of choice would be a hard one to make: it would involve considerable conscious thought and a careful weighing of the available alternatives. If we were forced to make all our choices under these conditions, we would have little time to do anything other than evaluate options and make decisions. Once again, though, our unconscious mind comes to the aid of its conscious counterpart: it skews our choice points by creating an imbalance between fears and prices. In the real world, therefore, most of our choice scenarios tend to look either like this:

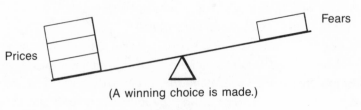

Prices · Fears

(A winning choice is made.)

Figure 17

or like this:

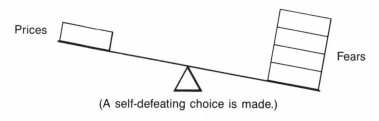

(A self-defeating choice is made.)

Figure 18

The relative balance of the price-fear equation, in other words, determines whether we will choose a self-defeating behavior or a winning alternative. In situations in which prices outweigh fears, we will choose a healthy thought or action. But when our mythical fears loom larger than the potential consequences of a particular behavior, we'll tend to make self-defeating choices.

How Minimizing Works (but Really Doesn't)

Minimizing is a conscious attempt to keep the price-fear equation in a state of imbalance that makes self-defeating choices seem appropriate. When we minimize, we use our conscious minds to reduce in severity or number the prices we must pay for practicing our self-defeating behaviors. In essence, we use an advanced technique to make a winning choice point (see the first diagram above) look like a losing choice point (see the second diagram). We say to ourselves something like this:

> I know that if I engage in this certain behavior, I'll have to pay a price. But that price is nothing compared to the fear I'll have to deal with if I choose not to practice the self-defeating behavior that has kept me safe for so long.

Using this or a similar notion as a basis, we then proceed to spin off elaborate rationales for our self-defeating choices. We tell ourselves that we aren't really paying prices, that we won't have to pay our prices until some point in the distant future, or that someone else will pay our prices for us. Bit by bit, these rationales rob our prices of their weight, significance, and instructive power, until we finally manage to create within our minds a scenario in which self-defeating thoughts and actions seem to have no consequences at all.

People who persistently minimize the consequences of their behavior are engaging in complex and difficult mental gymnastics. Their efforts would be impressive, save for one fact: *minimizing simply doesn't work.* Why not? Because *prices must be paid.* Those of us who minimize our prices are reducing not the prices themselves, but only our *perception* of the prices. What's more, in many cases minimizing increases the prices we must eventually pay. A person with a bad marriage, for example, may minimize by abusing alcohol or food. These techniques do little to improve the marriage, and more often than not this person must deal not only with a difficult relationship but also with a drinking or weight problem. We use minimizing techniques to convince ourselves that the costs of our actions are relatively small, but even as we minimize, those costs are increasing. Sooner or later, we all must pay the prices associated with our self-defeating behaviors. When we minimize, all we do is ensure that we'll pay these prices under less instructive—and, often, more destructive—terms.

Common Minimizing Techniques

Those of us who practice self-defeating behaviors must minimize if we are to perpetuate our cycles of distress. As soon as we fail to minimize, the full implications of our prices hit home, and we are directed toward healthier and more productive behaviors. If we insist on nourishing our faulty conclusions, however, we must continue to disrupt the price-fear equation by way of one or more of the following advanced techniques:

- Ignoring
- Comparing
- Joking
- Numbing
- Martyring

- Being chronically busy
- Nihilizing
- Making others pay
- Therapizing
- Adapting

A brief look at each of these minimizing techniques can provide us with an understanding of how far many of us are willing to go to hang on to the very behaviors that are responsible for our pain and unhappiness.

Ignoring

An obvious way of refusing to acknowledge the consequences of our thoughts and actions is simply to ignore these consequences when they arise. We are reminded here of Alice, a client of ours whose self-defeating behavior centered around the virtually promiscuous use of checking and charge accounts. When bills from creditors and overdraft notices from banks arrived in the mail, Alice simply shoved them into an infrequently used drawer in her kitchen. Before long, this technique inflicted financial ruin upon her family; a credit counselor who worked on the case with us reported that the unpaid bills and overdrafts in the drawer added up to over $37,000 of debt. During one of our sessions we asked Alice what she hoped to accomplish by hiding and ignoring these reminders of her prices. "I'm not really sure," she replied. "It's like that old saying—'Out of sight, out of mind.' So long as I didn't have to look at the bills, I could keep on shopping."

Comparing

Many people find it comforting to compare their own prices with the consequences that people with similar self-defeating behaviors have to deal with. Hence, the smoker or overeater who develops hypertension looks at his or her price as minimal in comparison to the lung cancer or heart attack that a friend or acquaintance suffers. People who use this minimizing technique try to convince themselves that they aren't really paying that steep a price for their self-defeating behaviors; they can recall on a moment's notice several examples of friends or acquaintances who are paying much more dearly for a related (if not identical) behavior. Like lawyers preparing for an important case, they collect evidence that would seem to prove that their cycles of self-defeat are taking a fairly minimal toll.

We spoke earlier of Celia, the young woman who began to starve herself because she feared that her husband was about to leave her. When we asked Celia to acknowledge her prices—when we literally placed a mirror in front of her emaciated face and told her to look at the consequences of her destructive actions—she stared into the glass for a moment and shrugged her shoulders. "Okay, so I don't look that great," she said. "But you should see my friend Carol. When her husband took off, she slashed her own throat and almost died. At least I don't have a scar."

Joking

Joking is an especially popular means of minimizing the results of a self-defeating behavior. This technique not only robs a personal price of its power and meaning but also enables the person who chooses it to win the approval of others. So obsessed is our culture with resilience, pluckiness, and good humor in the face of adversity that it encourages us to laugh or make jokes when confronted with our prices. We are taught from an early age to feel a measure of grudging admiration for the jolly overeater, the smiling victim, and the sardonic wit who snaps off puns in the wake or his or her own ill fortune. It's not surprising, therefore, that many of us learn to use humor to minimize our prices. Joking helps take the sting out of our hurts. What's more, it can bring us the grudging admiration of friends and relatives, who are often more than happy to reinforce the notion that we are "good sports"—and, therefore, attractive despite our destructive conduct.

We once worked with a client named Albert who was a master of this particular minimizing technique. Albert's self-defeating behavior had put him in a wheelchair; at age twenty-two, he had been diagnosed as diabetic, but he had continued to drink alcohol and eat sugary foods. For over ten years he practiced these behaviors, all the while refusing to see doctors or to medicate himself properly.

Finally, his actions caught up with him: as a result of complications resulting from his disease, Albert lost both his feet and a part of his lower right leg. Even after his surgery, he persisted in his pattern of self-defeat, missing scheduled medical checkups and continuing to have several drinks each day.

Albert, as we discovered during our first meeting, had developed a virtual comedy routine around the consequences of his self-defeating behavior. (We pointed this out to him, and he agreed heartily: "I'm the world's first sit-down comic," he said.) When we asked Albert how he felt about losing his feet as a result of an ongoing self-defeating behavior, his response was typical of the person who minimizes through humor. "Well," he said with a deadpan expression, "it sure cuts down on what I have to spend for shoes."

Numbing

An especially common—and, sadly enough, an often deadly—means of minimizing prices is to numb or deaden our responses to the consequences of our actions. We can accomplish numbing in a variety of ways: we can abuse alcohol, drugs, or food, we can smoke cigarettes, or we can lapse into depression and allow our internal chemistry to perform the desired anesthesia. When we numb ourselves to avoid the pain associated with our prices, we attempt to tell our minds and bodies that this pain does not in fact exist. What we fail to see is that we are transforming the healing pain of prices into a different sort of agony: an absence of sensation that can lead eventually to the death of the spirit.

For people who abuse alcohol and other substances, numbing is a favorite minimizing technique. Roger, who told us many times that life is a party and there's no point in going to a party if you can't drink, used alcohol to minimize the pain to which his overindulgence frequently led. "Sometimes I drink just for the sake of having a few," he told us, "but a lot of the time, I go on a binge because something bad has happened to me, like when a girl has dumped me or I've lost a job. Then, when that pain goes away, I have a hangover, and the best way to get rid of it is to have a drink or two. Not to get drunk again, you understand, but just to get rid of the hurt to the point where I can function again."

Martyring

We have all known people who seem to derive a perverse pleasure, or even a sense of nobility, from the suffering brought on by their self-defeating behavior patterns. We call these people *martyrs,* although they are not to be confused with people who endure pain or persecution in the service of a legitimate faith or cause. The would-be martyr minimizes the consequences of his or her actions by claiming that these hurtful results are a burden that must be borne in the name of some higher goal or purpose. People who consider themselves especially sensitive or artistic are prone to fall into this sort of minimizing, as are people who have built their lives around distorted religious doctrine.

A client of ours named Anna was raised in a family where martyring was practiced, encouraged, and, at times, required. The family held deep fundamentalist religious convictions, one of which was that no pleasure should be experienced until the afterlife. As a result, Anna grew up repressing her healthy inner self; she shunned any thought or action that might conceivably lead to self-esteem or joy. Within her family, this behavior earned her approval. When she tried to function outside this environment, however, her downcast eyes, frequent praying, and bizarre manner of dress brought her nothing but ridicule. Unable to find either a job or friends, she twice attempted suicide, and she spent parts of five consecutive years in a state mental institution.

Still, Anna clung to her obscure and largely distorted religious beliefs. During one session we asked her to try to feel the pain that she had experienced as a result of her deep convictions. We asked her to try to experience, at that moment, the prices she had paid in the form of loneliness, rejection, scorn, and mistreatment. After several minutes of silence, Anna began to weep. "Yes, I feel pain," she cried. "I hurt through and through. And it's a blessing, because I know I am feeling just the way God wants me to feel."

Being Chronically Busy

People who work for large business organizations often complain of colleagues or subordinates who are always "busy" but who never seem to get anything done. This sort of chronic busyness, we've found, is often simply a technique that is used to avoid paying prices. Just as people in work environments often remain frantically occupied to avoid facing up to the fact that they aren't accomplishing much, people also build rituals and chores into their personal lives to minimize the consequences of self-defeating behaviors.

Consider, for example, the case of Rachel. To avoid dealing with her sexuality, she arranged to be constantly "busy": when she came home from work in the evening, she assigned herself certain chores and would not relax until these tasks were completed. Each night she vacuumed the rug in her living room, scrubbed the kitchen floor, cleaned the mirrors in her bathroom, and did her laundry. "I don't have any sexual feelings at all," she complained to us. "I think it's because I'm tired all the time. I have so much to do in my apartment that I don't have time to worry about sex. As a matter of fact, I don't even have time to think."

Nihilizing

Nihilizing—a relatively sophisticated thought process by which people attempt to convince themselves that all beliefs, actions, rules, and standards are meaningless—is, in reality, an advanced technique for minimizing prices. Nihilists argue that because life is without purpose and the human predicament hopeless, it makes little difference whether they choose to behave in a self-defeating manner. These people contend that all behaviors are inconsequential—that while winning choices do not bring happiness, neither do self-defeating choices lead to misery. They minimize prices by denying, in effect, that the prices exist.

Intellectually sophisticated people often use this minimizer to avoid paying their prices, as do young people who emulate the nihilistic poses of their negative role-models. Chad, for example, acquired his self-defeating behavior by imitating the dress, manner of speech, and outward attitudes displayed by members of a nihilistic rock group. He then used the group's professed nihilism to minimize the consequences of his behavior. "Why should I put on clean clothes and work hard in school?" he once asked us. "After all, sooner or later someone's going to drop the bomb, and we'll all end up as radioactive dust. It won't make any difference who studied, who had a good job, or who played by society's stupid rules. Everyone will just be dead."

Making Others Pay

As we suggested in the previous chapter, some of the prices associated with our self-defeating behaviors are inevitably distributed to those around us. Some people who practice self-defeating behaviors recognize this tendency and use it as a means of escaping the brunt of the consequences to which their actions lead. When we consciously (and, in extreme cases, intentionally) force others to pay our prices, we are clearly using an advanced technique to minimize the cost of our actions. We can use this technique, however, only in situations in which a friend, relative, or colleague is willing and available to assume our prices as his or her own.

A client of ours named Phil made effective use of this means of minimizing his prices. Phil practiced a series of self-defeating behaviors that some would refer to as *hypochondria*. He managed consistently to find or imagine some physical ailment that kept him from holding a job. He spent his time and energy running from doctor to doctor, trying to elicit a definitive diagnosis of one of the illnesses from which he claimed to suffer. The consequences of this behavior fell largely on his wife, who worked two jobs to pay Phil's medical bills and spent much of her limited time away from work picking up prescriptions and arranging for transportation to and from clinics and hospitals. "It's hard on her, sure," Phil told us, dismissing casually the prices his wife was paying for him. "But I never asked to be as sick as I am. Besides, she's a good woman. She doesn't seem to have any problem in dealing with our situation."

Therapizing

We've had more than a few clients who have entered counseling not because they wanted to stop practicing their self-defeating behaviors, but rather to find a way to practice these behaviors without paying the associated prices. We've come to think of these clients as *therapizers:* people who move from counselor to counselor, or therapy program to therapy program, in search of the alchemy that will allow them to rid themselves of prices without changing their basic self-defeating behavior. Clients of this sort will frequently tell us how long they have been in therapy, or how many different counselors they have worked with, in an attempt to demonstrate how hard they have tried unsuccessfully to change. Consider Eva, whom you met in the first section of this book. She claimed she wanted desperately to stop smoking. Yet her voice had an almost prideful tone as she told us how many different programs she had enrolled in to eliminate this self-defeating behavior. She showed unmistakable signs of being what we view as a therapizer.

Therapizers do not consciously dislike their self-defeating behaviors; in fact, they are often quite fond of them. They claim to want to stop procrastinating, overeating, smoking, alienating people, or drinking too much—when, in reality, they want very much to continue practicing these behaviors, but without having to deal with the consequences to which such unhealthy patterns inevitably lead.

The first time we met Barbara, for example, she was quick to tell us that we were her "last hope" for changing a pattern of perfectionist behavior that was making life miserable for her and her family. "I really mean that," she added emphatically. "I'd be ashamed to admit to you how many different people I've gone to. None of them has been able to turn things around for me—I can't seem to get better, no matter how hard I try. This is the seventh clinic I've been to, and I'm still driving myself and my family crazy."

Adapting

Because minimizing techniques never work, people who continue to practice self-defeating behaviors are forced to make use of several minimizers, either in sequence or simultaneously, in order to deal with the consequences of their actions. When people refuse to change their self-defeating behavior patterns and choose instead to develop or refine multiple minimizing techniques over extended periods of time, they eventually adapt to their prices. They join the ranks of those unfortunate individuals for whom "the cycle is life": they become so inured to pain, anxiety, ill health, and self-reproach that they cannot imagine what life without these prices would be like. Perhaps more accurately, they cannot imagine that life does not bring with it harsh prices, or that there are alternatives to defeating themselves regularly. Once such people have effectively adapted to their prices, they find it extremely difficult to make winning choices and, as a result, to escape their cycles of self-defeat.

It's extremely difficult, however, to build an entire life around minimized prices. Each time we minimize the consequences of a self-defeating behavior, we violate our healthy inner self. This inner self is strong and resilient under repeated assault, however, it can be silenced or buried. Take, for example, the case of Sonia. When Sonia first came to us, she had been working as a prostitute for two years. Her life was fraught with prices that most of us find difficult to imagine: the threat of disease, regular physical abuse, frequent legal difficulties, a loss of self-esteem, the ongoing abuse of alcohol and drugs. Yet Sonia had managed to adapt to these prices; not only did she see them as essential parts of life, but for her they had *become* life. "It's not as bad as you think," she said to us. "Russell [her pimp] sees that we get regular medical checkups, and his friend Zack [a bail bondsman] takes care of the cops and the judges. You take care of the customers, and your people take care of you. It's 'The Life'— it's just what you do to keep yourself together."

Minimizing Leads to Disowning

We'd like to emphasize here that none of the minimizing techniques we've described enable us to escape the consequences of self-defeating behavior. A minimizing technique may alter for a limited time our perception of the prices we are paying for our unhealthy choices, but in the end, these prices make themselves known. Minimizing defers prices and, in some cases, increases them. Most people who enter into counseling programs do so because their minimizing techniques have already begun to fail. At this point, they are ready to make healthy changes in the way they behave—provided that they do not resort to disowning, an advanced technique that completes and perpetuates all cycles of self-defeat.

People develop disowning techniques when their minimizing techniques have failed to reduce to an acceptable level the consequences associated with a self-defeating behavior—when, in other words, they are no longer capable of using minimizers to skew the price-fear equation in a direction that seems to validate self-defeating choices. At this point in the cycle of self-defeat, people can choose either to pay in full the prices associated with their behavior or to abandon control over their own behavior. If they choose the latter option, they disown the behavior and assign responsibility for it to another person, the culture, or a part of their own being that functions independently of conscious choice.

Once a person has disowned his or her behavior, as we'll discuss in the final chapter of this section, that person completes a cycle of self-defeat. When minimizing fails, disowning results; and once disowning is accomplished, the negative experience that results is treated not as an aberration resulting from faulty choices, but rather as firm evidence that supports a faulty conclusion about the self or life. Under these circumstances, people cannot learn from their experiences; they can only repeat the behavior that led to unpleasant consequences in the first place. This unhealthy repetition is frustrating. It causes people to search for someone or something to blame for their own ongoing misery. Such people are virtually forced to disown their behavior and to live with the frustration and rage that disowning techniques often produce.

Chapter 13

Advanced Techniques II: Disowning Our Behavior

Even the most effectively minimized prices cause us to feel some degree of pain or psychic tension. The minimizing techniques we use to escape our prices inevitably fall short of their purpose; they fail to purge us completely of the toxic messages or memories that our psychic subsystems are trying to process. Some residue of these toxins remains within us and causes us to feel tense, unhappy, or incomplete. When we experience these discomforts, our conscious minds need to find a way to account for them, to explain why we feel bad when, on a conscious level, at least, we want to feel healthy and fulfilled.

Disowning is the advanced technique that we use to provide ourselves with the required rationale for our continued self-defeating behavior. To disown our behavior effectively, we must find a cause for our unhappiness and then assign responsibility for our choices to that cause. When we successfully complete this process, we link the prices of our actions not with the behaviors that led to these consequences, but, rather, with the faulty conclusions that cloud our choices. In making this connection, however, we complete the cycle of self-defeat and ensure that we will remain caught in a behavioral pattern that keeps us from making progress toward health and wholeness.

While minimizing inevitably fails, disowning almost always works. This is why disowning techniques serve as a sort of fail-safe mechanism for perpetuating a cycle of self-defeating behavior. But although effective, disowning is an extremely dangerous process—perhaps more dangerous than any of the inner, outer, or minimizing techniques that make it necessary. If practiced frequently, disowning forces us to think of ourselves as helpless victims. And once we have come to think of ourselves in this way, we have, in essence, abandoned our capacity for making winning choices and, hence, for changing our behavior patterns.

Why, then, do we disown our behavior? One reason, as we suggested earlier, is to provide ourselves with a superficially logical explanation of why we continue to think and act in ways that we know will lead to self-defeat. A second reason for which we develop and apply disowning techniques is that on some level of consciousness, we want to continue to practice our self-defeating behaviors. At the same time, however, we do not want to assume responsibility for these thoughts and actions. To do so would be to admit to ourselves that we somehow enjoy our suffering.

What Is Disowning?

Disowning is a systematic process of blaming some person, institution, or factor outside of our control for our own self-defeating behaviors. When we blame parents, friends, jobs, religious backgrounds, or cultural institutions for our behaviors, we tell ourselves that we are powerless over our personal cycles of self-defeat. What we are doing when we disown our behavior is to remove the element of choice from the basic model for human behavior. Once we've convinced ourselves that the concept of choice is invalid, however, we have removed our only access to winning behavior and eventual breakthrough. We have concluded that we do indeed practice self-defeating behavior and that we must continue to practice this behavior for as long as we are alive—or until the person or factor responsible for our behavior changes to allow us think and act in different ways.

People who practice disowning techniques are adept at diagnosing the alleged cause of their self-defeating behaviors. "My father treated my mother and sisters badly," such a person will say, "so how can I be expected to relate to women in the way they expect me to?" Or: "I know I'm impatient with my kids. But this job of mine doesn't allow me the time or energy to be a good parent." Some people even go so far as to blame parts of their own minds or bodies for their cycles of self-defeat. These people assure us that they could stop practicing their self-defeating behaviors if only their "nerves," "minds," "stomachs," or "heads" would cooperate.

The problem with these and similar diagnoses of the causes of self-defeating behavior patterns is that they themselves are faulty conclusions. When people continue to cling to this sort of incorrect assessment of their difficulties, they are bound to continue to make behavioral choices that lend credence to a faulty conclusion. The net result of disowning, therefore, is to complete a cycle of self-defeat and to close off avenues of escape from this cycle.

Disowning Links Prices with Conclusions

The process of systematic blaming that we call *disowning* links the consequences of our actions with the faulty conclusions on which these actions are based. This is a dangerous connection to make, because it distorts the cause-effect relationship between our actions and the results they bring about. It forces us to see our prices as natural consequences of the "truths" expressed in our faulty conclusions. In terms of our basic model for self-defeating behavior, disowning works like this:

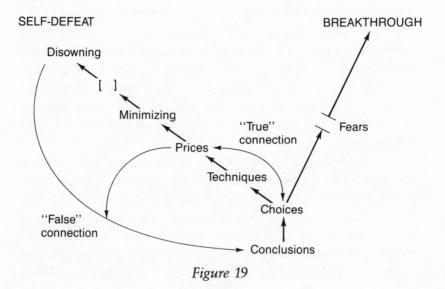

Figure 19

As this version of the model shows, disowning steers us away from the valid connection we must make if we are to change our behavior. Disowning enables us to elude the very basic truth that *the prices we pay are a direct result of the choices we make.* Until we acknowledge this truth, we cannot learn to make the clear and healthy choices that lead us to winning behaviors.

A short example might help clarify these concepts. Suppose that you have been having some problems at work and, as a result, have formed a faulty conclusion that goes like this: "My boss is a bad person who doesn't like me." You wake up one winter morning and prepare to depart for work, only to find that a heavy snowstorm is in progress outside. You turn on the radio for a traffic report and hear that the highways are in a miserable condition, and that no travel is advised.

At this point, you have a choice: you can either depart for work despite the warning or wait to see if the weather and road conditions improve. But in making this choice, you retrieve your faulty conclusion, telling yourself that your oppressive and hostile boss will punish or fire you if you arrive late. So you decide that you must get to work at any cost. After traveling a few miles along a slippery highway, however, you get into an accident with another vehicle. Your car sustains several hundred dollars' worth of damage, only some of which will be covered by insurance. Attempting to minimize this situation, you tell yourself that things could have been much worse; after all, you could have been injured, or even killed. But somehow this line of thinking doesn't help you to feel much better. Your car is badly damaged, your bank balance is low, and you're going to be late for work, anyway.

Then, while you are standing in the snow along the shoulder of the slick highway, a thought comes to you. "It's that boss of mine who's responsible for this mess," you say to yourself. "If he (or she) weren't such a jerk, none of this would have happened. I could have stayed home and driven to work later, and my car wouldn't be ruined. Not to mention the money this will cost me."

There you have it: by disowning your behavior and blaming it on your tyrannical supervisor, you have effectively linked the consequences of your behavior (a damaged car and a diminished savings account) with your faulty conclusion (that your boss is, in fact, an insensitive jerk who will punish you for lateness despite the adverse weather conditions). This connection makes you feel better, but it obscures the truth of the matter, which is that had you not *chosen* to ignore the traffic warnings and your own common sense, you would still be the owner of an undamaged car.

Your use of a disowning technique, in other words, keeps you from learning anything from this unpleasant experience. The accident that resulted from your unwise choice has served only to confirm your conclusion about your boss. If you continue to nourish this conclusion, chances are that the next time you wake up to a blizzard, you'll start out in your car again. After all, you'll be even more convinced that your boss is the source of your difficulties: wasn't it because of him (or her) that you smashed up your car? You'll see no point in aggravating him (or her) by failing to arrive at the office on time. If only he (or she) liked you . . . well, *then* you'd be in a position to make a better choice.

Major Disowning Techniques

Opportunities for disowning abound in our culture and present themselves regularly during our lives. Other people hurt, manipulate, and ignore us; our bodies do not always serve us the way we want them to; our cultural and religious institutions promote attitudes that discourage us from taking responsibility for our actions. These basic facts of life encourage us to develop and practice such disowning techniques as:

- Blaming other people
- Fragmentizing our minds and bodies
- Capitalizing on social, political, or economic inequities
- Embracing fatalistic conclusions

If you recognize one of your own attitudes in any of the examples that follow, chances are that you've been using a disowning technique to avoid responsibility for your personal behavior patterns.

Blaming Other People

Perhaps the most common disowning technique that people use is to blame others for their own self-defeating behaviors. The most frequently blamed people are, naturally enough, parents. Chad, the young punk-rock impostor whom we worked with, was not hesitant to blame his father and mother for his outrageous conduct. "They never paid any attention to me," he complained. "They ignored all the positive things I tried to do. They taught me that it's never good enough to do your best. The last thing I want to do is to turn out like them." Daniel—who, as you'll recall, drew a connection between his persistent depression and his father's precarious health—also blamed his parents for initiating his cycle of self-defeat. "If Dad had taken care of himself, he wouldn't have had a heart attack at forty-six," he told us. "And Mom is just as much to blame. They created this whole mess, and now I have to deal with it."

Aside from our parents, we most often tend to blame spouses and children for our self-defeating behaviors. "My husband beat me," Greta told us. "How can I ever be expected to have a healthy relationship with a man again? Hank showed me what men are all about, and I don't want anything to do with their violence and hatred." And Molly, whose abusive behavior caused her to lose custody of her children, to an extent blamed the children themselves for violence to which she subjected them. "I may have learned to be abusive from my father," she remarked in a moment of angry candor, "but those two kids helped things along. It was as if they saved their worst behavior for the moment I walked in the door. If only they could have been quiet and well-behaved at least once or twice a week, I could have stopped this trouble before it got out of hand."

In addition to blaming parents, spouses, and children, we often blame siblings, friends, enemies, colleagues, and supervisors for our patterns of self-defeat. When it comes to disowning, anyone who has any sort of ongoing relationship with us is fair game for blame. Evan, who remained at a college where he could not explore his interests or potential, blamed his roommate for his failure to transfer to another school. "Every time I started to talk seriously about leaving," Evan told us, "Charlie would go into this long speech about the good times we'd had, the friends we'd made, and how hard it would be to start over at a new school. He kept convincing me I should stay in residence, even though he knew I wasn't getting the kind of education I wanted."

When we find ourselves blaming others for our own misfortunes, it's important that we remember that although family members, friends, and people in positions of authority often cause us to *develop* self-defeating behavior patterns, we ourselves must bear the responsibility for *perpetuating* these behaviors. No one would, for example, absolve a parent who abused his or her child from responsibility for the self-defeating behavior that the child developed in an attempt to cope with the abuse. But at some point, that child, in order to escape the cycle of self-defeat, must recognize that he or she is choosing to perpetuate the behavior. Our point here is that while it is often helpful to identify the person whose actions led to our self-defeating behaviors, it is futile to continue to blame that person for our thoughts and actions. If we persist in blaming someone else for our behavioral choices, we give that person control over our behavior and, hence, surrender our capacity for making healthy and positive changes in the way we think and act.

Fragmentizing Our Minds and Bodies

When we fragmentize our minds and bodies, we deny that our internal human subsystems are integrated components that are designed to nourish and protect the healthy inner self. People who use this disowning technique contend, in so many words, that one or more of these efficient subsystems has taken on a will of its own and has "chosen" to work against the best interests of the integrated self. Such people often blame their "minds," their "nerves," or any one of their internal organs for a thought or action that leads to self-defeat. Sally, for example, who came to us after failing all her courses during her freshman year at college, was fond of saying that when it came time to take a test, her "mind went blank." When we asked her to explain what she meant, she said, "It's weird. It's like, all of a sudden, I have no thoughts in my head—it goes completely empty. I can see and hear, but I can't think or remember." We asked Sally if she had this experience on any occasions other than those when she had to take a test. "Never," she replied. "I guess my mind has decided to be dumb at the worst possible times."

People who suffer from chronic physical ailments often fragmentize themselves as a means of disowning responsibility for their behavior. "I'm a diabetic," Albert told us. "It's hard to think about the future when you know you have a disease that will probably kill you." When we told Albert that many people who suffer from diabetes lead long and productive lives despite the disease, he said, "Yeah, but the diabetes I have is the meanest kind. Bit by bit, it's eating me up. Why make changes or think about the future? This thing I have inside of me is going to kill me, regardless of what I think or do."

Capitalizing on Social, Political, or Economic Inequities

There's no denying that entire groups or classes of people— blacks, native Americans, Asian-Americans, and women, to name only a few—have had more than their share of suffering inflicted on them by our cultural system. As we discussed earlier in this book, our cultural system produces numerous toxic by-products. These by-products include such lamentable but real facts of life as racial prejudice, social stratification, poverty, and economic deprivation. Our cultural system has, over the years, tended to inflict these inequities on its least numerous and powerful members, who have found traditional routes to dignity and prosperity largely blocked off to them.

People who belong to oppressed or ignored groups, however, often fall prey to a particular kind of disowning. They associate the personal consequences of their self-defeating behavior not with the faulty choices they have made but, rather, with a well-documented social, political, and economic inequity. Hence, the perfectionist (who happens to be black) may attribute his or her failure to receive a promotion at work not to the perfectionist behavior that keeps him or her from meeting deadlines, but instead to a company policy of systematic racial discrimination. Similarly, the procrastinating sculptor (who happens to be female) may blame her failure to gain recognition on our culture's sexist biases, while at the same time overlooking the fact that her self-defeating behavior has kept her from finishing the work that is required to attract attention.

When we capitalize on a social, political, or economic inequity to justify our unhappiness, we disown responsibility for the thoughts and actions that, more often than not, brought about the unhappiness in the first place. We ignore the fact that many blacks, women, Vietnam veterans, and Mexican-Americans lead successful and productive lives, despite the culture's acknowledged prejudice. We once worked with Jamie, a twenty-seven-year-old black man who had been convicted of burglary three times. "Don't talk to me about self-defeating behavior," he said to us. "When you're black, society is just looking for a reason to lock you up." We then asked Jamie if he had ever been arrested and convicted for being black—or if his problems with the law had stemmed from his criminal and self-destructive actions. "Oh, I stole, all right," Jamie replied. "They caught me fair and square. But the judge would never have sentenced a white man to the kind of time I had to serve." In response, we pointed out to Jamie that while statistics might well bear out the truth of his statement, it was his own behavior—not societal prejudice—that had put him at the mercy of a system that might or might not have treated him fairly.

Embracing Fatalistic Conclusions

If we look hard enough, almost all of us can find a piece of religious or scientific dogma that would seem to explain our self-defeating behaviors. We can discover within certain religious writings the conclusion that we are born to be miserable and that we must bear our suffering in silence. Or we can pore over psychological and medical texts until we find passages that tell us that certain psychic or physical maladies are genetic and, therefore, inescapable. But when we focus our attention and energy on conclusions about things we cannot change, we shirk the responsibility for those aspects of our life that we can modify. In this way, we embrace fatalistic conclusions as a means of disowning responsibility for our choices and the consequences to which they lead.

When Rachel came to us, for example, she was convinced that her lack of sexual feeling was a genetic condition that she'd inherited from her mother. She had done considerable research in the area of sexual dysfunction; she brought to our first meeting photocopies of passages from several books and articles. Each passage seemed to prove that the condition Rachel referred to as her "frigidity" was a hereditary condition that had been passed on to her by her mother. "There it is, in black-and-white," Rachel announced to us. "Frigidity runs in my family. I'm not here to try to change that. I just want to find out how to cope better with the problem."

In working with Rachel, however, as well as with other clients who used fatalistic conclusions to disown their behaviors, we've discovered that these people do not really *believe* in the evidence they draw upon to justify their actions. We've found that what they want us to do is to help them *disprove* the conclusions on which they have come to base their choices. Rachel, for example, was in her own way asking us to provide her with information contrary to the evidence she had already accumulated. But as we explained to Rachel and others, the only way to disprove a faulty conclusion is to make winning choices and experience the healthy and positive results to which these choices lead. The conclusions these people have embraced are grounded in past experiences. Only through new experiences can people challenge their fatalism and break out of the cycle of self-defeat.

The Frustration-Rage-Helplessness Continuum

Although it works effectively to keep us from having to make changes in the way we think and act, disowning has serious side effects that make it a less than ideal means of coping with a self-defeating behavior. Once we've assigned the blame for our pattern of self-defeat to a factor outside our control, we often allow ourselves a period of psychic relaxation during which we continue to practice our self-defeating behaviors and reap whatever dubious benefits these behaviors afford us. Soon enough, however, the prices associated with our behavior reappear, and we are forced again into a cycle of minimizing and disowning. We grow increasingly frustrated, because we're reminded that something is wrong in our lives. But because we have disowned responsibility for our behavior, we have given away the power to change what troubles us. We are caught in a trap that we have set for ourselves.

At this point, *rage* enters the picture. Because we are miserable, and because we have long since concluded that someone or something outside ourselves is responsible for our misery, we become enraged at the alleged source of our discomfort. We grow furious with the parent who instilled in us a low level of self-esteem, at the boss who refused our request for a promotion, or at the society that classified and treated us as a second-class citizen. We feel a compulsive need to express our anger toward whoever or whatever is causing our distress—a need, if you will, to give back some of the toxic input we've received.

Many therapists believe that it's therapeutic to cultivate and express rage. We, however, are not among them. We believe that the expression of self-defeating rage (as opposed to immediate and appropriate anger) is unhealthy for two reasons. First, it can complicate or aggravate situations that are already volatile. If, for example, a person who is having problems at work decides suddenly to confront his or her supervisor with an outburst of pent-up rage, this confrontation will in all likelihood compound the difficulty. And in extreme cases, such as those in which women are enraged at their abusive spouses, angry confrontations can be downright dangerous.

We believe, moreover, that any relief a person experiences after venting this rage is, at best, temporary. Jack, the advertising executive who defeated himself by jumping from job to job, told us that he once worked with a therapist who advised him to "get in touch" with the rage he felt toward his mother. Jack did this and was directed to call his mother on the phone and express his feelings to her. He made the call, during which he accused his mother of instilling in him the belief that he had no right to be successful. "Sure, I felt better when I hung up the phone," Jack admitted. "A week later, though, I was angry all over again. The counselor suggested that maybe my problem had nothing to do with my mother. He suggested that I try to identify who I was really angry with, and then confront that person. I decided to cut things short then and there, because I knew that screaming at people wasn't the answer."

Rage, regardless of whether it is expressed openly or held in, often leads to *helplessness*. At this point in the cycle, people feel that they have exhausted all options for escape from their self-defeating behavior. They have blamed someone or something else for the behavior, grown frustrated with their perceived inability to change, and, finally, become enraged over their predicament. Yet none of these techniques have worked. So these people continue to practice their self-defeating behavior, and the consequences of this behavior continue to make themselves known. At this point, people typically give themselves up to the cycle of self-defeat. They become *victims* — people who say, in so many words, "I know what I'm doing, and I hate it. So I'm giving up. If only the world were a different place, or if people were less callous and abusive, then, maybe, I could find the energy to do things differently. But as it stands, there's nothing for me to do but live in misery for as long as I can hold out."

In this sense, victims are not people who enjoy their suffering or who use it as a means of feeling superior to their alleged persecutors. Rather, they are people who have traveled the frustration-rage-helplessness continuum to its logical conclusion. They have tried to accomplish a difficult psychic task: they have attempted to hang onto their self-defeating behaviors while refusing to take responsibility for them. As a result of repeated disowning, victims have depleted their conscious resources and lapsed into a state of perpetual discontent.

We Disown Behaviors So We Can Keep Them

When we blame our behavior on factors outside ourselves, we accomplish a clever bit of self-deceptive business. We not only give up control over our self-defeating behaviors, but we also deny to ourselves that, at some level of consciousness, *we want to continue to practice these behaviors.* Once we've deceived ourselves to this extent, we have completed and nourished a cycle of self-defeat and, in the process, blinded ourselves to the possibility of healthy change.

Why, you might ask, would people want to continue to practice a behavior that they have consciously acknowledged as self-defeating? If you'll recall the process by which self-defeating behaviors are born, the answer to this question will become fairly obvious. We develop self-defeating behaviors when our healthy psychic subsystems are unable to cope with toxic input from the cultural system; we adopt patterns of thought or action that reduce the pain and tension brought on by negative experiences. At a subconscious level, we associate these thoughts or actions with any subsequent reduction in our level of anxiety or discomfort. We form, as you'll recall, a faulty conclusion that tells us that our self-defeating behaviors are appropriate responses to certain new moments of life.

This faulty conclusion is stored within the unconscious component of the psychic subsystem. At this level of thought, the conclusion is protected from challenges that arise in the form of conscious thoughts or insights. Hence, the individual may be consciously aware that his or her behavior is destructive but at the same time may want to continue to practice the behavior.

Consider, for example, the alleged alcoholic. This person may be well aware—at a conscious level, at least—of the consequences to which excessive drinking inevitably leads. At an unconscious level, however, he or she may continue to associate this self-defeating behavior with the ostensible benefits it once afforded: reduced anxiety, social acceptance, a sense of glibness or sophistication, and so on. If the alcoholic continues to make this connection, he or she will, at an unconscious level, *want* to drink, despite a conscious awareness of the ruin to which drinking will lead.

When we disown our behavior, we create a psychic environment that allows for this sort of contradictory thinking. Disowning provides us with a perfect means of claiming to deplore a self-defeating behavior while continuing to practice it. We can deplore the behavior because we have consciously linked it with certain painful prices. But despite this awareness, we feel we must keep on practicing the behavior, for we have no control over it. By disowning a self-defeating behavior, we can satisfy the demands of both the conscious mind, which wants to be rid of the behavior, and the unconscious mind, which wants to perpetuate the cycle of self-defeat.

Disowning, in other words, allows us to lie to ourselves. It creates a sort of psychic chaos where cause and effect are confused, where what is right becomes indistinguishable from what is wrong. It creates a psychic environment in which clearheaded choices are difficult—and, in extreme cases, impossible. As long as we continue to use disowning techniques, our chances of making healthy changes in the way we behave are slim: behavioral changes, as we have said many times before, depend on winning choices at new moments of life. The first step toward changing our behavior, therefore, is to own it. In assuming this responsibility, we acknowledge our capability to choose the ways in which we think and act. Once we have availed ourselves of this capability, we can begin immediately to make good use of it. We can start to make the kinds of choices that will enhance, rather than deny, our sense of control over our thoughts and actions and, ultimately, over the way we live our lives.

Part Four

How
Self-Defeating
Behaviors
Can Be Replaced

*. . . The man who had been thrown overboard sat in a
bed of rocks on the bottom of the ocean, his arms
wrapped tightly around the anchor that he believed had
saved his life. He knew he could not hold his breath
much longer: his chest ached, and his head felt as if it
would explode. Finally, he gave in. He let out his breath
in a great burst, and when he did, his mouth filled with
sea water. He tried to swallow, but the salty fluid seeped
down his throat and into his lungs. He coughed vio-
lently. He knew he was drowning.*

*He looked to the anchor that had been his salva-
tion. Somewhat tentatively, he loosened his hold on the
iron shaft and felt his body float away. "Maybe if I let
go completely . . ." he thought. "It might not help, but I
am going to die anyway."*

*Nearing unconsciousness, the man saw that his
only hope was to let go of the anchor. He relaxed his
arms and let them float free. At that moment, his body
began to rise up from the floor of the ocean. He felt
himself being carried upward by the weight and flow of
the water. Above him he saw a light, which grew
brighter as he continued to float up. He used his arms
to push himself toward the brightness; he knew now*

that he might survive. With a burst of energy, he thrust his arms downward and, as he did, his face broke the surface of the water. He drew in a great breath of brisk sea air. As his vision cleared, he saw the cruise ship from which he had fallen, and, on its deck, a party of anxious rescuers. And all around him, he saw the light of the sun: directly overhead, in all its brightness, shone the sun.

Chapter 14

The Road to Breakthrough

We've spent a lot of time so far describing how self-defeating behaviors work without offering specific suggestions on how they can be replaced or eliminated. There's a reason for this. We believe that in order to change a pattern of self-defeat, you must first understand exactly what it is that you want to change. Without an understanding of how self-defeating behaviors are created and practiced, it's very difficult to determine precisely what needs to be done to change these behaviors. Trying to change a self-defeating behavior without this understanding is a little like deciding to move to a new city without knowing what it is you dislike about your current location. In each case, you're contemplating a major decision without knowing precisely what has caused you to want to make a change. Your only basis for making the decision is a vague sense of discontent with where you are now. You may want to move, but you don't know where you want to go.

An understanding of the basic model for self-defeating behavior is a necessary prerequisite for a clearly focused change program. If you attempt to change without an understanding of this model—without an awareness of your conclusions and fears, as well as of the techniques you use to carry out your choices, minimize your prices, and disown your behavior—you'll find yourself relying heavily on willpower or excessive self-control. You'll develop unrealistic expectations with regard to how the change process works and will experience frequent disappointments. Uninformed attempts at change often lead to the development of perfectionist or rigid attitudes that may cause people to fail despite their best intentions.

We're suggesting here that an understanding of how your self-defeating behavior works can provide you with the basic mental tools you need to build a flexible and dependable program for personal change. Therefore, if you do not at this point have a clear sense of why and how you continue to practice behaviors that ensure unhappiness and discomfort, we urge you to review the previous sections of this book. It's necessary at this point for you to have an understanding of your behavior, because in the following chapters, we'll be asking you to identify the things you do to perpetuate your cycle of self-defeat. We'll be asking you also to develop healthy alternatives to these destructive techniques and choices, and to combine these alternatives into a program that can produce a behavioral cycle based on healthy choices and productive actions.

To open our discussion of how you can eliminate your self-defeating behavior, we'll present and discuss an enhanced version of our basic behavior model—one that specifies the milestones you'll encounter on the road that leads to breakthrough. We'll then provide an outline of a program that we feel can be used to replace or eliminate unhealthy and destructive behavior patterns. We'll emphasize, too, why it is so crucial for you to *own responsibility for your behavior* so that you can begin to change it and, perhaps more important, so that you can take credit for the progress you make along the road to breakthrough.

The Model for Breakthrough Behavior

In thinking about the versions of the basic behavior model that you've seen so far, you may have asked yourself why the road to breakthrough appears less cluttered than the road to self-defeat. One reason for this is that winning behaviors are less complicated and cyclical than their self-defeating counterparts. Another reason is that up to this point, we have purposely omitted from our representations of the model the activities and milestones that lie along the road to breakthrough. These elements are best understood, we believe, in the context of their self-defeating counterparts. Now that you understand the road to self-defeat, you're ready to appreciate fully how winning behavior works. Here, then, is what breakthrough behavior looks like in terms of our basic model:

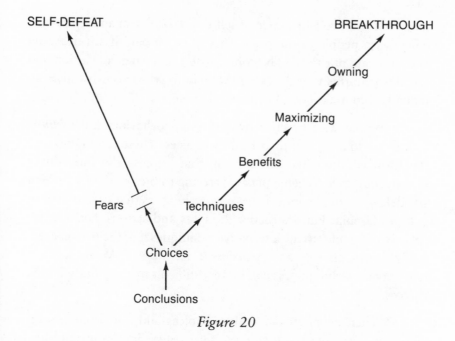

Figure 20

As you've probably noticed, the road to breakthrough contains a series of elements that are similar to those along the road to self-defeat. This does not mean, however, that the two roads are alike. It simply suggests that both paths are shaped by the same principles of behavioral logic. People who travel the road to self-defeat habitually distort and misapply these principles, while those who practice winning behaviors use them in a clearheaded and appropriate manner.

How does the model for breakthrough behavior work? Here's a brief summary of the steps that people who practice winning behaviors tend to follow to accomplish their goals and achieve their potential:

• Like those of us who practice self-defeating behaviors, people who practice winning behaviors make *choices* based on their *conclusions* and *fears*. Unlike the conclusions on which self-defeating behaviors are based, however, the conclusions that lead to winning behaviors are valid; they express fundamental truths about life and how it should be lived. Conclusions of this sort bring with them certain fears, but these fears—unlike the mythical fears that play such a key role in a cycle of self-defeat—are real and legitimate. They warn people of the prices that must be paid if self-defeating behaviors are practiced. The combination of a valid conclusion and a real fear in this way closes off the road to self-defeat. It causes an individual to make sound behavioral choices.

• People who practice breakthrough behaviors use *winning techniques* to carry out their healthy choices. These techniques take the form of thoughts and actions that express the individual's healthy inner self. When a person is trying to break out of a cycle of self-defeat, he or she must learn new techniques that can be used in place of familiar but destructive thoughts and actions. For this reason, we often refer to the alternative techniques that the person eventually learns to use as *replacement techniques*. Without these replacement techniques, it can be very difficult to carry out winning choices.

• When people make healthy choices and use winning techniques to carry out these choices, they realize important and life-enhancing *benefits*. These benefits are diverse: they may occur in the form of financial rewards, new opportunities, more meaningful relationships, or simply as an increased sense of inner peace and fulfillment. Regardless of the form they take, however, these benefits are crucial to the ongoing practice of winning behaviors. They validate both the behavioral choices that the individual has made and the conclusions on which these healthy choices are based.

• While those of us who practice self-defeating behaviors minimize the consequences of our thoughts and actions and, eventually, disown responsibility for them, people who practice winning behaviors *maximize* the benefits they receive and then *own* the successful results they have achieved. These people do not feel guilty when they accomplish the tasks they've set for themselves but, rather, take full credit for the choices, thoughts, and actions that have led to their success. What's more, they're able to share this success with others and hence to make a positive impact on the individuals, institutions, and organizations with which they interact.

• Winning behavior, like self-defeating behavior, is cyclical. Both types of behavior lead to experiences that validate the conclusions on which they are based. This enables people who practice winning behaviors to perpetuate with relative ease their patterns of healthy thought and action. These people make winning choices, which bring important benefits. These benefits, in turn, are maximized, owned, and shared. This entire positive experience is then stored within the unconscious mind to nourish and support the life-enhancing conclusion from which the experience itself originated.

Winning behaviors are every bit as systematic as their self-defeating counterparts. For some people, these winning thoughts and actions seem to come naturally. Most of us, however, need to take conscious and purposeful steps to put winning behaviors into action. We need to think about our choices and techniques, as well as about how we can maximize the benefits we receive when we act in accordance with our healthy inner selves. But once we've learned them, winning behaviors soon become incorporated into our psychic subsystems. At this point, we can practice them without conscious thought or effort.

A Program for Change

In helping our clients rid themselves of self-defeating behaviors, we've developed what we believe is a practical and effective program for change. This program encourages the individual not only to understand the self-defeating behavior that he or she currently practices but also to develop alternative patterns of thought or action. The program consists of either six or seven general steps, depending upon how thoroughly a person's cycle of self-defeat has been incorporated into his or her daily life. In the remaining chapters of this book, we'll discuss in detail each of these steps. We'll also suggest exercises that can help you complete each step and prepare for your journey along the road to breakthrough.

Here, then, is a general overview of the program that we recommend as a workable means of eliminating persistent patterns of self-defeat. When a client comes to us with a problem that has its roots in a self-defeating behavior, we suggest that he or she do the following:

Identify specifically the behavior that is causing the problem. The first step toward the development of a winning behavior pattern is for the individual to identify as specifically as possible his or her present pattern of self-defeat. By the time they decide to seek help, many people already understand clearly what they are doing to hurt themselves and those around them. Others, however, need to consult checklists, solicit feedback, analyze their personal histories, or examine the environments in which they were raised to identify clearly the behavior that they are using to defeat themselves.

Identify when, where, and/or with whom the behavior is practiced. It's extremely rare for a person to practice his or her self-defeating behavior during every moment of the day. Virtually all self-defeating behaviors are practiced selectively: at certain times of the day, month, or year, in certain types of situations, or only in the company of certain individuals. To help our clients understand why and how they practice their patterns of self-defeat, we ask them to keep a detailed record of the circumstances in which they resort to self-destructive thoughts and actions.

Identify the specific inner, outer, minimizing, and disowning techniques that are used to put the behavior into practice. In the previous section of this book, we described and provided examples of the techniques that people use to carry out their patterns of self-defeat. We did this to illustrate the range of thoughts and actions that are employed once a self-defeating behavior is put into practice. An essential part of behavioral change, we believe, is for people to acknowledge and specify the things that they do to carry out their self-defeating choices. Once these techniques are recognized, they can be observed and, with practice, modified or eliminated.

Catch the behavior while it is being practiced. Once you have identified the techniques you use to perpetuate a pattern of self-defeat, you can catch the behavior while practicing it. This step, we believe, is the key to successful behavior change. We tell our clients to observe their self-defeating behaviors while they are practicing them and to try to catch these behaviors at successively earlier points in the overall cycle of self-defeat. They can start, for example, by becoming aware of the times when they minimize and disown a particular behavior. Gradually, they can learn to catch the behavior at earlier points in the cycle: when they use an inner or outer technique to carry out a behavioral choice, for example, or when they make this choice. Our goal here is to teach people to become familiar with the thoughts and feelings that indicate that they are on the verge of making an unhealthy choice.

Develop replacement techniques. Replacement techniques are the precursors of winning behaviors. If you have not identified healthy alternatives to your self-defeating techniques, you will find it very difficult to escape the cycle of self-defeat. We encourage our clients, therefore, to pair each of the techniques they use to practice their self-defeating behaviors with a healthy alternative. These alternatives form a set of replacement behaviors that an individual can draw upon at new moments of life. Without them, people are forced to rely on willpower or rigid abstinence to see them through difficult circumstances that tempt them to return to their old habits.

Analyze conclusions and fears. For the majority of people, the five steps we've just described are sufficient to bring about the desired changes in behavior. But every now and then, we work with a client who needs to do additional work to eliminate his or her self-defeating behavior. This sort of client is caught in the interplay between faulty conclusions and mythical fears. To make winning choices, such a person must first work with a counselor to identify and analyze the conclusions and fears that are behind his or her thoughts and actions. Once these conclusions and fears have been exposed and challenged, the individual can move on to complete the other steps that make up the change program.

Acknowledge setbacks and breakthroughs. Any person who attempts to get rid of a self-defeating behavior needs to recognize that he or she will experience occasional setbacks. We teach people to anticipate and recognize these relapses and to interpret them not as indications of failure, but instead as evidence that the change process is working. At the same time, we emphasize the importance of acknowledging each successful step along the road to breakthrough, no matter how small it seems to be. Without this sort of self-monitoring, people tend to develop unrealistic expectations about how behavior change should work. They assume that break-throughs are dramatic and that setbacks are inevitably catastrophic. Under these conditions, it's extremely difficult for the change process to begin, let alone succeed.

We've found that people who follow these six (or perhaps seven) steps are able to bring about significant changes in how they behave and, just as important, in how they feel about their behavior. This program is effective, however, only for people who have begun to own their behavior. It's extremely rare for a program of change to work for people who continue to disown their thoughts and actions. As we explain to our clients, change begins where disowning ceases.

The Importance of Honest Ownership

By and large, people who seek counseling have already begun to assume at least partial ownership of their self-defeating behaviors. More than a few of these people, however, are not completely honest in the way they take responsibility for their behaviors. They acknowledge that they are responsible for the choices they make, *but only after these choices have already been made and acted upon.* They own their behaviors only after the fact and, in so doing, fall into a pattern of *disowning through ownership.* People who practice this sort of disowning use superficial ownership as a smoke screen behind which they can continue to indulge their self-defeating impulses. With feigned remorse, they appear to accept total responsibility for their behavior—but only after they have yielded to their unconscious desire to hang onto it. They present themselves to the world as chronic confessors or smiling failures; they're willing to take their medicine, just as long as they're allowed to keep infecting themselves with the disease.

Such people frequently attempt to use their counselors or support groups as sources of validation for their cycles of self-defeat. Their pattern is to practice a self-defeating behavior, admit to it *after the fact,* and then promise to make a better choice the next time they are tempted to lapse into their destructive habits. They expect their counselors or support groups to congratulate them for their honesty and to absolve them of their recent mistakes. They confuse confession with ownership. They accept responsibility for their behaviors only so that they might continue to practice them.

This process of disowning through owning serves only to delay the point of reckoning at which the individual must honestly choose either to change his or her behavior or to continue to practice it. Consider, for example, habitual gamblers. They might consciously acknowledge a need to stop gambling, and may even go so far as to seek help in the form of counseling or a program of group support. But if they do not honestly own their behavior, they will find it easy to continue to gamble while using a counselor or support group as a source of absolution. Their enhanced pattern of self-deception might take the following form: (1) place a wager; (2) go to a meeting or support session and admit to the behavior; (3) seek and receive reassurance that they are only human, and that mistakes are inevitable; (4) promise to do better the next time they are tempted to gamble; (5) believe that they have made amends for lapsing into an old pattern of self-defeat; and (6) repeat this sequence of events the next time an opportunity to gamble presents itself. If the counselor or support group does not intervene in this process, this person will be able to sustain a self-defeating behavior while claiming to own it and to want to be rid of it.

Our suggestion is that you get into the practice of owning your self-defeating behaviors *before* you carry them out and *while* you are carrying them out. This, we feel, is what true ownership is all about. Until you are honest with yourself in accepting the notion that you and you alone are responsible for your thoughts and actions, you'll find it difficult to make winning choices at new moments of life. You'll find yourself playing the "I want to change but can't" game, in which confession and apology are substituted for honest ownership. And because this game helps to minimize the prices you pay for your destructive actions, you'll find that it will serve only to perpetuate your cycle of self-defeat.

How to Use This Section

In the chapters that follow, we'll be guiding you through each of the steps you'll need to take if you wish to get rid of a troublesome self-defeating behavior. We'll be asking you to analyze when, how, and with whom you practice this behavior; we'll be suggesting, too, that you work on developing replacement behaviors that can be used in place of self-defeating techniques. To help you through this process, we've included a series of exercises for you to complete. The first time you read this section of the book, you may wish to skip over the exercises and read straight through to the end of the program. It's okay to move through the material in this manner, especially if you're anxious to find out where the program leads. Keep in mind, though, that change requires time and effort. We believe that to receive the full benefit of the program outlined here, you must at some point complete the recommended exercises.

One more point before we move on: It's important for you to know that our program for change is designed to bring about permanent but gradual changes in the way you think, act, and feel. If you believe that you're in a crisis situation that demands an immediate remedy, however, we recommend that you seek counseling at the earliest possible opportunity. Once you've dealt with your crisis, you'll be in a position to take full advantage of our guidelines for healthy and lasting behavioral change.

Chapter 15

Identifying Your Self-Defeating Behaviors

The crucial first step to breaking out of a cycle of self-defeat is to identify the behavior on which the cycle is based. We use the term *behavior* here to refer to the complete sequence of thoughts and actions that are used to respond to and reinforce faulty conclusions. You should not be concerned at this point with identifying or analyzing the specific techniques that you use to initiate your particular cycle. Neither should you attempt to articulate the conclusions that underlie your behavioral choices. Your goal here is to develop a simple but accurate description of the behavior pattern that you use to defeat yourself.

To help you achieve this goal, we'll suggest several approaches that can help you identify what it is that you do to bring on the problems that plague you. We'll provide a checklist that you can use to narrow down the potential sources of your discontent. We'll suggest also that you listen to feedback from others, chart your personal history, and analyze the environment in which you were raised. Each of these approaches can help you get a firmer grasp on the behavior pattern(s) you want to change.

As you move through this chapter, keep in mind the importance of describing your self-defeating behavior in your own words. You can use the suggestions you'll find here as guidelines, but ultimately you'll want to phrase your description of how you behave in terms that are natural and comfortable to you. If you get into the pattern of thinking and talking about this behavior in terms or labels that someone else has imposed on you, you'll eventually begin to regard it as something outside of you or beyond your control. This way of thinking, as we've indicated earlier, makes it easy to disown the behavior and to lapse into a cycle of blaming, helplessness, and continued self-defeat.

A Behavior Checklist

For some people, the process of identifying personal patterns of self-defeat is relatively simple. The person who wants to stop smoking, overeating, or spending excessive amounts of money, for example, probably does not need to perform an extensive analysis to discover what it is that he or she needs to change in order to escape the cycle of self-defeat. For others, however, the process of identifying a specific self-defeating behavior is less straightforward. People who want to change because they feel caught up in a general pattern of discontent, discomfort, or failure often need to take a close look at the possible sources of their problem. Having done this, they can move on to identify more specifically the pattern of thought or action that is at the root of their difficulties.

To help those who fall into this second category, we've provided a checklist of commonly practiced self-defeating behaviors. We ask you now to read through the list and to check any behaviors that you regularly practice and—perhaps more important—that you want to change.

_____ Procrastination	_____ Shyness
_____ Defensiveness	_____ Overeating
_____ Abuse of alcohol/other substances	_____ Smoking
_____ Depression	_____ Hostility
_____ Worrying	_____ Suspiciousness
_____ Compulsive/ritualistic actions	_____ Impotence/frigidity
_____ Dependency	_____ Prejudice
_____ Perfectionism	_____ Inferiority
_____ Alienation	_____ Abusiveness

Studying this checklist and checking off the behaviors you feel you need to change can be an instructive process. After completing this exercise, Barbara—who, as you may recall, came to us seeking relief from her perfectionist tendencies—discovered that chronic worrying, not perfectionism, was the behavior that was giving her the most trouble. "Making demands on myself and others is a way of expressing my concern," she told us. "I worry all the time about everything, especially the health and future of my family. I worry myself sick. I'm demanding because I'm so concerned about things."

You may find that you've checked off more than one self-defeating behavior on the list. If this is the case, you'll find it helpful to choose one or two behaviors to work on initially and to work on the remaining behaviors later. Some of our clients have successfully worked on two or three behaviors simultaneously, while others have found it necessary to concentrate on one behavior at a time. We suggest that you choose the approach that best fits your needs. Keep in mind, though, that trying to change multiple behaviors all at once can become a complicated task, especially in the latter phases of the change program.

Now that you've identified the behavior(s) that you believe is (are) causing you to defeat yourself, you need to describe each behavior *in your own words*. There are two reasons why you need to do this: First, we recognize that our checklist of general behaviors cannot possibly apply accurately to all people in all circumstances. It's important, therefore, that you describe the behavior in a way that accurately reflects your specific situation. Second, we feel that at this point you need to describe your self-defeating behavior as something that you actively practice, as opposed to some general condition that has been imposed on you.

A format that works well for this is to identify first what your self-defeating behavior is, and then to rephrase it in a way that describes specifically what you think or do when you are practicing the behavior. "My self-defeating behavior is dependency," you might say, "which means that I make a lot of annoying phone calls that alienate people." This format allows you to describe your self-defeating behavior accurately and, at the same time, to own it honestly.

Take as much time as you need here to rephrase the behavior(s) you identified earlier in your own words. Try to come up with an accurate but comfortable description of what it is that you do to bring about difficulties for yourself. If you're tempted to rush through this exercise, keep in mind that the identification statements you come up with will serve as the basis for subsequent steps in your change program. An inaccurate identification statement can lead you astray as you attempt to move along the road to breakthrough.

My self-defeating behavior is—   *Which means that I—*

Don't be concerned if at this point you cannot precisely describe the form that your self-defeating behavior takes. We'll be suggesting a variety of approaches that you can use either to identify your particular pattern of self-defeat or to refine your description of it.

Listening to Feedback

Another approach that can help you identify your self-defeating behavior is to listen to the feedback that you receive from others. Jack, the advertising executive who moved from job to job without career advancement, had trouble picking out his self-defeating behavior from the list we provided. So we suggested that he listen to the feedback he received from colleagues he respected and trusted. He returned to our office one day and said, "I think I've got a handle on this now. I was talking to my art director last week, and he asked if I was having any problems. When I asked what he meant, he said,

'You've always seemed like a confident, take-charge guy. But lately it's seemed like you're a little overwhelmed—like you don't feel you're up to the job anymore.' I was ticked off at first, but then I realized that this guy had helped me put a finger on what it is I do to get out of an agency. I start feeling inferior, and I convince myself I have to leave before the bosses find out how inadequate I am."

We believe that listening openly and carefully to the feedback you receive from others can help you identify and describe your self-defeating behavior. But a word of caution is in order here: We suggest that you choose carefully whom you listen to and that you take what they say with reservation. Because self-defeating behavior is so rampant in our culture, the people who give you feedback may be telling you more about their own difficulties than about your behavior. If you choose this approach to help you identify your pattern of self-defeat, we suggest that you solicit the advice of someone who appears to be relatively free of self-defeating behaviors. We also suggest that if what this person tells you doesn't seem to fit with your sense of the way you're behaving, you should *get a second opinion*. It's always risky to rely on a single evaluation, particularly with regard to matters that can affect the way you think about yourself.

We suggest also that if at all possible, you exercise caution when asking members of your immediate family for feedback about your behavior. There are two reasons why we say this. The first is that because we learn from our environments, a parent, sibling, or spouse might well be caught up in the same pattern of self-defeat that you are; hence, he or she may not see this particular behavior pattern as a problem. The second reason for which family members are not always the best sources of feedback is that these people may, at either a conscious or an unconscious level, want you to continue to practice your self-defeating behavior. They may have a stake in your behavior; your perfectionism or chronic worrying may, for example, make it possible for them to be careless or irresponsible. Or, to cite another common example, your drinking or drug abuse might enable them to think of themselves as martyrs and, hence, to minimize the prices of their own self-defeating behaviors. If you want objective and accurate feedback about the way you behave, it's best to consult a person who knows and respects you but who will not be intensely affected by any behavioral changes you make.

Charting Your History

For most of us, life does not consist of a series of unbroken triumphs or defeats. Instead, it's a sequence of relative high and low points. Certain years, months, and weeks are better than others: there are times when everything we do seems to produce positive results, and there are times when nothing seems to work. An analysis of the relative high and low points of our lives can give us insights as to the kinds of winning and self-defeating behaviors we have practiced.

You can perform this sort of analysis by charting your personal history. To do this, you must first identify a period of time to work with. We recommend that this period be at least one year but no more than four or five years long. We recommend also that you exclude the recent and distant past from this sort of analysis. Your memory of the past year or six months may be unduly influenced by the difficulties you're currently experiencing, just as your recollection of the remote past may be clouded by nostalgia. For the purpose of this exercise, it's best to work with a period that falls within the previous ten years.

Once you've identified a period to work with, you should move on to represent graphically how you felt about yourself and life in general during that period. We've found the following format to be effective:

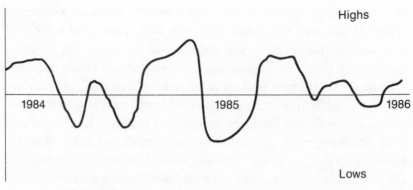

Figure 21

After you've set up the format for the period you want to chart (in this example, we've used the years 1984–1986), identify your high and low points relative to the norm represented by the time line. Try to represent these highs and lows accurately; avoid making it seem as if your good times were all equally good, or your bad times equally bad. The more jagged and uneven your pattern, the more accurately you're probably remembering the period under consideration.

Next, look at the low points on your chart. Exclude for the purpose of this exercise any low points that represent a misfortune over which you had no control: a death in the family, a serious illness, or a catastrophic accident. (These events are "natural" lows that do not necessarily suggest the practice of a self-defeating behavior.) Then consider the low points that remain. Ask yourself if you were practicing any particular kind of behavior during each of these lows. Were you defensive or manipulative at these points in your life? Were you acting out of a sense of your own inferiority? Were you shy or withdrawn? Were you open to the actions and suggestions of other people, or were you closed to new possibilities and options? The answers to these and similar questions can give you a good indication of the kinds of self-defeating behavior you've practiced in the past—and may continue to practice in the present.

Working on a chart of your personal history can give you valuable insights about how you think and act, as well as about what you need in order to feel comfortable with yourself. Remember Ted, the Vietnam veteran who found it difficult to get a job and assume a productive role in society? When Ted first came to us, he viewed his time in the military as a period of unbroken misery and terror. (This was understandable, given the ordeal to which he'd been subjected.) Upon completing this exercise, however, Ted realized that during his military service, he had also experienced some of the highest moments of his life. "Before combat, things went pretty well," he told us. "I had a place to go each day, things to do. I kept in shape and I learned new skills. I worked, I met new people, and I got paid." Ted was then able to contrast these relative highs with the low points that followed: points when his actions were guided by a sense of inferiority and purposelessness. By charting his history, he was able to identify not only his self-defeating behaviors but also the winning behaviors he practiced at those points at which he felt most comfortable about himself and his place in the world.

Analyzing the Environment
in Which You Were Raised

Another approach that can help you identify your self-defeating behaviors is to look closely at the environment in which you were raised. One of the ways in which we acquire self-defeating behaviors is to watch the people closest to us and then replicate their actions. And the people who are closest to us when we are developing our self-defeating behaviors tend to be family members: parents, grandparents, siblings, aunts and uncles. Recalling how these people behaved when we were young can often help us identify our own patterns of self-defeat.

For some people, the relationship between the environment in which they were raised and their self-defeating behaviors is extremely clear. "In our house people prayed aloud several times a day, asking for God's forgiveness," Anna told us. "But when I prayed that way at school, I was labeled as mentally disturbed. I didn't understand it, because I was only doing what I had been taught to do." For others, however, the link between their current behavior and their early environments is not as direct. Rachel, for example, at first found it difficult to see the similarity between her frantic housekeeping and her mother's obsession with games and rituals. "I didn't get my behavior from my mother," she told us. "Mom never cleaned house or washed dishes. For her, it was Bingo—night after night, five, six, sometimes seven days a week. Once we'd finished eating, she couldn't sit still until my aunt came by to drive her to the Bingo parlor. I think she did it to avoid spending time with my father."

When you analyze the environment in which you were raised, try to identify general patterns among family members, as opposed to specific self-defeating behaviors. Behaviors that on the surface appear to be dissimilar are often different manifestations of related patterns of thought and action. It is these general patterns that can help you identify your own self-defeating behaviors. The behavior we call "dependency," for example, may appear in many forms within the same family environment; it may take the form of alcoholism, drug abuse, chronic overeating, smoking, or a tendency to depend on other people for approval and support. If you can identify a set of related—but not necessarily identical—behaviors that were practiced by members of your family, you'll increase your understanding of why you think and act the way you do.

If You Still Need Help

If none of the approaches we've suggested help you to identify your self-defeating behavior, we encourage you to seek the assistance of a professional counselor. Being caught up in an ongoing cycle of self-defeat often makes it difficult to identify specifically what it is that you're doing to bring about your difficulties. In situations such as this, it's wise to seek the assistance of an objective professional who can look at your circumstances from the outside and help you evaluate your patterns of thought and action.

As we mentioned earlier, it's very hard to change your behavior if you do not have a clear sense of what it is that you want to change. So if at this point you have no idea what you are doing to defeat yourself, we advise you to begin to pay careful attention to the things that you say and do. Again, we suggest that you look for patterns of thought and action. Ask yourself *when* you're most likely to practice your self-defeating behavior, as well as *where* and *with whom* you activate your cycle of self-defeat. The answers to these questions will not only help you identify your specific self-defeating behavior— they'll also prepare you for the next step in your program for healthy change.

Chapter 16

Your Trigger Patterns

Most of us practice our self-defeating behaviors selectively. We do not, in other words, practice these behaviors from the time we get out of bed in the morning until the time when we retire for the night. Instead, we choose to carry out our cycles of self-defeat only under certain circumstances. These circumstances, which we interpret as threats to our health, safety, or emotional well-being, form patterns of experience that tell us we had better start behaving in self-defeating ways if we want to maintain equilibrium. Each of us has such a *trigger pattern:* a set of events and/or conditions that causes us to move away from the road to breakthrough and to carry out a familiar cycle of self-defeat.

A trigger pattern usually consists of three components. If we analyze our trigger patterns carefully, we can discover (1) at what time of day, week, month, or year we are most likely to practice a self-defeating behavior; (2) in which situations or locations we are apt to practice the behavior; and (3) in whose company the behavior is most likely to occur. An understanding of this *when–where–with whom* pattern can help us avoid lapses into destructive patterns of thought and action.

Some people maintain that they practice their self-defeating behaviors constantly or under a variety of conditions. What these people are really saying is that their self-defeating behaviors are associated with *multiple trigger patterns.* Our response is that, yes, it is possible for a person to respond to more than one trigger pattern. As a matter of fact, most people do respond in related self-defeating ways to a variety of different conditions. What's more, many people practice more than one self-defeating behavior, each of which is associated with two or more trigger patterns. For this reason, the task of identifying trigger patterns is often not a simple one. It's a task that becomes easier, however, once a specific self-defeating behavior has been identified. When a behavior itself is clarified, the conditions under which it is practiced often become surprisingly apparent.

In this chapter, we'll be asking you to think about when you resort to your self-defeating behavior, where you resort to it, and with whom you most often practice the behavior. As you answer these questions, you'll be establishing a personal trigger pattern: you'll be describing the specific circumstances under which you carry out your personal cycle of self-defeat. Once you recognize these circumstances, you'll be in a position to develop better and healthier responses to them.

When Do You Practice Your Patterns of Self-Defeat?

After taking a close look at their patterns of thought and action, many people find that they practice their self-defeating behaviors primarily at certain times of the day, week, month, or year. Why is this the case? Because, as we indicated earlier, it requires a lot of work to override the healthy inner self and enact a cycle of self-defeat. A person who attempted to practice a self-defeating behavior constantly would soon be exhausted. Self-defeating behaviors make tremendous demands on the individual; they require numerous choices and extensive conscious thought. Hence, many people choose to practice these behaviors only at selected times.

Alice, for example, brought her family close to financial ruin by using credit cards to charge items she didn't need or particularly want. In looking through the dates listed on her billing statements, she discovered that she tended to go on shopping sprees on Tuesday or Wednesday evenings. Roger, whose drinking cost him more than a few jobs and personal relationships, was able to determine that he was most likely to abuse alcohol after seven o'clock on weekday evenings, and also on Sunday afternoons. And Daniel, who initially claimed to be depressed "day in and day out," eventually came to realize that he was most often "down" during the periods that preceded holidays and birthdays, and, particularly, late in the spring—a time that coincided with the anniversary of his father's heart attack. By identifying *when* they were most likely to enact a cycle of self-defeat, these people acquired a measure of control over their destructive thoughts and actions.

Identifying when you most often practice your self-defeating behaviors provides an insight into what your personal trigger pattern looks like. We ask you now to consider each of the behaviors you identified in the previous chapter and to analyze when you tend to practice them. Try to be as specific as possible in determining the time of day, week, month, or year when you put each of your self-defeating behaviors into practice. We've provided a chart on which you can record your insights.

Behavior	Time	Day	Month	Year
_____	____	____	____	____
_____				
_____				
_____	____	____	____	____
_____				
_____				
_____	____	____	____	____
_____				

Don't be concerned if you find it difficult to specify precisely when you practice your self-defeating behavior. It may well be that this behavior is associated more closely with a particular location or situation than a specific time. An analysis of *where* you practice the behavior can help you develop a fuller understanding of how your personal trigger patterns work.

Where Do You Defeat Yourself?

It's not unusual, we've found, for a person to practice a self-defeating behavior only in a particular location and environment. Some people are shy, nervous, abusive, or suspicious at school or the office, yet function as open and caring human beings at home or in social situations. Some abusers of alcohol indulge themselves only in bars and restaurants, while others drink to excess only within the private confines of their living rooms. Similarly, certain highly intelligent people choose to "become stupid" or blank their minds when they are asked to take tests, write letters or memos, or speak in front of groups of people.

Our experiences with people who behave according to these and related patterns have caused us to conclude that many individuals selectively practice their self-defeating behaviors in specific settings or circumstances. These locations or situations may be (and often are) relatively neutral in terms of the threat that they pose to the individual; an environment that triggers a cycle of self-defeat is not necessarily one in which the person is in danger of being harmed, shamed, or overwhelmed. It is, however, a location or situation in which the individual for some reason feels that his or her ability to cope will be taxed beyond its limits.

Rachel, for example, practiced her compulsive and ritualistic behavior only inside her apartment, and only at the end of a workday or during the weekend. At the office, she seemed the very model of composed efficiency. But once she entered her apartment, she flew into a frenzy of housework; she scrubbed floors that she had washed and waxed the night before, removed clean dishes from the cupboard and washed them before they had been used, and vacuumed her spotless carpet. "At work I don't think too much about how empty my life is," she told us. "But once I walk through the door into that apartment, I get tense. It's as if I'm face to face with my loneliness and the lack of sexual feeling that has made my life a mess. That, I guess, is the mess I'm really trying to clean up when I do my housework."

Try now to look at your self-defeating behavior in the way that Rachel looked at hers. See if you can list any particular locations, environments, or scenarios that seem to cause you to behave in self-defeating ways. If you have trouble getting started, look back at the analysis you did earlier of *when* you practice your pattern of self-defeat. The times you've specified might give you an insight about the kinds of environments or situations that trigger your unhealthy thoughts and actions. And try to be as specific as possible in describing your trigger environments. If, for example, you practice your shyness or inferiority during department meetings at the office, make a note of this tendency. Don't simply write down that you practice your self-defeating behavior "at work," "at home," or "at parties." The more specific you can be about these environments, the more control you'll eventually be able to develop over your trigger patterns and, ultimately, over the self-defeating behaviors to which these circumstances lead.

Behavior	Location (and/or) Situation	
_____	_____	_____
_____	_____	_____
_____	_____	_____
_____	_____	_____
_____	_____	_____

Once you've filled out this chart, you'll have an idea of *when* and *where* you're most likely to initiate a personal cycle of self-defeat. You'll have identified two of the three key components that make up your trigger pattern and will be ready to look at the individuals or types of people who seem to cause you to behave in self-defeating ways.

With Whom Do You Practice Your Self-Defeating Behaviors?

Many of our clients have found that they tend to practice their self-defeating behaviors only with certain individuals or types of people. Ted, for example, withdrew into his shell of shyness and suspicion primarily in the presence of strangers who appeared to have authority over him: doctors, nurses, government administrators, and potential employers. Jim, on the other hand, felt at ease with strangers and casual acquaintances, but lapsed into his pattern of withdrawal and rigidity when he was in the company of friends and co-workers. And Molly, who physically and verbally abused her son and daughter, would never have thought of lashing out at another adult, or even at a child who was not her own. Each of these people had incorporated specific individuals or groups into his or her personal trigger pattern.

We need to explain here—just as we explained to Ted, Jim, Molly, and thousands of others—that the people who become incorporated into a trigger pattern *are not the cause* of the self-defeating behavior to which the pattern leads. Ted's potential employers, Jim's colleagues, and Molly's children were not responsible for the self-defeating behaviors that these people chose to practice. More often than not, they were neutral and unknowing participants in patterns that had been arbitrarily configured within another person's mind. The point here is that the people with whom we are most likely to practice our self-defeating behaviors have little or nothing to do with why we carry out these behaviors. To believe otherwise is to disown responsibility for our thoughts and actions, and to ensure that our cycles of self-defeat will be perpetuated.

We should add, too, that many of our clients, in analyzing the *with whom* component of their trigger patterns, come to the realization that they practice their self-defeating behaviors primarily when they are alone. This, we feel, is an insight that can be put to good use when an individual is trying to develop alternative ways of responding to his or her trigger pattern. We suggest that if you discover that your cycle of self-defeat is initiated primarily when you are alone, you note this tendency as a key component of your overall trigger pattern.

Take some time here to identify the individuals and/or types of people with whom you most often practice your self-defeating behavior. You might find it helpful to look at the triggering environments and situations you listed earlier and to think about which people or groups you tend to be with in these circumstances. For each of your self-defeating behaviors, list the person(s) or types of individuals in whose company you practice the behavior. And if you carry out your cycle of self-defeat mostly when you are alone, make a note of this tendency.

After you've analyzed this third and final component of your trigger pattern, you'll have a clear picture of what your pattern looks like. You'll be using this information as you begin to develop healthy alternatives to your self-destructive habits and tendencies.

Behavior	Whom You Practice It With
_____	_____
_____	_____
_____	_____
_____	_____
_____	_____

Putting Your Insights to Work

A knowledge of the situations and circumstances in which you practice your self-defeating behavior is essential if you want to eliminate this kind of behavior. But how can you use this knowledge? Or, perhaps more to the point, what can you do with the insights you've gained by analyzing your trigger pattern? How, in other words, can you put your insights to work in a way that leads to the elimination of a behavior that brings you unhappiness, pain, and failure?

We've found that people can use their understanding of their personal trigger patterns in one of two ways. They can simply attempt to avoid those circumstances and individuals that they have associated with their cycles of self-defeat. Although this approach can be effective, it is in many cases impractical or impossible. If, for example, you have associated your self-defeating behavior with a work environment or the company of a spouse or child, your trigger pattern will probably be inescapable—unless, of course, you are willing and able to take drastic measures to avoid your triggering circumstances. Most people, however, are unwilling to change jobs, get divorced, or terminate friendships simply to escape situations that are likely to lead to continued self-defeating behavior.

Fortunately, there is a less dramatic and more effective way for people to deal with their personal trigger patterns. This approach involves the development and practice of *replacement techniques* that can be used in place of self-defeating thoughts and actions when triggering circumstances arise. These replacement techniques are healthy ways of responding to trigger patterns. Over time, they can be learned and incorporated into the individual's habits of thought and action. They are a vital part of a program for positive and permanent change.

Before you look at how replacement techniques can be developed and put into practice, however, you need to consider in greater detail the techniques you use to carry out your cycle of self-defeat. You also need to have the experience of "catching" yourself while you're practicing your self-defeating behaviors. These two steps will help you see how you respond to your trigger pattern and, perhaps more important, what you might do differently in situations in which you have traditionally practiced your self-defeating behavior.

Chapter 17

Know Your Techniques

Over time, each of us develops a set of techniques to carry out the habits of thought and action that together form a self-defeating behavior. We develop primary inner and outer techniques to enact the self-defeating choices we make at new moments of life; we learn and apply advanced minimizing techniques to deal with the consequences of our destructive actions; and we practice disowning techniques to escape responsibility for our behavior and to avoid making changes in the ways we respond to new moments. The sequence in which we apply these techniques, along with the interplay that exists among them, defines our individual cycles of self-defeat. To understand these cycles, we must identify the specific techniques that are used to implement our self-defeating choices.

So far, we've asked you to identify the behavior pattern that you want to change or eliminate and to describe the circumstances in which you practice this behavior. At this point, we'll suggest that you look closely at the techniques you use to carry out and perpetuate your self-defeating behavior. We'll ask you to clarify in your own mind the specific inner and outer techniques you draw upon in new moments of life. We'll also ask you to become familiar with the minimizing and disowning techniques that you rely upon to temper the consequences of your behavior and to escape responsibility for it. At the conclusion of this segment, you should have a clear sense of what it is you do to bring about your own unhappiness, discontent, and sense of incompleteness or failure.

Your Primary Inner and Outer Techniques

People who practice self-defeating behaviors, as you'll recall from chapter 10, use some combination of inner and outer techniques to carry out the self-defeating choices they make at new moments of life. Inner techniques are thought processes that support self-defeating choices; outer techniques, on the other hand, are observable actions that enact misguided behavioral decisions. Some people use only inner techniques, and, as a result, learn to live with a considerable amount of internal tension. Others relieve this tension by way of an external act or gesture. When people use both inner and outer techniques, they subject themselves to the consequences of a "one-two punch." They suffer not only the tension created through the use of the inner technique but also the very real consequences that result from an overtly destructive action.

We've provided lists of the most common inner and outer techniques that people use to carry out their self-defeating choices. You'll find it helpful to read through these lists and check the techniques that you draw upon to implement the self-defeating behaviors you identified earlier in this section. Don't be surprised if you find yourself checking more than one or two techniques. Self-defeating behaviors are complex structures that often manifest themselves in many different ways. If the inner and outer techniques that you use are not listed, describe these techniques in the spaces that have been provided.

Inner Techniques

_____ Comparing the self to others

_____ Forming unrealistic expectations

_____ Anticipating negative results

_____ Holding back honest feelings

_____ Distorting feedback

_____ Creating false limitations

_____ Blaming oneself or others

_____ Others: _____

_____ Imposing guilt on the self or others

_____ Reviewing past hurts

_____ Labeling the self or others

_____ Blanking one's mind

_____ Fantasizing

_____ Intellectualizing

_____ Selective forgetting

_____ Magnifying real problems

_____ Rationalizing

_____

Outer Techniques

_____ Attacking others, verbally or physically	_____ Failing to meet obligations
_____ Throwing temper tantrums	_____ Engaging in promiscuous or unloving sexual acts
_____ Manipulating others	_____ Lying
_____ Laughing when it is not appropriate	_____ Making sarcastic remarks
_____ Being late for appointments	_____ Crying at inappropriate times
_____ Arguing for the sake of argument	_____ Drinking too much
_____ Withholding sexuality in loving relationships	_____ Spending money you do not have
_____ Pouting	_____ Racial or religious bigotry
_____ Analyzing problems or situations when action is required	_____ Using drugs
_____ Acting rashly in situations where thoughtful analysis is required	_____ Smoking or chewing tobacco
_____ "Nervous" tics or habits	_____ Acting "crazy" to acquire or maintain a diagnostic label
	_____ Stealing
	_____ Gambling

_____ Others: _____

_____

Minimizing Techniques

If you are currently practicing a self-defeating behavior, you are to some extent using minimizing techniques to make sense of your thoughts and actions. These advanced techniques, as we discussed in chapter 12, skew the price-fear equation in a way that makes self-defeating choices seem logical. When you minimize the consequences of your destructive thoughts and actions, you attempt to convince yourself that these consequences are more manageable than are the mythical fears that prevent you from making winning choices.

Although you must minimize on a regular basis to continue to practice a self-defeating behavior, you may not be aware of the specific minimizing techniques you use. If this is the case, we suggest that you consider the following list of common minimizing techniques and mark those that you draw upon to justify your self-defeating behavior. (If you have developed a personal minimizing technique that does not fit within one of the listed categories, describe this technique in the space provided.) Again, don't be surprised if you discover that you use more than one of these techniques. Because minimizing always fails, most people who practice self-defeating behaviors need to resort to more than one minimizer in order to sustain their cycles of self-defeat.

_____ Ignoring   _____ Being chronically "busy"

_____ Comparing   _____ Nihilizing

_____ Joking   _____ Making others pay

_____ Numbing (with alcohol,   _____ Therapizing
drugs, food, sex, etc.)
    _____ Adapting
_____ Martyring

_____ Others: _____

_____

Disowning Techniques

To complete your personal cycle of self-defeat, you must eventually disown responsibility for your behavior. This advanced technique removes your thoughts and actions from your control and serves ultimately to convince you that you cannot change. Through disowning, you cast yourself not as a free and intelligent human being who is capable of healthy choices, but rather as a victim caught up in a cycle of rage and helplessness. Disowning thus completes the cycle of self-defeat: it gives you someone or something to blame for your misguided choices.

We've provided a list of the most common techniques that people use to avoid taking responsibility for their behavior. As you read through the list, note which of these techniques you use to complete your cycle of self-defeat and support your faulty conclusions. You might also find it helpful to describe your disowning techniques more specifically: you may want to make a note of who or what it is that you blame for your behavior, or to write down the specific words you use to construct your disowning statements.

Disowning Technique	How You Use It
Blaming other people	_____
	_____
	_____
Fragmenting the mind and body	_____
	_____
	_____
Capitalizing on social, political, or economic inequities	_____
	_____
	_____
Embracing fatalistic conclusions	_____
	_____
	_____

Why It's Important to Know Your Techniques

Making a healthy and permanent change in how you behave is a gradual process. It requires knowledge, initiative, and experience. It is not simply a matter of saying, "I know my behavior is self-destructive, so tomorrow I'm going to start acting differently." Rather, it's a process of discovering precisely what you do, watching the way you behave, and learning from the results that your thoughts and actions bring about. Until you understand where you are now, it will be difficult for you to determine how to get to the place where you want to be in the future.

It's important that you avoid the temptation of trying to make changes in your behavior without looking in detail at the techniques you use to carry out your self-defeating choices. Tempting though this shortcut may be, we've found that it almost always leads to failure and disappointment. Without a clear understanding of your techniques, you'll find it difficult to catch yourself practicing your self-defeating behavior, and as a result, you will come to think of this behavior as something that simply "happens" to you without cause or warning. From this perspective, behavioral change will seem too formidable to deal with; it will seem to demand constant alertness, rigidity, and willpower. You'll be left with the choice of either returning to your self-defeating behavior patterns or exhausting yourself in an effort to keep these threatening but amorphous patterns from overwhelming you.

The work that we did with Ted brought this point home dramatically. Ted's experiences in Vietnam had left him with the conclusion that he was crippled, inadequate, and psychologically damaged in a way that was obvious to everyone he met. Although he was able to see that his particular form of self-defeating behavior took the form of displaying a sense of inferiority to those people who might help him, he was at first unwilling to look closely at the techniques he used to put this behavior into practice. He decided instead to martial his inner resources in an effort to be "a different person" when he met with potential employers and administrators of government programs.

We met with Ted soon after he had attempted to put this approach into practice during a job interview. "How did things go?" we asked him. "Were you able to convince the interviewer that you were calm, even-tempered, and ready to go to work?"

"I messed up," he replied glumly. "I tried to steel my nerves, look the guy straight in the eye, and let him know I'm as good as anybody else. But I was nervous right from the start. I felt as if I might start coughing or trembling. I used all my strength to try to stay calm, but I got caught up in the effort. I barely heard a word the guy said.

"I'm sure I won't get called for the job," Ted concluded. "The guy probably thought I was a total basket case."

We then talked for several minutes about the things that Ted had done to ensure that he would fail. He admitted that he had overslept on the day of the interview and that, in his haste to be on time, had forgotten the potential employer's address. As a result, he had to stop at a pay phone to call the interviewer and explain that he might be "a few minutes late" for the appointment. When he arrived at the office (in plenty of time, as it turned out), he was frantic over the possibility of being late and concerned that the interviewer would be put off by his disheveled appearance. With all of this behind him, Ted rushed into the interviewer's office determined to present his "new" self for inspection.

"Can you see now why you had trouble during the meeting?" we asked him following our discussion of the events that had preceded the interview.

"I guess so," Ted admitted. "You're saying that I set myself up for failure."

"No," we replied, "you did the best you could. But you didn't know enough about the techniques you use to defeat yourself. Had you been more aware of how your pattern works, you might have been able to make better choices. Why don't we look closely at all of your techniques, including the ones you use to make yourself feel better when things don't go well?"

We spent the remaining time going over a series of checklists and specifying exactly what Ted did to carry out his cycle of self-defeat. We talked about his tendency not to give himself enough time to do what he needed to do; about his obsession with his appearance and what others were thinking about him; and about his tendency to become confused and inarticulate when attempting to "explain" himself. We told Ted to keep track of how often he used these techniques—not only when he was faced with a job interview, but also during the course of his daily activities.

The next time we met with him, Ted had recently been through still another job interview. "How did it go this time?" we asked him.

"Not bad," he replied. "I didn't get the job, but it was because I don't have the required background—not because the guy thought I was a bomb ready to go off. I can't say that I behaved any differently during the meeting; I just tried to be myself. But I was on time, I looked okay, and when I felt myself getting nervous, I sort of sat back and watched myself. I saw that the interview wasn't going too terribly, and I felt better about myself."

What Ted had done during this second interview was to catch himself practicing his self-defeating behavior. He used his knowledge of his techniques to accomplish this important step. He wasn't quite ready to develop and implement healthy replacement behaviors, but he was clearly moving toward the road that opens up when informed and winning choices are made.

Our experiences with Ted and other clients have convinced us that it's essential for people to recognize and understand the techniques that they use to carry out their cycles of self-defeat. This knowledge enables people to "catch" themselves when they are in their cycles and to learn from the experience of consciously practicing a pattern of destructive thought or action. This catching process is a transitional step in the process of healthy change. It provides people with a conscious awareness of the progress they are making and, at the same time, relieves them of the struggle that is required to prevent or ward off a sequence of thought and actions that is feared but not completely understood.

Chapter 18

Catching Yourself

Many people try to eliminate a self-defeating behavior by deciding abruptly to stop practicing the behavior and then mobilizing their psychic resources in the attempt to break a habit or interrupt a behavior pattern. This approach is not very effective. It creates a great deal of internal tension and, even if successful, often leads to the replacement of one self-defeating behavior with a different (but equally destructive) pattern of thought or action. A more practical and less taxing strategy, we believe, is to phase the behavior out of your life gradually, replacing it over time with one or more life-enhancing responses to new moments. This approach allows your healthy inner self to emerge naturally, in step with your increasing capacity for making the kinds of choices that lead to breakthrough and personal growth.

Catching yourself while you're practicing the behavior you want to eliminate is an essential part of this program for gradual and lasting change. Once you are aware of your personal trigger patterns and your favorite techniques, you'll have the information you need to complete this step: you'll know when you are most likely to practice your self-defeating behavior, how you practice it, and what it feels like, both physically and emotionally, to make a series of self-defeating choices. If you remain attuned to these signals, they'll alert you to the fact that you are in the process of initiating and perpetuating an unwanted behavior that yields undesirable results.

At first, you may find it difficult to catch yourself in the earlier stages of a cycle of self-defeat. In the initial stages of your program for change, it may seem that you can consistently catch yourself only when you are minimizing the consequences of your actions or disowning responsibility for your behavior. With practice, however, you'll develop the ability to catch yourself at successively earlier points in the cycle of self-defeat. Eventually, you'll learn to catch yourself *before* you make the choice that initiates your cycle. You'll be able to catch yourself while your self-defeating behavior is being *formulated,* rather than when it is being *implemented.* When you've developed this ability, you'll have arrived at the phase of your program in which behavioral change is truly possible.

This is not to say that the time you spend learning to catch yourself will be wasted. Even when you are catching yourself only in the latter stages of your cycle of self-defeat, you are acquiring important insights as to how and why you choose to hurt yourself. These insights are invaluable. You'll be able to use them to contrast the results of the replacement behaviors you eventually develop with the prices you pay for your self-defeating behaviors. You'll find, too, that the insights you gain through catching yourself are essential in the event that you need or want to challenge the conclusions and fears on which your destructive habits are based.

Consciously Practicing Your Self-Defeating Behaviors

To catch yourself is simply to practice your self-defeating behavior while maintaining a conscious awareness of what you are doing. It's a matter of recognizing your trigger patterns as they emerge, spotting your techniques while you are using them, and seeing clearly the results that your behavior will yield. This process will not of itself eliminate a self-defeating behavior—at least, not at first. In time, however, it can provide a means by which you can replace a self-defeating behavior with a healthy alternative. It can give you a new pattern to follow at those moments when triggering circumstances arise.

We recommend to our clients that when they are preparing to eliminate their self-defeating behaviors, they allow themselves a period of time during which they seek only to develop a conscious awareness of these behaviors as they are being practiced. We suggest that during this transitional period, they make no effort to change what they think or do but, rather, that they simply pay close attention to the choices they are making to carry out their cycles of self-defeat. We recommend, in other words, that they catch themselves in the act of practicing a self-defeating behavior, but that they not be overly concerned with changing the behavior at this point.

What does this catching process accomplish? For one thing, it teaches people through experience that they are, in fact, choosing to think certain thoughts and carry out specific actions. People who make purchases they can't afford, for example, can say to themselves, "Well, here I go—I'm about to walk into this store, and that will get things rolling. I'll lose control over what I buy, I'll get into an argument with my spouse when I get home, and I'll feel terrible in the morning. That's the way things will go if I walk into the store." In the early stages of their change program, such people might well choose to enter the store and make an unnecessary purchase at this point. But later, when the prices of this destructive choice come due, they will be able to see that the consequences of overspending—the arguments, the unpaid bills, the feelings of guilt—were brought on by a chosen action, not by fate, circumstance, or any other external factor.

The catching process also serves to slow the rate at which behavioral choices are made. One of the major reasons people fall into the habit of making self-defeating choices, as we pointed out earlier, is the speed at which the majority of these choices are made. When people have learned to recognize their trigger patterns and their favorite self-defeating techniques, however, they begin to reduce the speed at which they make decisions about how they will behave. (We often recommend that in this stage of their change programs, our clients write down their self-defeating choices once they are made, but before they are carried out. The act of describing the choice in writing forcibly slows down the speed at which the choice is made.) As the speed of making the choice is slowed down, more options become evident; as options multiply, self-defeating behavior starts to seem less and less of an automatic response to a particular set of circumstances.

People whose favorite technique for avoiding required tasks at the office is to make personal phone calls, for example, might catch themselves reaching for the receiver and say, in so many words: "I know I have work to do, but right now I am choosing to make an unnecessary call. Instead of dialing the phone, though, I could pick up the report on last month's sales and read it. Or I could dictate the memo that needs to be sent to headquarters tomorrow. If I did either of these things, I could avoid the hassle of trying to do everything this afternoon. Maybe that's the way to go." In catching themselves at a key choice point, these people not only slow the speed of choice; they also open up other options. For the present, they might continue to procrastinate. But having seen that alternative actions are available, they can pursue them at some future time and, in the process, short-circuit a cycle of self-defeat.

Alice's knowledge of her trigger pattern and self-defeating techniques enabled her to catch herself just as she was about to embark on a destructive shopping spree. "I figured out that I tended to go to the mall after work on Tuesdays and Wednesdays," she reported, "and only when I didn't have to be home to fix dinner or to give one of the kids a ride somewhere. In studying my pattern, I was also able to see that on those days, I would search my mind for some small item we needed: toothpaste, light bulbs, thread, whatever. I would drive from the office to the mall, and I would park as far away from where I planned to shop as possible. That way, I'd have to walk past all the shops and boutiques, and before I knew it I would be charging a set of expensive candlesticks or a new blouse or a food processor.

"But," Alice continued, "then I started catching myself while I was playing out this scene. I began to realize that I was setting myself up for defeat and that, sooner or later, I'd have to pay for what I was doing. At first this didn't come to me until I was standing at a cash register with my credit card in hand, but after a few weeks I started catching myself when I was sitting at my desk on a Tuesday or Wednesday afternoon, racking my brain for something I absolutely 'needed' to pick up at the mall. I saw what I was doing, and it helped me stop."

What Alice did was to learn to catch herself at successively earlier points in her cycle of self-defeat. She moved from a level of awareness that allowed her to catch herself while she was enacting her self-defeating behavior to a level of awareness that enabled her to recognize the behavior while it was being formulated. The catching process taught her through experience that she was choosing to carry out actions that would cause her to feel guilty and irresponsible. With this experience behind her, she was able to learn to make better choices and to use these choices as a basis for eliminating her destructive behavior patterns.

Catching Yourself at the Formulation Stage

The progress that Alice was able to make by learning to catch herself points to the outcome toward which the catching process should be directed: people should strive to catch themselves while they are formulating a self-defeating behavior, as opposed to when they are practicing it or after they have carried it out. This is not as easy to accomplish as it might seem. When people are first trying to catch themselves, they most often become aware of a self-defeating behavior at the minimizing or disowning stages—the stages that require the greatest amount of conscious effort. Catching a self-defeating behavior in these latter stages, while it can be helpful during an individual's initial attempts at behavioral change, does little to help eliminate the behavior.

It is possible to change or eliminate a behavior that has been caught at the minimizing or disowning stage, but few people, we've found, are able to do so on a regular basis. "It was easy to catch myself when I was making excuses for my compulsive behavior, or rationalizing it away," Rachel told us. "It was too late to do anything about it, though. I had already arranged things in my mind so that I would behave in a certain way, and I had little choice but to carry out the 'plan' I'd made for the evening." Other clients have described similar experiences with the catching process. They have told us that trying to eliminate a behavior that is not caught until its later stages is a little like trying to stop a speeding train on a downhill grade.

Our recommendation is that, after an initial practice period, you use your knowledge of your trigger patterns and favorite techniques to catch your self-defeating behavior at earlier and earlier points in its cycle. Ideally, your goal should be to catch this behavior in its formative stage—in other words, when the interplay between your faulty conclusions and mythical fears is creating a framework within which the resulting destructive behavior will seem logical and appropriate. Those of our clients who have developed the ability to catch their self-defeating behaviors at this crucial stage have been successful at eliminating the unwanted behaviors. They have used their self-awareness and personal experiences to terminate cycles of self-defeat before these cycles acquire momentum or a sense of inevitability. They have learned that if the initial choice to practice a self-defeating behavior is not made, then the behavior and its consequences will, without further effort, be eliminated.

Learning from Your Experiences

It's likely that while you're in this catching phase of your change program, you'll have more than a few experiences that will seem to underscore your apparent inability to rid yourself of a self-defeating behavior. Naturally enough, you'll tend to view these experiences as further evidence of your "failure" to respond to new moments of life in healthy ways. We encourage you, however, not to interpret the results of these self-monitoring exercises as indications of your inability to change how you think and act. You are still in the early stages of your program for change: you're learning to understand your trigger patterns and techniques, and to create in your mind a clear picture of what your personal cycle of self-defeat looks and feels like. Moreover, you haven't yet developed a set of replacement techniques that can be used to fill the vacuum that is created when a self-defeating behavior is first eliminated.

So how should you respond to the frustrations that arise when you are in this early phase of your program? One way of dealing with these frustrations is to keep in mind that at this point your goal is to observe and learn from your behavior, not to change it. If you are able to see clearly what you are doing to defeat yourself, do not make additional demands on yourself. Avoid the trap of trying to combine the catching and replacement steps of your program into a confused and premature attempt at permanent change. Keep in mind that you have acquired and perpetuated your self-defeating behavior because this behavior has made perfect sense to you. Until you discover through experience that a self-defeating behavior is neither logical nor appropriate, you can't really expect to eliminate or change it.

Another way of dealing with the internal discord that may arise during the catching process is to be aware that although you are still practicing your self-defeating behavior, you are now practicing it *consciously.* You might not think that this makes a difference in terms of how you think and feel, but it does. Why? Because if you practice a self-defeating behavior with an awareness of what you are doing, it is unlikely that you'll use the results of the behavior to nourish and strengthen faulty conclusions about yourself and life. Remember that a cycle of self-defeat is not completed until the consequences to which it leads are used to validate the conclusion on which it is based. The conscious practice of a behavior, however, interrupts this cycle; it prevents you from using your experiences to support a misguided notion or belief. In catching yourself while you practice a self-defeating behavior, you are undermining its internal logic. You are cutting off its source of nourishment and, hence, weakening its hold on you.

Let's listen to what Jack, the successful-but-unsuccessful advertising executive, had to say about how the conscious practice of his self-defeating behavior helped him change it:

> This business of catching myself while practicing a self-defeating behavior struck me as just another mind game at first. But I thought, what the hell, nothing else has worked for me, so I might as well give it a try. I'd figured out my trigger pattern—I knew I was most likely to start feeling hostile toward my job on Monday and Friday afternoons, before regularly scheduled staff meetings. I knew also that at those times I would be late for the meetings, that I'd act bored during the discussions that followed, and that, afterward, I'd make sarcastic remarks about the time we had wasted during the session.
>
> So last Friday, I watched myself play out this scene. I observed how I waited to fill out an expense report until ten minutes before our meeting was scheduled to start; I saw myself walking in late and taking a seat near the door. I was aware that I sat through the meeting with a dazed, disinterested expression on my face—I knew I was showing the other people in the room how pointless I felt the meeting was. And afterward, before I left the office, I stopped by Rob's desk, and we joked about how much money it was costing our clients to subsidize sessions like the one we'd just been through. We had a few laughs, and then I left.
>
> It was a Friday, so I should have felt good while I was driving home. But I didn't: I had this sense of déjà vu that made me nervous. I knew that I was setting things up so it would make sense for me to

resign, and the thought of having to look for another job depressed me. I asked myself why I was doing this to myself—did I think that anything would go differently at a new agency? I've worked at too many places to believe that. It came to me then that I was planning to act out my script in a new setting and that two, three years in the future, I'd be thinking the same thoughts and doing the same things. I saw how futile it was to continue in this cycle. I needed to find a new way of thinking about myself and my job.

Thinking back over the afternoon, I saw that I had chosen to be late for the meeting and, once there, to make my boredom evident. I could have chosen to do otherwise, and had I done so, I might have felt a lot better. I guess that was when I first realized that I could control the direction in which my career went. I didn't need to play out the same scene at another agency with a new audience—I could determine through my actions whether things went differently for me this time. The change wouldn't happen overnight, but I was convinced that I could learn from my mistakes and not keep repeating them.

In Jack's words we find evidence of how the catching process paves the way to healthy and permanent behavioral change. To be sure, Jack was still practicing his self-defeating behavior even while he was working at catching it; his colleagues and superiors at the agency probably perceived no difference in the way he was acting. But within Jack, the process of change was under way. He was beginning to call into question the faulty conclusions upon which he had based his career decisions. He had also begun to recognize an important truth: his future was less governed by "the way things work" in the business world than by his own choices. This truth, as hard as it might have been to accept, gave him a sense of control over his actions and enabled him to open his thinking to the possibility of lasting change.

The process of behavioral change begins within us. When we begin to catch ourselves in the practice of our self-defeating behaviors, we begin to change inside. At this point (and not earlier), we are ready to discover how we can display this internal change to the outside world. We are ready to work on the kinds of replacement techniques that will enable us to put into practice the winning choices we are learning to make.

Chapter 19

Developing
Replacement Techniques

Many of the people we've worked with have decided, after experiencing the patterns and consequences of their self-defeating behaviors consciously, that they want to stop practicing these behaviors immediately. Although it is healthy, this reaction tends to draw people into an attempt to eliminate a self-defeating behavior without first developing healthy alternatives to their destructive patterns of thought and action. This approach is often doomed from the start. The elimination of a self-defeating behavior almost always creates a sizable vacuum in a person's life. If the person has not decided on an alternative behavior to fill the void, he or she will be tempted by uncontrollable events to return to familiar ways of thinking and behaving. Therefore, we tell our clients that as they are preparing to let go of their self-defeating behaviors, they'll need to develop a set of replacement techniques to fill the vacuum that is created when a self-defeating pattern is abandoned.

Replacement techniques are thoughts or actions that you can use in situations in which you would otherwise resort to a self-defeating behavior. To discover and develop these techniques, you must be open not only to the possibilities that life offers but also to your own feelings and instincts, and to the workings of your healthy inner self. This openness will enable you to see that even though your life is complicated by one or more of these self-defeating behaviors, you are in fact capable of making winning choices and engaging in life-enhancing thoughts and actions. You'll become reacquainted with your own special talents and abilities, which, in turn, will direct you toward healthy replacement techniques.

The replacement techniques that you eventually choose to work on should be specific but simple. They should also be a natural extension of your healthy inner self. You'll find it difficult to make use of replacement techniques that are too general to work with. If, for example, you decide that your replacement technique will be to "take positive actions," you'll probably find yourself at a loss as to what you should do when your triggering circumstances arise. Similarly, replacement techniques that are overly complex—"writing an opera," for example, or "finding a new career"—will tend to leave you without workable alternatives in situations in which you are tempted to return to your old patterns of self-defeat. Your replacement techniques should consist of thoughts and actions that reflect your particular abilities and attitudes, rather than a misguided notion of what an ideally healthy person would do if he or she were in your shoes.

Your replacement techniques should also be flexible enough to accommodate changing circumstances. If they aren't, you may find yourself abandoning them when uncontrollable events force you out of the pattern you've planned to follow. Furthermore, inflexible replacement techniques can easily be transformed into self-defeating behaviors. Techniques that require you to be rigid, uncompromising, or obsessive can be quite effective—in the short run, at least—in eliminating self-defeating behaviors. But if you use these kinds of techniques, you run the risk of falling into new patterns of self-defeat. Rigidity is rarely a healthy attribute, even when used in place of a destructive thought or action.

When you are cultivating your replacement techniques, it's essential that you avoid the trap of replacing one self-defeating behavior with an equally harmful way of thinking or acting. The trap of faulty replacement has been the downfall of many potentially healthy change programs. Many people fall into this trap, for example, when they try to quit smoking or drinking. Instead of developing healthy replacement techniques, they substitute another destructive habit—overeating and taking medication are two of the most common ones—for the self-defeating behavior they are trying to eliminate. As a result, they successfully abandon one unhealthy behavior only to discover that they've acquired another. This pattern of faulty replacement leads eventually to minimizing and disowning and, as a result, the creation of a new cycle of self-defeat.

Once you've identified and worked on your replacement techniques, you must learn to use them when your trigger pattern emerges. Just as you learned at an earlier time to practice your self-defeating behaviors in response to specific situations or people, you must now learn to use your replacement techniques when triggering circumstances arise. At first, this may seem uncomfortable; it will require a conscious effort on your part to carry out your replacement techniques at the appropriate moments. With practice, though, you'll find that when you need them, these techniques will be triggered automatically. Your unconscious mind, in response to the winning choices you have learned to make, will see to it that you think and act in accordance with the renewed vitality of your healthy inner self.

You Can't Replace Something with Nothing

Whether you're aware of it or not, your self-defeating behavior most likely plays a significant role in your daily life. It makes sense that if you suddenly cease to practice this behavior, you'll run into spots of emptiness as you go about your activities. These empty spaces in your daily or weekly routine are potentially dangerous; upon approaching them, you'll need to do something that will replace the self-defeating behavior that you're trying to eliminate. In some cases, people find it helpful to replace self-defeating behaviors with external actions or activities. In others, it is more appropriate simply to counteract a destructive pattern of thought with a different and more productive way of thinking. If you've not identified replacement techniques such as these, you're apt to find yourself dwelling on the unwanted behavior you've left behind — and perhaps even returning to it.

This is why it it so important for you to develop and practice at least one replacement technique before you attempt to eliminate a self-defeating behavior. Your conscious mind abhors a vacuum and will try to fill it by any available means. If you have a replacement technique at hand, chances are that you'll use it. But if you don't, your conscious mind will lure you in the direction of an undesirable but familiar pattern of self-defeat.

"Last week I decided to stop being a hypochondriac," Phil reported to us during a session. "I resolved to quit reading medical texts and to ask my doctors to withdraw me from pills I've been taking." Here Phil paused and slowly shook his head. "My 'new life' lasted about a day and a half. I started to get bored; I had nothing to do, nothing to think about. Before long, I was worrying about my health, thinking maybe I'd acted too rashly in asking my doctors to cut off my prescriptions. I convinced myself I was getting sick, I guess. Anyway, I phoned one of my doctors, and he agreed to refill a prescription for the low blood sugar I claimed to be suffering from. I seem to be stuck with my thoughts of illness, pain, and death."

"What would have happened if you had planned out a series of activities to keep you busy for those first few days?" we asked. "We've talked about some alternatives you need to pursue, like going to the library and doing research on the procedures for starting your own business."

"I know, I know," Phil replied. "I thought about that particular task, but to tell the truth, it seemed like too much to take on all at once. I can't withdraw from medication, stop thinking about my health, and plan for the future at the same time."

"But what you tried to do last week is much more difficult than replacing a self-defeating behavior with a productive alternative," we explained. "Your concern for your health has dominated your life for a long time now. You can't simply drop that concern and leave nothing in its place. You have to have a project or a series of activities that you can use to fill the hole you leave behind when you no longer have your unproductive worries to occupy you."

"You might be right," Phil conceded. "Maybe if I had something to occupy my time, I wouldn't need to work so hard at trying not to think about my health."

Phil came to realize, in short, that he needed a set of replacement techniques to absorb the energy that he had spent calling doctors, reading medical texts, and going to clinics for tests and consultations. Without these replacement techniques, he would continue to battle himself and his desire to return to the behavior that had governed his life for so long.

Finding Effective Replacement Techniques

It's one thing to know that replacement techniques are essential, but quite another to find and practice them. Because effective replacement techniques are often specific to an individual's talents, schedule, past experiences, and current circumstances, they are difficult to prescribe or impose. While singing or exercising might be ideal replacement techniques for the homemaker who is trying to stop watching so much television, these same techniques might be totally ineffective for the office worker who is learning not to procrastinate. And while meditation might be a sound replacement activity for the harried and unfeeling executive, this same technique might prove disastrous if used by a person who was trying to deal with an obsession with religious theory or doctrine. Our point here is that we cannot tell you which replacement techniques will work for you. We can suggest patterns of thought and action that our clients have used to replace unwanted behaviors, but, beyond that, we'll have to leave you to your own resources.

How can you find the replacement techniques that will work for you? We recommend that you first look inside yourself. Keep in mind that your self-defeating behavior is itself a sort of replacement pattern: it is what you have learned to do in situations in which you feel that an honest expression of your healthy inner self will be met with hostility or censure. So ask yourself what it was that you did before you learned to practice your cycle of self-defeat. Were you expressive and friendly before you developed your self-defeating behaviors of shyness and withdrawal? Did you ask a lot of questions before you learned through painful experience that a pose of suspicious hostility would serve to protect you? Did you actively seek out tasks and projects before you learned to procrastinate? And what did you do in social situations before you took up smoking, drinking, or drugs? The answers to these and similar questions can suggest the kinds of replacement techniques that can help you deal with new moments of life without resorting to your habits of self-defeat.

Two other points of reference can help you find the replacement techniques that are most likely to work for you. It is important to consider the winning behaviors that you currently practice. Although many people contend initially that they do not practice any such behaviors, odds are that if they are alive and conscious they must make certain winning choices simply to survive. It's quite possible, for example, for a person who acts destructively in his or her role as a parent to function as a model of efficiency on the job. It's equally possible for a destructive abuser of drugs or alcohol to act creatively and benevolently when sober, or for a person who withdraws in social situations to behave warmly and expressively within the confines of his or her family or work group. Your healthy inner self demands expression and no doubt makes itself known in some aspect of your life. Look to that aspect when you are trying to develop alternatives to the unhealthy behaviors you practice at other times or in other environments.

Still another source of guidance about potential replacement techniques is any person you view as both healthy and successful. We've seen how negative role models often provide us with examples of the kinds of self-defeating techniques we use to carry out our destructive choices. There's no reason why you can't reverse this pattern to your advantage. Find a person who appears to accomplish with relative ease the kinds of goals and objectives you'd like to achieve yourself. Then observe how this person behaves; try to discover how he or she reacts in new moments of life and what techniques he or she uses to enact healthy and productive choices. The person you choose as a positive role model won't be perfect, but you should nevertheless be able to benefit from watching how he or she moves through moments of life similar to those in which you experience difficulty and discomfort.

An unlikely but helpful source of clues as to the replacement techniques you might use during your time of change is your self-defeating behavior itself. Several of our clients have identified effective replacement techniques as a result of the work they did when analyzing unwanted patterns of thought and action. Alice, for example, noted that her tendency to go on shopping sprees was triggered on weekday afternoons when she had no obligations to her children. Near the end of one of our sessions with her, we remarked in passing that Alice seemed to put a lot of effort into her mothering activities, and that she seemed to have a special talent for getting along with her children. A few weeks later she reported that she had found her replacement technique. We asked her to explain.

"It came to me when I was thinking through my trigger pattern after our last meeting," she told us. "I mentioned how I tend to go to the mall when I'm not scheduled to pick up one of the kids. So I asked myself, 'What would happen if you arranged to take the kids out to eat or to a movie on a Tuesday or Wednesday afternoon?' I decided this might keep me away from the mall, so I gave it a try: last Wednesday I told the kids I'd take them to a show when I got off work.

"I drove straight from the office to the kids' school. We went to the earlier show and afterward we stopped and had dinner. I had a great time; I never thought for a moment about going shopping. And the whole evening cost about a tenth of what one of my trips to the mall usually does."

Alice's story confirmed our belief that replacement techniques are highly personalized and are often found through an examination of the inner self. Effective replacement techniques are often *discovered*, rather than developed. They tend to be revealed when a person focuses on a capability, desire, or interest that has been a part of his or her life all along.

Specific, Simple, and Flexible Replacement Techniques

Above all, the replacement techniques that you decide to use in place of your self-defeating behavior must be *practicable*. They must be things that you can do with a minimum of effort and on relatively short notice, and that you can modify when necessary. We've watched many well-motivated change programs go awry because the individuals involved tried to implement replacement techniques that were complicated or difficult, or that required a degree of rigidity that was at odds with daily life.

How can you be sure that your replacement techniques are workable? The first question you should ask when you're evaluating a potential replacement technique is whether or not it defines a specific course of action. If it doesn't, then it probably won't serve your needs. We've found that when looking for replacement techniques, people tend simply to invert their descriptions of their self-defeating behaviors. Hence, the smoker decides that his or her replacement technique will be "not to smoke"; the anxious person plans to "stay calm"; and the chronic procrastinator resolves to "get things done on time." But none of these potential replacement techniques describe a specific action these people can take in situations that tempt them to return to a self-defeating behavior. We believe that general goals or desires are not specific enough to see an individual through times of change or crisis.

You should also ask yourself whether the replacement technique you are considering is *simple* enough to be put into practice on a regular basis. Many potential replacement techniques—especially those that require substantial investments of time or money, or that require the cooperation of more than one or two people—are simply too complicated to be relied upon. Jack discovered this the hard way. One of his self-defeating behaviors was to participate in exchanges of negative gossip with his colleagues at the agency. To replace this unproductive habit, he decided that when he was tempted to exchange sarcastic remarks with his co-workers, he'd instead call a meeting of four department heads to discuss ways of improving the agency's relationship with its customers. The problem with this approach, as Jack soon discovered, was that it required too much effort and involved too many people. The second time he tried to put his replacement technique into practice, it simply didn't work; there were deadlines to be met, and neither he nor his colleagues had the time or energy for a meeting. As a result of trying to implement a replacement technique that was too complex to be practicable, Jack soon returned to his habitual gossiping.

Finally, you should ask yourself whether each replacement technique that you plan to incorporate into your change program has enough built-in flexibility to be workable. A replacement technique that requires you "always" or "never" to behave in a certain way is probably too rigid to serve your interests. If, for example, your goal were to stop wasting time at home, it would be unwise to adopt a replacement technique that required you to stop watching television completely or to complete a productive task each and every evening. These approaches might work for a while, but sooner or later you would have a strong desire to watch a television program. At that point, you would need either to expend precious psychic energy to overcome your feelings or to give into temptation and deem yourself a failure. You would find yourself in what therapists often call a "lose-lose" situation; you would have no option that would allow you to do what you wanted and yet feel good about yourself. Inflexible replacement techniques will tend to put you in this sort of predicament more often than you like. We suggest that you not adopt rigid replacement patterns unless you're willing to fight a prolonged series of psychic battles with yourself.

The Trap of Faulty Replacement

It almost goes without saying that you should avoid replacing one self-defeating behavior with an equally destructive pattern of thought or action. It *would* go without saying, were it not for the fact that so many people make this mistake. It's rare, we've discovered, for a sincerely motivated change program to fail completely. But when it does fail completely, faulty replacement techniques are almost always to blame. The trap of faulty replacement is tempting but treacherous. It often leads people not only to continue to practice their original self-defeating behavior but also to incorporate new patterns of destructive thought or action into their lives.

Faulty replacement tends to occur when people want to eliminate their self-defeating behavior but do not understand the behavior completely. These people decide that anything they choose as an alternative to a self-defeating behavior will somehow be an improvement over their current cycle of self-defeat. This general conclusion underlies the confused actions of the smoker who becomes a compulsive overeater, the thief who turns to another type of crime, and the procrastinator who changes into an unproductive workaholic. In each case, one self-defeating behavior is replaced with another. More often than not, however, the victims of faulty replacement not only return to their old self-defeating behavior but also continue to practice the misguided replacement technique.

Before she decided to seek counseling, Molly made the mistake of faulty replacement. She had been abusing her children to relieve her own discomfort, and she knew she had to escape the resulting cycle of tension, rage, and guilt. Without understanding why she chose to attack her son and daughter, she decided that she could stop this pattern of abuse by drinking a tumbler of brandy when she returned from work in the evening. Before long, she found herself drinking even earlier in the day. She told herself that if she managed to calm her nerves before she left the office, she wouldn't need to drink as much when she got home.

"That was how I got into trouble with alcohol," Molly explained sadly. "I thought the brandy would keep me from screaming at my kids, or at least from hitting them. It worked for a while, but pretty soon I was drinking at lunch, in the office, in my car. . . . I ended up knocking the kids around pretty badly. I fell apart around that time. I'd become the worst kind of drunk, and my kids were still terrified of me."

We realize that your current circumstances are unlikely to become as catastrophic as Molly's. Still, we advise you to be extremely wary of the trap of faulty replacement. It can undo the results of any healthy choices you've made and can lead you into a truly tenacious cycle of self-defeat.

Triggering Your Replacement Techniques

The key to putting your replacement techniques into practice is to teach yourself to use them in triggering circumstances or situations. At first, this process might seem difficult. After all, your replacement techniques, even if they reflect your natural instincts and talents, are like muscles that you haven't used regularly; they can be developed and brought to full strength only through frequent exercise. Learning to use these techniques will initially require that you expend what will seem like a considerable amount of psychic energy. Eventually, however, you'll find yourself practicing these techniques automatically, as your unconscious mind gradually comes to a new conclusion about the kinds of behavior that are likely to bring success and fulfillment.

Earlier, you analyzed both your trigger patterns and the self-defeating techniques you rely upon to deal with new moments of life. Once you've decided on the replacement techniques you plan to implement, we suggest that you make a conscious attempt to use these techniques each time you realize that a set of triggering circumstances has arisen. If, for example, your trigger pattern tended to emerge on weekday afternoons, when you would begin to think about going to a bar and drinking the evening away, we'd suggest that you use your ability to catch yourself at this stage and make alternative plans immediately. Your replacement technique in this situation might be to go to a gym and work out, or to stop at a library and do some reading in an area that interests you. Your goal here would be to associate the thoughts and feelings that come to you in the afternoon with the subsequent action of going to the gym or the library. Gradually, your subconscious mind would learn to link your trigger pattern with the appropriate replacement technique — at which point, the act of exercising or reading after work would come to seem a natural and productive part of your life.

Through this process, you'll be able to build within your mind a healthy connection between your trigger pattern and the kinds of winning choices that will satisfy the needs of your inner self. This is why it is important that you develop replacement techniques that are natural ways of expressing your true interests and desires. The people who have the most difficulty learning to trigger their replacement techniques are those who attempt to think and act in ways that do not accurately reflect their inner selves. Quiet and contemplative individuals who try to implement a replacement technique that requires them to be aggressively gregarious, for example, are setting themselves up for failure. Their replacement technique will always be at odds with their inner nature and will probably never be effortlessly triggered.

Daniel learned of this difficulty through a process of trial and error. He had decided to attend concerts and plays instead of becoming worried and depressed. He failed to take into account, however, that he had little natural interest in music or the theater. Despite persistent efforts, he continued to find it a strain to implement his proposed replacement technique when he was about to worry or become depressed.

"This program isn't working for me," he complained to us. "I can tell when I'm worrying or getting down, but the thought of sitting through a concert or a show makes me even more depressed. Isn't this replacement thing supposed to get easier and easier?"

"It should," we replied. "But maybe we haven't found a good fit between your replacement techniques and your innermost thoughts and feelings. We may want to look at those thoughts and feelings to see if we can't find a better pattern of replacement for you."

We talked for a while about the basic fears on which Daniel's self-defeating behavior was based. We discussed again his fear that his father might suffer another heart attack—perhaps a fatal one. We agreed with Daniel that at the root of his difficulty was his concern for the well-being of his family. We then suggested that he put this essentially healthy feeling to work for him.

"The love you feel for your father is a strong and valid expression of your inner self," we told Daniel. "The next time you notice that your cycle of self-defeat is about to be triggered, why don't you call him on the phone. Ask how he feels, when he has last visited his doctor, and so on. Find out if there's anything you could do that might help him or bring him comfort. If you don't go overboard with this approach, it might provide you with a workable alternative to worry and depression."

About a month later, Daniel returned for a follow-up session. He reported that he felt his life was on the upswing. "I'm going over to the house a couple times a week now. It turned out that my dad needed an extra pair of arms to help him remodel the basement. He explains what should be done and shows me how to do it, and I handle the heavy lifting and reaching. I like the work, and when I'm with my father I don't fantasize so much about how sick he might be."

"Does it seem like a chore to visit your parents' house so often?" we asked Daniel.

"Not at all," he answered. "Actually, it takes a load off my mind. It's become something that I do because it makes me feel good, not because I have to."

Daniel's discovery of an appropriate replacement technique made it relatively easy for him to eliminate from his life an ongoing pattern of self-defeat and unhappiness. We've found this to be true for the majority of our clients: once they've successfully replaced an undesirable behavior with a healthy and natural alternative, they are soon able to free themselves from their cycles of self-defeat. The message we want to underscore here is that you should select your replacement techniques carefully. They must reflect your best impulses and capabilities, and you must derive satisfaction from them. If you remain on the road that leads to breakthrough, you'll be putting these techniques into practice regularly. As you move closer and closer to breakthrough, your replacement techniques will shape your thoughts and actions; as a result, they will play a significant role in determining how you live the rest of your life.

Chapter 20

Analyzing Your Conclusions and Fears

For the majority of the clients we work with, the five steps discussed so far—identifying their self-defeating behaviors, understanding their trigger patterns, recognizing their techniques, catching themselves, and developing replacement techniques—are sufficient to bring about healthy and enduring behavioral change. In completing these steps, people learn gradually to make winning choices at new moments of life and, as a result, begin to experience the benefits associated with breakthrough behavior. The experience of making winning choices and recognizing the positive results to which these choices lead helps to undermine faulty conclusions and, eventually, instills within a person's mind a new equation about the kind of behavior that brings success. The conclusion that has caused the person to develop a self-defeating behavior is, in effect, effortlessly replaced by a new and more accurate belief about life and how it should be lived.

But it would be untruthful to claim that these five steps work for everyone. We've found that the faulty conclusions upon which some people base their thoughts and actions are too powerful and pervasive to be undermined without additional work. These people, we've learned, need to complete a thorough analysis of their faulty conclusions before the process of change can begin to move forward. They must discover which of their beliefs about themselves and their lives are impeding their progress. They must come to realize why they continually choose to behave in ways that lead to self-defeat; they must learn what it is they hope to gain or accomplish through the ongoing practice of a self-defeating behavior. They must come to terms with the inherent falsity of the promises contained in their conclusions and must experience on an unconscious level the connection between the choices they make and the prices they eventually pay for their destructive thoughts and actions.

Analyzing faulty conclusions and the mythical fears they produce can be a difficult and time-consuming process. Therefore, we would like to offer some suggestions that can make this process less of an uphill battle and more of an exercise in personal growth and understanding. We'll begin by talking briefly about how conclusions work, and we will suggest how you can articulate and clarify your faulty conclusions and mythical fears. We'll move on to recommend a simple exercise through which you can expose the falsity of the promises that your conclusions seem to offer. We'll discuss also the role that counseling can play in helping you examine the faulty conclusions that govern your thoughts and actions.

How Conclusions Work to Prevent Healthy Change

Because it's been a while since we discussed faulty conclusions and how they work, it might be helpful here to summarize briefly the role such conclusions play in perpetuating patterns of self-defeat. A conclusion is formed, you'll recall, through a combination of experiences and behaviors: an individual encounters a new moment of life, chooses a behavior that he or she believes is an effective response to the moment, and, on an unconscious level, links the behavior and the experience to create a belief about the self or the outer world. This belief—or, as some would call it, this feeling—subsequently gives rise to mythical fears about what will happen if the individual does not continue to practice the behavior. In terms of the basic diagram we've been using, our conclusions play the role illustrated in figure 22.

The mythical fears contained in our conclusions keep us from making the kinds of choices that can lead us to breakthrough. As a result, we come to believe that we have no choice but to follow the road to self-defeat. The subsequent experience of practicing our self-defeating behaviors, in turn, provides evidence that seems to validate our conclusions. The result is a cyclical pattern of thought and action that guarantees our unhappiness.

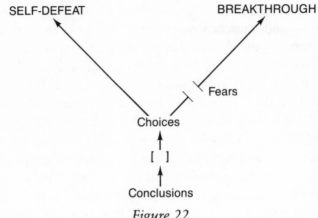

Figure 22

We begin to feel a need to change when the prices of our destructive thoughts and actions tell us that something is wrong with the way in which we've chosen to think and act. These prices block the road to self-defeat, much in the way that mythical fears block the road to breakthrough. An awareness of these prices is often motivation enough to keep us from creating the mythical fears produced by our faulty conclusions. Under these circumstances, it's relatively simple to develop effective replacements for our self-defeating behaviors and to use the results brought about by our winning choices to invalidate faulty conclusions and eliminate mythical fears.

In some cases, however, people's faulty conclusions are so strong, so pervasive, or so much a part of their lives that healthy changes are difficult to make. Such people have usually developed their self-defeating behaviors as a result of numerous painful experiences during childhood. When attempting to make winning choices or implement replacement techniques, these people find themselves trapped between the prices associated with a self-defeating behavior and the mythical fears of what will happen if the behavior is not practiced. The trap in which such people are caught looks like figure 23.

This diagram illustrates the experience of people who believe that despite their best efforts, they simply cannot alter established patterns of thought and action. On the one hand, they see the prices that must be paid if a self-defeating behavior continues to be practiced; on the other, they see the fears that seem to make it impossible to do anything but practice the unwanted behavior. And each alter-

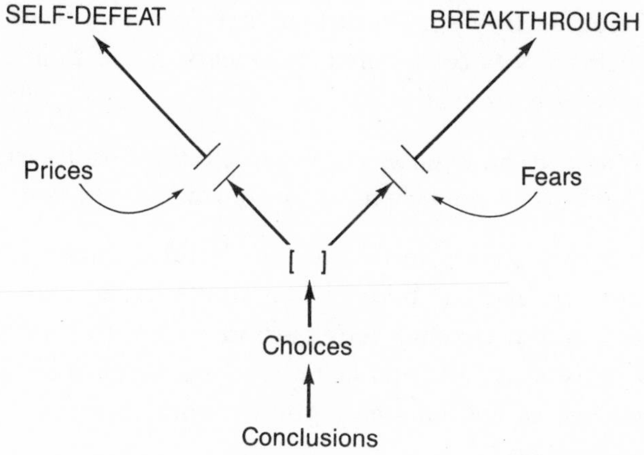

SELF-DEFEAT   BREAKTHROUGH

Prices   Fears

[ ]

Choices

Conclusions

Figure 23

native they consider seems to support and point back to the faulty
conclusion on which the entire problem is based. These people are
faced with a tenacious psychological dilemma. They want to change
but can't. They know what is wrong but don't know how to fix it.

If you find yourself in this situation—or if, in other words,
none of the steps we described earlier seems to help you change the
way you behave—it becomes essential that you analyze the conclusions on which your patterns of thought and action are based.
Exposing these conclusions for what they really are will limit their
ability to generate the fears that impede your progress toward change
and breakthrough.

Stating Your Conclusions

Faulty conclusions, on the unconscious level at which they are
formed, promise us that if we practice our self-defeating behaviors,
we will be safe from pain or anxiety. They also tell us that if we
behave in certain ways, then nothing that happens will take us by
surprise. In this sense, all of our conclusions are conditional statements: they seem to tell us what will happen if we think or act in
accordance with our patterns of self-defeat. To understand our conclusions and, as a result, to render them invalid, we must first learn
to state them in a way that reveals the false promises they contain.

There's a fairly simple format that you can use to articulate your conclusions as conditional statements, rather than declarative expressions of basic truths:

If I (describe how you practice your self-defeating behavior), then (describe what you believe will or won't happen to you).

When you state your conclusions in this format, you describe clearly the unconscious bargain that you've made with yourself to avoid growth and change. Your purpose here is to transform what you believe is a fundamental fact about yourself into a statement of what you believe will happen if you continue to practice your self-defeating behavior.

You might wonder why you should bother to articulate your conclusions as conditional statements. The reason is that if you view your conclusion as a description of fact, it will be extremely difficult to prove or disprove. If, for example, your conclusion is stated in a simple declarative form — "I am ugly," for example — you really have no means of testing its validity. By whose standards are you ugly? Are you prepared to interview every person in your community, state, or country, and then to compile the results either to support or refute your conclusion about yourself? And what if these results turned out to be ambiguous? What if you interviewed a thousand people, only to discover that three hundred found you unattractive, three hundred found you attractive, and four hundred deemed your appearance to be average? You would really not have accomplished much in terms of establishing the truth or falsity of your self-defeating conclusion.

A conclusion that is stated as a conditional statement, however, contains within itself a basis for testing and evaluation. All you need to do is to ask if the results promised in the "then" part of the statement indeed occur when you practice your self-defeating behavior. Suppose, for example, that your conclusion goes as follows: "If I behave in a shy, withdrawn manner, then I will be protected from the pain of being rejected by others." You can use this statement to test the validity of your conclusion. How? Simply by continuing to be shy and withdrawn, and then asking yourself honestly if you are not, in fact, experiencing the pain of rejection. If you go to a party and stand alone in a corner of the room with your eyes cast down, do people rush to embrace you and include you in their conversations? Does every person you might want to get to know come over to you and initiate a relationship? Do you leave the party feeling confident, elated, and accepted by the other guests? Probably not; you probably leave the party with feelings of isolation, depression, and unworthiness—the very feelings that are most often associated with rejection.

Here are some examples of common faulty conclusions that are stated in conditional form. Read through this list, then try to cast your own faulty conclusion in a format that allows for testing and evaluation.

- "If I am a perfectionist, then I will always win the approval of others."
- "If I am withdrawn, then I won't be rejected by others."
- "If I display hostility, then I'll be perceived as a strong person."
- "If I behave defensively, then I'll be protected from hurt."
- "If I procrastinate, then I'll never make a mistake."
- "If I attempt to control everything and everyone around me, then I'll never be disappointed or surprised."
- "If I remain closed-minded, then I'll never have thoughts or feelings that might lead me astray."
- "If I worry constantly, then I'll always be prepared for whatever life throws my way."
- "If I believe that I'm inferior to others, then I'll be able to escape the pressures of competition."
- "If I act lazy or unambitious, then I'll always be excused from difficult situations or tasks."

Now take one of your own destructive beliefs about yourself—preferably, the one that you see as the source of your primary self-defeating behavior—and write it down as a conditional statement. Once your conclusion is stated in this way, you can test it against your actual experiences and, ultimately, evaluate its validity.

"If I _____,

(describe your self-defeating behavior)

then _____."

(describe what you believe will happen to you or the results you'll achieve)

When you have the time, you might want to restate all of your faulty conclusions this way. Then, as you move through your program for change, you can step back every now and then and ask yourself if your experiences have tended to support or undermine each of these conclusions.

Facing Your Fears

Along with faulty conclusions, mythical fears form the death embrace that seems to immobilize those of us who practice self-defeating behaviors. In the absence of mythical fears, we would naturally make winning choices, and the resulting experiences would lead us to doubt our faulty conclusions. These conclusions, however, are the source of our mythical fears, and so the two elements—fears and conclusions—work to perpetuate each other and, in the process, lead us away from the road to breakthrough.

The best way to deal with mythical fears is not to create them in the first place. To do this, we need to avoid the tendency to retrieve faulty conclusions at new moments of life. But for those of us who are caught between our prices and fears, this can be difficult. So if we find ourselves in this position, we need to learn to face our fears if we are to make positive changes in the way we think and act.

To face our fears, we must first become aware of the form that they take. Most mythical fears, as we suggested earlier, fall into one of two categories: the fear of what we might discover about ourselves or the fear of what others might say about us or do to us. On a more specific level, we might carry within us the fear of success or failure, which makes us apprehensive about what will happen if we cease to practice our self-defeating behaviors. The nature of our individual fears depends, to a large extent, on the conclusions we have formed. If we believe, for example, that there is something inherently "wrong" with us, we'll do whatever we can to avoid facing the mythical flaw or defect that we believe will appear if we allow our inner selves to emerge. Similarly, if we believe that others will reject our healthy inner selves, we'll develop self-defeating behaviors designed to make sure that our best and most natural responses to new moments of life are suppressed or distorted.

Like faulty conclusions, mythical fears are essentially bargains that we strike with ourselves. As such, they, like faulty conclusions, are best expressed in conditional statements. But while conclusions describe what you believe will happen if you practice self-defeating behaviors, mythical fears describe what you believe will happen if you *don't* enact your personal cycle of self-defeat. "If I don't drink," the alcoholic may decide on an unconscious level, "then I'll lose my friends and be alone in the world." "If I don't put off doing things to the last moment," the procrastinator thinks, "then I'll do something wrong and will fail at my assigned task." Conditional statements such as these provide people with an illusion of control. They seem to tell people what dire fate they can avoid if only they continue to practice self-defeating behaviors.

Once mythical fears have been expressed as conditional statements, they, too, can be tested. If you believe, for example, that your friends will desert you if you stop making witty but destructive remarks, there's a simple way to test this assumption: you can simply choose to withhold your sarcasm for a few weeks, and, at the end of that time, ask yourself how many of your friends have disappeared and turned away. If none of your friends have abandoned you, you can safely conclude that your fear was groundless, and that your talent for sarcasm is not, after all, the quality that causes people to be attracted to you.

We suggest that you pause here and try to describe your primary mythical fear in terms of a conditional statement. You'll find it helpful to use the following format:

"I'm afraid that if I don't _____,

(describe your self-defeating behavior)

then _____."

(describe what you think will happen)

Here are some examples of how mythical fears can be stated to express the conditions of the inner bargains they represent:

- "I'm afraid that if I don't display hostility, then people will attack me."

- "I'm afraid that if I don't withhold love from my spouse or companion, then he or she will take me for granted."
- "I'm afraid that if I don't worry compulsively, then a disaster or tragedy will take me by surprise."
- "I'm afraid that if I don't overeat, then I'll be overwhelmed by the problems in my life."
- "I'm afraid that if don't procrastinate, I'll produce substandard work."
- "I'm afraid that if I don't sabotage myself, then I'll succeed and be unable to deal with the demands that will be imposed on me."

Use these examples as guidelines as you describe your primary mythical fear in conditional terms:

"I'm afraid that if I don't _____ *,*

then _____ *."*

You'll find that virtually all of your mythical fears can be expressed in this format. If you find yourself unable to make healthy changes because a mythical fear is blocking the road to breakthrough, articulate that fear in conditional terms. Once you've done so, you can test the fear by breaking the destructive bargain on which it is based. You can stop practicing the self-defeating behavior that the fear assumes and then see if what you fear does indeed happen.

Using Your Prices to Test Your Conclusions and Fears

An effective way to break the death embrace between your faulty conclusions and mythical fears is to analyze all the prices you pay for the continued practice of your self-defeating behavior. These prices will tell you if the bargains expressed in your fears and conclusions are being kept. Your conclusions and fears are telling you that if you perpetuate your cycle of self-defeat, you'll be spared certain consequences. You owe it to yourself, therefore, to take a hard look at whether or not your self-defeating behavior is delivering on its promises.

We've developed an exercise that has helped many of our clients clarify the prices that they pay for thinking and acting in destructive ways. To complete this exercise, you'll need a large sheet of plain white paper. In the center of the paper, draw a circle, and in the center of the circle, write your description of the self-defeating behavior that you want to eliminate. Next, draw a line from this main circle and write down what happens to you when you practice the unwanted behavior. Circle this consequence, then draw another line and describe in writing still another of the results to which your self-defeating behavior (or its initial consequence) leads. Continue in this fashion until you've either exhausted all the results of your self-defeating behavior or run out of room on your sheet of paper. In describing and connecting these various consequences, be sure to take into account how your unwanted behavior affects you in the following ways:

- Physically
- Emotionally
- Professionally
- Sexually
- Financially
- Spiritually
- Intellectually
- Educationally
- Socially

When you've finished listing and connecting the consequences and results of your self-defeating behavior, you should have before you a diagram that resembles the example shown in figure 24.

Now look at the consequences you've associated with your self-defeating behavior, as well as those that appear to be the extended results of more immediate consequences. Each of these is a price that you pay in order to keep on practicing your self-defeating behavior. The diagram you've drawn should suggest clearly what you are doing to yourself in hanging on to this particular behavior. It should show what you're actually getting in return for your destructive thoughts and actions.

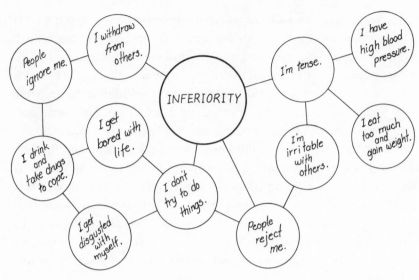

Figure 24

To carry the exercise a step further, compare the results your self-defeating behavior is producing to what you have promised yourself in forming your faulty conclusions. We've provided a format that can help you compare the conclusion and fear statements you developed earlier with the results that your self-defeating behavior actually yields.

"I believe that if I _____ **,**
            (describe your self-defeating behavior)

then _____
            (describe what, according to your conclusion, you believe will happen or

_____ **, and I'm afraid that if**
  what results you think you'll achieve)

I don't _____ **,**
            (again, describe your self-defeating behavior)

then _____ **.**
            (describe what you think will happen if you stop defeating yourself)

But what really happens when I practice my self-defeating behavior is

_____

  (list the consequences you identified in the circle exercise)

_____ **."**

It shouldn't take long for you to see that the bargains implicit in your faulty conclusions aren't being kept: your self-defeating behavior is not protecting you from failure, disappointment, rejection, anxiety, or loneliness. You may well realize—and, rest assured, many people have—that the consequences brought on by your self-defeating behavior are exactly those that you've attempted to avoid by practicing the behavior.

Exposing the Falsity of the Promise

Rachel was making little headway in her change program. It wasn't that she had failed to work hard: she had expended a considerable effort to identify her self-defeating behavior and her trigger pattern, and had spent a good deal of time developing replacement techniques to carry out the healthy choices she was learning to make. Still, she found herself retreating to her apartment at the end of each workday and nervously performing her ritualistic chores.

"I suspected it all along, but now I know it for sure," she reported glumly at the start of one of our sessions. "I can't change, and I'll never be able to. There's something inside me that isn't quite right. It's too strong for me to overcome."

After congratulating her for the hard and earnest work she had done to try to change her behavior, we suggested that Rachel needed to analyze her basic beliefs about her innermost self. We asked her to spend some time over the next few days working out, in writing, the fundamental conclusion on which she based her thoughts and actions. She was to bring this conclusion to our next meeting, where we'd analyze it and see if together we could discover what was impeding her progress.

At the start of our next meeting, Rachel reached into her purse and brought out a folded piece of paper. She told us that she had pared her basic conclusion about herself down to its barest essence. We asked her to share with us what she had discovered. "I believe that at the innermost level of my mind and body," she read from the paper, "there is something wrong with me—a mental or physical flaw that I can't repair."

We saw that while Rachel was moving in the right direction, she needed guidance to state her conclusion as a conditional statement that would reflect accurately the bargain she had made with herself. "You're off to a good start," we told her. "But the faulty conclusions that mess up people's lives are usually based on the belief that if they continue to practice self-defeating behaviors, they can be sure of what will happen to them. So why don't you try rephrasing your conclusion like this: 'If I continue to think and act as if I had a basic physical or mental flaw, then . . .' Fill in the last part of your statement with a description of what you think will happen if you act out the notion that you're damaged or flawed."

Two weeks later, Rachel returned to our office and told us she had completed this assignment. "I think I've got it now," she said. "My conclusion is that if I think and act as if there were something fundamentally wrong with me, I'll be protected from all the problems that come with a social life and a sexual relationship."

"Now you've got it right," we told her. "So ask yourself: has your self-defeating behavior helped you avoid sexual and social difficulties?"

Rachel hesitated. "Yes . . . I suppose it has. I mean, I don't have to worry very much about getting dates or being attractive, or any of the other crap that goes along with the whole mating game."

"You might want to think that over," we said. "When you came here six months ago, you complained that you had no friends and that you were congenitally frigid. No friends, no sexual feelings: aren't those difficulties related to your social life and sexuality?"

"In a way, I suppose," Rachel replied. She thought about what we had been discussing. "So you're telling me that my conclusion is a way of lying to myself?"

"Not lying, really. You've been trying to protect your inner self from hurt, and you've tried to strike a bargain that will guarantee your safety. But the bargain isn't a good one, because you're not getting what you've been promised. That's the way misguided conclusions work."

"By making false promises?"

"You've got it," we said. "Conclusions promise one thing, then deliver the opposite. That's how people are tricked into hurting themselves. And that's why it's important to figure out what your conclusions are. Until these false promises are exposed for what they actually are, it can be difficult to carry out winning choices and see the results that healthy alternative behaviors can bring."

The Role of Counseling

Working on your conclusions can be difficult, especially if you have carried them within you for a long time and have based your life on the false bargains they imply. Conclusions operate at the unconscious level of our psychic subsystems; therefore, they may not be easy to identify and articulate. So if you have difficulty determining what your conclusions are and how they influence your thoughts and actions, we encourage you to seek professional counseling.

What can a counselor do for you? He or she can look at your situation objectively and can point out discrepancies between what you think you're achieving through your behavior and what you are actually doing to yourself in continuing to think and act in self-defeating ways. A good counselor will be able to empathize with your particular situation but will not get caught in the psychic traps you've ingeniously set for yourself. The counselor's observations will not be clouded by your personal history, prejudices, blind spots, or confusions. He or she can help you discover why the same things seem to happen to you again and again, despite your efforts to change the way you do things.

A counselor can, over time, guide you through the process of analysis and comparison we've presented in this chapter. A concerned and thoughtful professional can help you learn through experience that you need not continue to behave in ways that guarantee disappointment, anxiety, and defeat. This is a lesson well worth learning, but one that you may find difficult to learn on your own.

Be aware, though, that a counselor will not be able to help you change your life overnight, or even within a few weeks or months. Change is usually a gradual process; it takes place in small increments and tends to consist of repeated gains and setbacks. Some people, however, are ready to change and can make use of the approach we've suggested here to move ahead rapidly. If you fall into the latter category, trust yourself to make the required behavioral changes at your own pace. Don't let the idea that change takes a long time slow you down.

Usually, though, healthy and lasting change takes place only when you learn from personal experience what kinds of thoughts and actions produce the results you want to achieve. This sort of change tends to occur slowly, as the experiences born of conscious thoughts and actions reshape conclusions that are formed at an unconscious level. It occurs when you discover, on your own or with professional assistance, that you have the ability to break out of your cycle of self-defeat and to experience the sense of wholeness that comes to each of us when our beliefs, thoughts, choices, and actions are clarified and aligned.

Chapter 21

Traveling the Road to Breakthrough

To travel the road to breakthrough is to think clearly, make winning choices, and take advantage of the positive, life-enhancing experiences that result. This journey is continuous, but it is not without obstacles, detours, and setbacks. How well you fare as you move forward to experience life without your self-defeating behavior depends largely on the kind of expectations you bring with you, and also on your willingness to treat your emerging inner self with tolerance and compassion. No program for self-improvement can promise a future free of problems and disappointments. Even the great religions of the world acknowledge that the individual's true triumph is defined more by an ability to cope with defeat than by an unbroken series of successes.

The approach that we've described in this book does not propose to eliminate all stress, worry, or anguish from your life. What it can do is to reduce dramatically the amount of controllable distress you bring upon yourself. It may improve your life to stop smoking or drinking, to lose weight, to let go of your feelings of inferiority, or to leave behind the hostility and suspicion that have distorted your view of yourself and the world. But even if you successfully eliminate your self-defeating behaviors, you will still have to contend on a regular basis with the toxins sent out by our cultural system and with your own imperfections and relapses.

We'd like to offer a few suggestions that you can use to cushion your emerging inner self against the rough spots you'll encounter on the road to breakthrough. We'll talk about the kinds of expectations that are reasonable and will contrast them with some of the unrealistic hopes and demands that serve only to subvert winning choices. We'll consider, too, how you can deal with the setbacks that you'll inevitably encounter along the road to breakthrough and how you can avoid the trap of perfectionism. We'll describe the importance of maximizing the benefits that result when winning choices are made, and we'll remind you to take full ownership of the breakthroughs you achieve. And we'll emphasize the importance of regarding yourself with the kind of empathy and compassion you normally extend to those people for whom you have the deepest love and the highest admiration.

We hope you will take to heart our advice that you treat yourself with compassion. We hope, also, that you'll continue to follow the guidelines we've provided long after you've rid yourself of your unwanted and self-destructive thoughts and actions.

The Importance of Expectations

Barbara arrived at our office one afternoon in a downcast mood. She claimed that for the past month she had been depressed, irritable, and listless. She traced her current malaise to her decision to let go of the perfectionist behavior that had alienated her from her friends and family. "Nothing's changed since then," she complained. "My husband and kids don't seem to have noticed any difference in me, and they still aren't sensitive to my needs as a woman and a mother. My friends don't call up and ask me out more often. And when I do go out for lunch or a drink, I'm nervous because I'm afraid I might say or do something that I shouldn't."

"What did you think would happen once you got rid of your self-defeating behavior?" we asked.

"I'm not sure," Barbara replied. "I thought that maybe there'd be less tension around the house, or that my friends would notice the change I'd made. I guess I believed that things would just get better in general, or that I'd experience a sense of accomplishment. But none of this has happened."

"You might want to look at some of your expectations," we suggested. "The discomfort you've been feeling may have less to do with letting go of your perfectionism than with the fact that some of your hopes haven't been realized. Some of your expectations probably haven't been realistic, given the way people respond to change."

"I've thought about that," said Barbara. "But to be honest, the only way I could motivate myself to change how I think and act was to visualize what would happen once I got rid of my perfectionism. I kept telling myself that there would be a real breakthrough—that I'd finally be fulfilled in terms of what I'm doing with my life."

People who have successfully eliminated their self-defeating behaviors often find themselves in situations similar to Barbara's. After working hard to break out of destructive patterns of behavior, they expect that their efforts will in some way be rewarded: that friends and relatives will applaud them, or that they'll experience a flash of enlightenment or a heightened and perpetual sense of well-being. While they are in the process of learning to make better choices, they tell themselves that they'll soon receive credit for being wise enough or strong enough to change their behavior. These expectations take on a life of their own. They come to represent an altered reality that can be achieved through good intentions, vigilance, and hard work. They become, in effect, the deferred wages for the effort that is sometimes required to alter destructive behavior patterns.

The problem with these expectations is that they simply aren't realistic. It's entirely reasonable to assume that once you've eliminated a self-defeating behavior, the general quality of your life will improve: that you'll eventually feel more alive, that you'll experience your environment from a different perspective, or that your relationships with others will become healthier and more meaningful. But it's unrealistic to assume that because you've successfully altered a destructive pattern of thought or action, you'll be promoted at work, meet a special person who will change your life, or be unconditionally loved by those around you. Expectations of this nature set you up for a return to your old patterns of self-defeat. If you tell yourself that a certain unlikely event will occur after you've eliminated a self-defeating behavior, you'll have a convenient reason to go back to your old pattern when things don't work out as you've anticipated.

One of the most common unrealistic expectations that people nourish while they are working at changing their behavior is that others will recognize, respect, or reward their decision to change. They want their spouses, parents, children, friends, and colleagues to acknowledge the effort required to make behavioral changes. Even if they fail, they want to be lauded for their good intentions. Although it seems natural and reasonable, this expectation contains within it a rationale for relapse and eventual disowning. The person who wants credit from others for attempting to change is, in a subtle way, making others responsible for his or her behavior. This person is trying to strike a bargain. He or she is saying: "Okay, I'll change my behavior. But other people had better notice—and, furthermore, had better let me know that they notice. If they don't, I'll go back to my old way of doing things, and my failure will be their fault."

The approach reflected here doesn't work. If you base your change program on the eventual approval of others, you're bound to be disappointed. Other people will simply not be able to meet your expectations. They may acknowledge at some point the progress that you've made, but they will rarely reward you to the extent that you desire. The mother who expects to be embraced and praised by her children once she stops criticizing them is bound to be disappointed, as is the office worker who expects to be complimented by the boss every time he or she works late to meet a tight deadline.

So as you move along the road to breakthrough, pause every now and then to ask yourself what you expect will happen once you've eliminated your self-defeating behavior. If you find that the ultimate success of your effort is based on what other people will say or do, remind yourself that, in the end, you are making changes for your own sake. Your goal is to enable your healthy inner self to emerge—not to gain approval, love, respect, or wealth.

You're Healthy . . . but Not Perfect

As you leave your self-defeating behavior behind and begin to move forward along the road to breakthrough, you are going to make mistakes. We can virtually guarantee you that sooner or later you'll respond to a new moment of life in a way that resembles (or even is identical to) the self-defeating behavior you've worked to eliminate. How can we be sure of this? Because although your emerging inner self is healthy and versatile, it is by no means perfect. There will come a time when threatening circumstances arise, and in a moment of understandable weakness, you'll return to the destructive pattern of thought or action that has traditionally limited your potential for growth and fulfillment. Keep in mind that even though you've rid yourself of an unwanted behavior, the toxins that caused you to develop the behavior in the first place are still present in the world around you. You can't expect to avoid completely all of the people, places, and circumstances that remind you of your old ways of responding to toxic messages and perceived threats.

The important thing to remember when you find yourself straying from the road to breakthrough is that mistakes or relapses *need not be permanent.* It's impossible to undo by way of a single errant thought or action the work you've done in moving away from the road to self-defeat. Taking a single drink does not imply a full-scale return to an unwanted pattern of alcohol abuse; losing your temper in a crisis does not constitute a total relapse into a pattern of thought and action governed by hostility or rage. In situations such as these, rigid or perfectionist thinking is your greatest enemy. So don't tell yourself that any single incident is the forerunner of an inevitable and permanent relapse into a cycle of self-defeat. Mistake-free behavior simply can't be achieved. It's unrealistic to expect it of others and equally unrealistic to expect it of yourself.

If You Make a Mistake . . .

How, then, should you deal with the setbacks that will inevitably occur as you travel the road to breakthrough? We believe that it's important not to panic, to focus on prices associated with the mistake you've made, and to be tolerant in evaluating your behavior. If you treat your setbacks as *natural* (and, hence, neutral) occurrences, you're much less likely to form the kinds of catastrophic conclusions that can lure you back to your cycle of self-defeat.

Once you've experienced a setback, it's important for you to remain relatively calm and objective about what has happened. If you become overwrought or anxious, you'll tend to view the event in a false context; you'll see it as evidence that a bias toward self-defeat underlies your actions and can never be changed. Panic is the enemy of clear and compassionate thought; it causes us to see single events not simply for what they are, but rather as evidence of pervasive and unchangeable patterns. Say, for example, that you've been dieting successfully for several days. One afternoon, following a miserable day at work, you walk past a candy counter and, in a moment of weakness, buy a chocolate bar. You eat the chocolate, and almost immediately, you sense a threat: all the work that you've put into your diet is about to be undone. You can't walk past a candy counter without breaking down, you'll never be able to lose weight, it's part of your nature to eat candy, you might as well buy another chocolate bar and be done with it. . . .

If you allow yourself to fall into this state of psychological panic, you'll be unable to deal effectively with what is really a relatively minor setback. Before you begin to form conclusions about what eating the candy means, you need to stand back from the situation and describe for yourself what, in fact, has happened: you ate a bar of candy. This single event does not mean that you'll eat more candy tomorrow, that you'll never be able to lose weight, that you were born to be overweight, or that your diet is doomed to fail. What does it mean? It means only that you ate a candy bar. You felt a sense of weakness. You made a mistake. You'll know better next time. Now, on to the next moment of life. . . .

This is not to say that you should totally ignore the consequences of any setbacks that occur. On the contrary, we feel it's important for you to call to mind directly the prices associated with the mistake you've made. So if you've broken your diet and eaten a candy bar, you need to be aware that it will be difficult to stay within your calorie limits for the day. Difficult, yes; impossible, no. You can choose to eat less at dinner or to exercise and burn off the additional calories you've consumed. Alternatively, you can choose simply to accept the added calories and then resolve to do better tomorrow, because if you don't, you'll start to gain back the weight you've lost, which will cause you to think negative thoughts about yourself. Do you want to return to your old behavior of eating and thinking like an overweight person? Are you willing, in short, to accept the prices associated with your old self-defeating behavior?

Note that this sequence of thoughts is rational and measured. It allows you to make several choices about how you'll behave in the future. It's different from the anxious and confused series of assumptions that leads hastily to the conclusion that you'll never be able to change the way you behave. It allows you to evaluate objectively the consequences of your setback, but it does not end in a prediction of catastrophe. Rather, it concludes by offering you a *choice* about what you can do after experiencing a setback.

In addition to remaining calm and evaluating the consequences of your mistakes, it's important that you treat yourself with compassion and tolerance. Ask yourself how you would react if a beloved relative or acquaintance—one of your parents or children, or a close friend—made a mistake similar to the one you've made. If, for example, your mother had successfully dieted for several weeks but had yielded momentarily to the temptation to eat a piece of candy, would you condemn her? Tell her that she might as well quit trying to diet, because she was born to be overweight? Advise her sternly that in a moment of weakness, she had completely undone several weeks' worth of good work? Probably not; instead, you'd tell her not to worry about this single insignificant incident. You would acknowledge all that she'd accomplished prior to her setback and encourage her to build on the success she'd previously achieved. You'd treat her with respect and affection, and you would make these feelings known to her.

Why, then, should you treat yourself any differently when you encounter an obstacle on the road to breakthrough? In making the decision to eliminate your self-defeating behavior, you acknowledged your imperfections and sought better ways of dealing with them. It should neither surprise nor disappoint you that you are still not perfect. A predictable setback is not just cause for harsh self-criticism. Rather, it's an affirmation of your flawed but healthy humanity. In moments of doubt, it's far better to err on the side of compassion and tolerance than to expose your emerging inner self to excessive punishment.

And don't forget that in acknowledging mistakes or setbacks, you are *catching yourself* in the practice of a behavior that might lead to a renewed cycle of self-defeat. When you catch yourself in this way, you greatly reduce the chance that a single incident might develop into a new pattern of destructive behavior. Alice, after several months of success, grew bored one afternoon and found a reason to visit one of her favorite shopping centers. Before she knew it, she'd purchased an expensive silk blouse and a new pair of sandals. The next morning, she called us on the phone, obviously distraught over what she had done.

"It's starting all over again," she told us. "I had nothing to do, so I invented a reason to drive by the mall. There was a sale at one of my favorite shops, and I hadn't bought myself anything for a long time. It seemed to be harmless while I was doing it, but later, when I got home, this terrible sense of guilt and failure came over me. I'm afraid that I'm out of control again."

"You're treating yourself too harshly," we told her. "It seems clear from what you've said — to say nothing of your tone of voice — that you realize you've made a mistake. That in itself is an indication of how far you've come. You've caught yourself doing something that might be destructive, and you're aware of what might happen if you do it again. We don't think you will. Do you?"

"No, I don't," Alice replied. "At least not right away. For now, I don't want to go near that shopping center. It's not worth the feelings I'm having today. What good are new things if you feel miserable over having bought them?"

"You're doing a good job," we said. "You've shown that you're capable not only of catching yourself but also of considering your prices clearly. That's what breakthrough is all about: using an awareness of the choices you make and the consequences to which they lead to avoid minimizing and disowning your behavior. You ought to congratulate yourself, because you've dealt with a setback and continued to move in the right direction."

We should mention that since this phone call, Alice has reported no additional setbacks. She has managed to pay off the debts she incurred while practicing her self-defeating behavior, and she is now able to spend hours at a shopping mall without making a single unnecessary purchase.

Nurturing Your Success

For many of us, the greatest obstacle to breakthrough lies not in the occasional setbacks we experience, but rather in our inability to acknowledge and build upon the success we achieve. The perfectionist and self-critical beliefs that cause us to exaggerate occasional mistakes can also blind us to the progress we've made. It's important, therefore, that as you travel the road to breakthrough, you consciously *acknowledge* the benefits of the winning choices you've made, that you *maximize* these benefits, and that you *own* fully the behavior that has led to these positive results.

Acknowledging Benefits

It had been over ten years since Ted walked out of an interview with a prospective employer feeling good about his performance. By his own admission, he brought this pattern of failure upon himself: he showed up late for interviews, failed to dress and groom himself in a way that would cause the interviewer to look favorably upon him, and created mythical fears that distracted him from the business at hand during the meeting. Eventually, Ted was able to see that he was setting himself up for defeat: he was focusing his thoughts not on making a favorable impression, but instead on the notion that his combat experiences had left him "damaged" and unworthy of employment.

"What do you want to accomplish when you go out on an interview?" we asked him.

"To get a good job," he replied.

"We agree that your ultimate goal is to get hired," we told Ted. "But maybe you'd be better off setting a more basic goal. What if you decided that what you wanted to accomplish immediately was to have a job interview that left you feeling good about yourself? Forget for the moment whether or not you're eventually hired, because you can't control that outcome. We think you should concentrate on making the best possible impression on the person you meet with. We want you to walk away from your next interview knowing that the interviewer talked to the true Ted—not some guy who seemed intent on defeating himself."

Ted worked hard in preparing for his next interview. He got a haircut, bought a new pair of shoes, and worked on keeping his thoughts focused on the goal he had set. Following the interview, he telephoned to report that things had gone well for him. "The guy seemed interested in me, and I was really curious about the business he was in," he said. "We talked for quite a while, and I felt like I'd handled myself well. I presented myself as a person who had skills to offer and who was a fast learner. I left the disabled Vietnam vet back at my apartment."

"Do you think you'll get the job?" we asked.

"It's hard to say, but it really doesn't matter," Ted replied. "What matters is that now I know I can show myself to employers and not be worried about what they'll think. If I can keep it up, it's only a matter of time before I find something."

We were quite pleased with the results Ted had achieved. He had not only managed to leave his self-defeating behavior behind, but he had also learned to acknowledge the benefits that resulted from his winning choices. He saw that healthy behavior brings positive results, and that these results need not take a form that most people would deem successful. He could have viewed his most recent interview as the latest in a long series of failures, but he chose not to. He linked his winning choices with his feelings of accomplishment and self-worth, which enabled him to move ahead on the road to breakthrough.

Maximizing Benefits

You've heard it before: nothing succeeds like success. To our way of thinking, this is simply another way of saying that people who travel the road to breakthrough have learned to maximize the benefits that their winning behavior brings. These people have discovered that successful results are not ends in themselves, but instead are starting points for new ventures, added enrichment, and further learning. While people who practice self-defeating behaviors expend precious time and energy trying to minimize the negative consequences of their thoughts and actions, those who travel the road to breakthrough are able to focus their attention fully on the potential that each new moment of life offers. They move from breakthrough to breakthrough, broadening their range of experience and increasing their understanding of themselves and the world around them.

How can you develop the ability to maximize the benefits that result from your winning choices? Once she left behind her self-defeating behavior, Rachel found that she was instinctively able to build on her initial successful results. In an attempt to find a replacement for the compulsive activities she carried out each evening, she enrolled in an art appreciation course. There she met a man named

Edward. He seemed to take an interest in her, and Rachel, to her credit, did not retreat into her customary pose of aloofness and hostility. As a result, she got to know Edward better. He and Rachel became friends and, eventually, began to meet after class for dinner. Edward also introduced Rachel to his sister Margo, and Rachel and Margo discovered they had several common interests. Both worked for large accounting firms, and both liked to shop for antiques. When Margo suggested that she and Rachel take a night class in minicomputer accounting applications, Rachel was receptive. She picked up some valuable information that she was able to apply to her job and, as a result, received a raise and a promotion.

"I can't believe what's happening to me," Rachel told us with a smile. "All of a sudden, I'm going out almost every evening, meeting new people, learning new things. I feel like someone has lifted a weight off of my shoulders: there are times when the rush of life seems to lift me off the ground. One thing has led to another, and I'm feeling alive and healthy."

"How about your sexual feelings?" we asked. "Or what you used to call your lack of them?"

"You're asking me if I've been to bed with anyone, right?" said Rachel. "The answer is no, not yet. But the feelings are there, and when it seems right to act on them, I probably will. To tell the truth," she continued, "I don't spend a lot of time thinking about that particular problem any more."

We told Rachel that she'd experienced the breakthrough we had talked about while she struggled to eliminate her self-defeating behavior and allow her inner self to emerge. "You're doing a good job of maximizing the benefits you've earned," we told her. "You're learning to build on your successes—to take what life offers and to use each experience to your advantage. That's what winning behavior is all about. It's about moving ahead to new moments, rather than cycling through a pattern based on destructive ways of thinking and acting."

Owning Your Breakthroughs

Earlier in this section, we talked about the importance of owning your behavior and the consequences it leads to. We pointed out that people who believe their behavior is governed by other people,

God, fate, or genetics essentially give up the ability to change and grow. In order to learn to make winning choices, you must acknowledge that the potential for such choices exists—or, in other words, that your life is not controlled by some external force or agent.

Ongoing breakthrough behavior depends heavily on ownership. Just as people who practice self-defeating behaviors must own their choices and prices in order to eliminate the unwanted behavior, people who travel the road to breakthrough need to give themselves full credit for the benefits that winning choices bring. There is little point in working hard to change your behavior only to attribute your eventual success to luck, chance, or the efforts of others. This way of looking at the results of your efforts is not only distorted—it's also dangerous. If you deny the cause-and-effect relationship between the winning choices you've made and the positive consequences of your actions, you undermine the role that choice plays in determining your behavior. And once the notion of choice is cast aside, faulty conclusions arise to provide explanations of why things happen the way they do.

We encourage you, therefore, to give yourself full credit for the benefits you realize and the breakthroughs you achieve. Own the results of your efforts on a regular basis. Set aside a few moments each week to review the progress you've made and to establish in your mind the direct connection between your choices and the consequences that these choices have brought about. Form in your mind short summaries such as this:

> Let's see . . . it's been two weeks since I last had a drink. As a
> result, I've been able to save some money: money we can set aside
> for the kids' Christmas presents. That means we won't feel such a
> financial pinch around the holidays, so there'll be less arguing and
> tension around the house. That's one major improvement I can
> take credit for. And since I stopped drinking, I don't come to work
> hung over or drowsy. I'm more on top of things, more interested in
> the things I need to do. My boss has noticed this: yesterday he
> complimented me for a report I turned in. All of a sudden, I seem
> to have a more interesting job and a more understanding boss. And
> this happened because of my choice not to drink. I'm making my
> life better, and I want to continue to do so.

Think for a moment how the person who made this ownership statement could have glossed over his or her successes and attributed them to arbitrary circumstances. Money not spent on alcohol is money saved: "So what, it'll just get spent on something else." Work is now more interesting and easier to complete: "Yeah, well, that last report was easy to put together. They won't all be that way." The boss complimented the report: "Oh, he was only in a good mood. Tomorrow he'll be his old self again, and I won't be able to do anything right." These distorted interpretations of positive consequences show how benefits can be minimized and disowned.

We urge you to avoid this way of thinking, even if you're tempted to minimize your accomplishments in the interest of seeming modest or unassuming. Let go of your belief that pride inevitably precedes a fall: own your success. Don't try to predict what will come in the future, but take honest ownership of what has happened in the recent past. You—and you alone—have chosen to eliminate your self-defeating behaviors and to allow your strengths and virtues to emerge. Your healthy inner self is responding appropriately to new moments of life, and you're realizing the benefits of the clear-headed choices you've made. This is how you were meant to function. It is how you were meant to live your life.

Where the Road to Breakthrough Leads

By now you're probably aware of this, but we'll say it anyway: The road to breakthrough is not a path you follow only when you need to eliminate a self-defeating behavior. It's a map for traveling through life—a set of guidelines that your healthy inner self will embrace once it is free of the restraints imposed by destructive patterns of thought and action. Once you've moved off the road that leads to self-defeat, you'll find yourself practicing breakthrough behavior with little conscious effort. You've known for a long time how to acknowledge and maximize benefits, and how to credit yourself for the results you achieve. This knowledge is a part of your healthy inner self. It is obscured only when you begin to rely on self-defeating behaviors to cope with new moments of life.

Where does the road to breakthrough lead? Everywhere and nowhere. It leads to no identifiable goal or result; it does not end when a self-defeating behavior is left safely behind, or when a long-sought goal is achieved. The road to breakthrough takes you only from one new moment of life to another. Each of these moments contains the seed of either a new breakthrough or a cycle of self-defeat. You can plant and nurture either of these seeds. In moments of doubt and crisis, the seed of self-defeat may seem attractive: it will promise to grow at an alarming rate, to repair what you believe is broken within you, and to provide an effective antidote to the toxins you've absorbed. It will ask only that you plant it, that you allow it to take root. But you know what will happen if you do. The seed of self-defeat will grow into a behavior that will soon cease to be a useful solution. This behavior will itself become a problem; it will branch out and entangle you, and it will demand that you continue to cultivate it. It will trap and limit you, leaving you to wonder what would have happened had you never planted it.

Your healthy inner self knows instinctively how to respond to the potential contained in each new moment of life. This inner self will turn its back on the seed of self-defeat. It will tell you to plant instead the seed of breakthrough, which, after an initial period of nurturing, will grow and flower on its own. If you heed the counsel of your healthy inner self, you'll plant the right seed: you'll make a winning choice. You'll send your best self forward to deal with each new moment of life and will face the next moment with the sense of peace and accomplishment that life-enhancing decisions inspire.

A Few Final Words

Our culture has benefited on an unprecedented scale from advances achieved in the physical, social, behavioral, and medical sciences. We know more about how our minds, bodies, and social structures work than any of our ancestors knew. Yet the practice of self-defeating behaviors is more rampant today than ever. In trying to eliminate these behaviors, we need first to ask ourselves why we insist on undermining our own best efforts and then to consider the implications of the answers we arrive at.

From this perspective, it seems apparent that self-defeating behaviors are perpetuated for two general reasons. First, these behaviors appear to make sense. Our modern minds have been inculcated with the principles of logic and rationality; we solve problems and avoid difficulties by linking causes and effects, actions and outcomes. We are also pragmatic. We place our faith, both consciously and unconsciously, in whatever appears to solve the problem at hand. So when we are confronted with a piece of information, a person, or a situation that threatens us, we make a speedy inventory of the thoughts and actions available to us and choose whichever option promises to resolve our inner tension directly and expediently. We light cigarettes, drink alcohol or take drugs, turn our backs on others, fill our mouths with food, or escape into fantasy. The option we choose becomes our tested and proven way of dealing with uncertainty and discomfort. We resort to it each time we are threatened, despite the fact that it is doing us far more harm than good.

Second, in addition to seeming sensible and workable, self-defeating behaviors are promoted and supported by our culture. This helps them endure in an era of enlightenment and self-awareness. Day in and day out, we are told in so many words that only the wealthy, the beautiful, and the fortunate are entitled to happiness. What's worse, we're encouraged to practice self-defeating behaviors in order to be more like the people we're supposed to admire. A few highly publicized celebrities, for example, spend money wantonly or abuse themselves and those around them. From this behavior we derive the notion that if we do likewise, people might think that we, too, are wealthy, carefree, and spontaneous. And as for prices—we are told on the one hand that they do not exist, and on the other that they even if they do exist, there is always a way to minimize or avoid them. Those of us who lack financial resources are urged to buy on credit. The lonely among us are told that there are miraculous agencies that, for a fee, will broker meaningful and lasting relationships. When we complain of the anxiety or physical pain brought on by our destructive ways of thinking, we're given medication. We are told not only that we can have our cake and eat it too, but also that we need not pay for the pleasure of the snack.

It's no surprise, therefore, that self-defeating behaviors thrive in our culture. As we grapple with the toxic and contradictory messages we regularly receive, our thinking becomes confused. The relationship between causes and effects becomes unclear: behaviors we instinctively recognize as wrong seem to be right, and the basic human truths in which we believe appear to be invalidated. Our conscious and unconscious minds work hard to reconcile the disharmony that exists between them, but more often than not they direct us toward modes of thought and action that guarantee further confusion.

But we carry within ourselves a sort of master blueprint for health and wholeness. By paying attention to this fundamental pattern, we can take conscious steps to neutralize the toxins to which we are subjected. Once we've learned consciously that self-defeating behaviors make no sense (despite what our culture may tell us), we can use this knowledge to shape the conclusions we carry within our unconscious minds. Simply put, if we cease to practice behaviors that lead to negative experiences, our unconscious minds will link the healthy choices we've made with the positive results we achieve. The process of eliminating a self-defeating behavior reverses the sequence by which the behavior was initially created. We acquire these behaviors unconsciously, and only with time do we become consciously aware of the problems we've created for ourselves. To leave our self-defeating behaviors behind, however, we must use our conscious minds to undermine the destructive but unconscious beliefs that cause us to defeat ourselves.

In reading this book, you've completed the crucial first step toward lasting behavioral change. You've become aware of what you do to hurt yourself, how you do it, and why you persist in acting contrary to your best interests. This awareness is bound to strike at the faulty conclusions that cause you to cycle through your pattern of self-defeat. Once these conclusions have been invalidated by the successes that will result from your winning choices, you'll be well on your way to healthy and permanent change. The road to breakthrough is now open to you. Make a conscious choice to travel it: it will lead you to yourself.

Index